D1462119

A New Species
of Criticism

A New Species of Criticism

Eighteenth-Century Discourse on the Novel

Joseph F. Bartolomeo

DELAWARE

Newark: University of Delaware Press
London and Toronto: Associated University Presses

Associated University Presses
440 Forsgate Drive
Cranbury, NJ 08512

Associated University Presses
25 Sicilian Avenue
London WC1A 2QH, England

Associated University Presses
P.O. Box 338, Port Credit
Mississauga, Ontario
Canada L5G 4L8

The paper used in this publication meets the requirements
of the American National Standard for Permanence of Paper
for Printed Library Materials Z39.48-1984.

Library of Congress Cataloging-in-Publication Data

Bartolomeo, Joseph F., 1958–
    A new species of criticism : eighteenth-century discourse on the
novel / Joseph F. Bartolomeo.
      p. cm.
    Includes bibliographical references (p.) and index.
    ISBN 0-87413-488-9 (alk. paper)
    1. English fiction—18th century—History and criticism—Theory,
etc. 2. Criticism—Great Britain—History—18th century.
I. Title.
PR851.B36 1994
823'.509—dc20   93-29770
                                                CIP

PRINTED IN THE UNITED STATES OF AMERICA

To Lydia, Julie, and Cara

Contents

Preface

Far from inhibiting further consideration of the issue raised in its definitive-sounding title, Ian Watt's *The Rise of the Novel* has instead prompted more than three decades of fascinating reconsideration of the subject, from a variety of historical, formalistic, and ideological stances. The last few years have witnessed provocative accounts not only of the social and cultural forces that fostered the emergence of the novel, but of the reciprocal impact of the genre on popular and political culture and of the relationship between fiction and other forms of cultural production. Addressing origins, Lennard Davis's Foucauldian approach has traced the development of a "news/novels discourse" and its eventual fission into the discrete categories of fact and fiction,[1] while Michael McKeon's more ambitious dialectical method has attempted to present the novel as resulting from and mediating profound instabilities in social structure and epistemology.[2] Among the effects of the genre, numerous critics have focused extensively on the centrality of gender in the production and consumption of fiction, on the opportunities and limitations that novel writing presented to women, and on the implications for authors of either sex of a substantial female reading public.[3] For Nancy Armstrong, the emphasis on "feminine" subjectivity in the domestic fiction addressed to women actually led to a transformation in conceptualizing political power, a move toward a feminized bourgeois ideology.[4] Granting the novel's equally significant influence in a very different context, John Bender has read the ordering of fictional narrative as an anticipation of—and a preparation for—the development of the modern penitentiary.[5] Other initially surprising, but often persuasive, connections include Terry Castle's study of the masquerade—a phenomenon that collapsed ideological and institutional oppositions—and its significance in four novels,[6] and Carol Kay's examination of the common issues and rhetorical strategies that inform fiction and political writing.[7]

As even a superficial survey reveals, these critics have concurred on the discursive nature of the novel and its potency as a cultural

9

force, and they have all proceeded—appropriately, given their purposes—"from the top down," premising their readings of texts upon contemporary theoretical assumptions. My study goes further toward examining the construction of a valorized notion of the novel—but moves in the opposite direction by focusing on the explicit commentary on the genre offered by the earliest novelists and critics. All too routinely, this critical commentary has been consigned to the footnote, the aside—or, occasionally, the chapter—and has been invoked largely for utilitarian purposes in literary histories, surveys of the genre, and critical biographies. Moving the discourse to the foreground will demonstrate the constitutive cultural role it played, its success in forging a place for the genre in literary and popular culture. In addition, I will demonstrate the extent to which eighteenth-century writers initiated discussion of many of the central concerns that occupy critics of prose fiction today, such as (a) the ethics of writing and reading, (b) historicity and the boundaries of fact and fiction, (c) narrative as a gendered phenomenon, (d) formal conventions and transgressions, (e) the limits of probability, (f) conflicts between popular and "high" culture, and (g) the role of the reader as both consumer and cocreator of literary texts. The often tentative, exploratory, and even visceral nature of early commentary on the novel also connects it to contemporary approaches to emerging genres. Similar apologies, moralistic condemnations, and attempts at canon formation attend the "rise" of the film and television media in our own era. All of these characteristics justify—indeed, invite—a thorough historical synthesis of eighteenth-century discourse on the novel.

Contemporary appreciation of the polysemous nature of language and writing also invites a skeptical, deconstructive approach to this early commentary—an approach that refuses to accept the commentary at face value but, instead, regards it as a series of often indeterminate texts within or about other texts. Both deliberately duplicitous rhetoric and unconscious contradiction commonly underlie the several modes of discourse that constitute "criticism" of the novel. Various intended audiences and varying degrees of fictionality characterize (a) the statements that appeared as constituent parts of the novels themselves, such as prefaces or introductory chapters, (b) the more "personal" comments within letters, (c) the sanctimonious polemics of popular journalism, and (d) the self-consciously "learned" approach of the avowedly critical periodical reviewers. Content and context, in other words, are inseparable.

My selection and structuring of materials proceed in part from a desire to devote substantial attention to context. I confine my attention primarily to comments by novelists about their novels or the genre and to reviews from the two leading organs of institutionalized criticism—namely, *The Monthly Review* and *The Critical Review*, which readily lend themselves to analysis of common formal conventions and rhetorical strategies. Representing the largest—and, in my view, most significant—channels of criticism, these two critical genres also demonstrate a significant change in the discourse over time. Commentary within novels—which was necessary to establish the legitimacy of the form and the authority of its practitioners—predictably diminished after the middle of the eighteenth century with the popular success of the genre and the critical success of individual authors and texts. Around the same time, another new and insecure genre, the review journal, undertook the task of regularly scrutinizing novels—in part, at least, to foreground a systematic and professional approach to judging fiction and, thereby, to win respectful attention. Taking this shift from novelists to reviewers into account, my organization attempts to extend reader-response theory to the construction of, problems with, and dialogues between individual authorial voices, communities of authors, and the professional critical community.

A number of other critical genres that explicitly or implicitly reflected upon the art and craft of fiction—such as parodies, histories of romance, and pamphlets about particular novels or parts of novels—resist this type of contextualization and often deal with issues that are also covered in authorial commentary or reviews. Therefore, as interesting as these other genres often are, I usually ignore them in this study. The major exception is Samuel Johnson's criticism. Despite a slender output that consists of a single essay and scattered bits of barbed conversation, Johnson not only offered the first significant comments on the comparative merits of Richardson and Fielding but also articulated most compellingly the moral possibilities and dangers of fiction that preoccupied so many of his predecessors and successors.

One issue that I have chosen to minimize is nomenclature—more specifically, the genesis, uses, refinements, and revisions of the terms *novel* and *romance*. This complex subject of naming, impinging as it does on the origins of a consciousness of genre among novelists and readers, has already generated considerable discussion. Yet eighteenth-century writers and critics themselves seldom devoted much sustained attention to the labels—and often used them interchangeably. Such neglect shown toward labels may, in fact, derive from one of the central critical preoccupations of the period—originality. It will become clear how certain generic conventions and expectations developed and became broadly accepted; but it will become equally clear how the genre remained open to innovation, experimentation, and continuous reinvention. Critical voices, whether belonging to novelists or to reviewers, tended to devote more energy to identifying and celebrating the new—and, consequently, encouraging it—than to demarcating and defending boundaries. The malleability of the genre made any apparent stability in labeling suspect or irrelevant.

Like the genre itself, critical and theoretical commentary can accommodate a strictly teleological or synthetic approach only through egregious selectivity and omission. When I began this project, I had precisely such an approach in mind, namely, tracing an orderly evolution of a set of assumptions about—and rules for—prose fiction. Confronting a mass of such diverse material convinced me, however, that the book I had originally intended would badly misrepresent the first century of narrative theory—the most prominent characteristic and greatest strength of which is resistance to dogmatism and closure. As a result, I have structured all but one of the chapters around competing voices and values; for while the criticism of the novel was certainly progressive—building from the start upon insights derived from earlier generations—it seldom resolved into finite or absolute positions. Division within and among authors, the divergence between theory and practice, changes over time, and the fragmentary nature of the critical enterprise—all militated against a consensus or even a synthesis. Even where agreement seemed almost unanimous—as in the insistence that fiction be morally correct and edifying—writers pursued different agendas and appealed to different audiences: the sincere moralist tried to reform the unwashed masses, the transparent poseur to provide cover for ethically or artistically suspect work, and the reviewer to emphasize the social responsibilities of an elite class of readers. Cultural elitism, as I will show, helped to account for the unique degree of consistency in reviewers' general estimates of the purpose and place of the novel, but it could not prevent frequent and serious disagreements among them about considerations of genre and narrative form.

Readers sensitive to the multiple implications of the concept of a discourse in contemporary theory—its rhetorical dimension, its self-defining and self-limiting activity, its hidden complexities and contradictions, and its relationships to other discourses—cannot but value the unresolved, multivocal character of the discourse examined here. By resisting uniformity and all its stultifying effects, this critical commentary not only mirrored but fostered the astonishing variety and vitality in the early English novel.

Acknowledgments

My longest-standing debt is to my parents, who encouraged the choices that made it possible for me even to think about attempting to write a book.

My interest in the subject of this book began when James Slevin introduced me to *Rambler* No. 4, and his advice and example persuaded me to pursue eighteenth-century studies. The earliest version of the book was a dissertation written under the direction of Walter Jackson Bate, for whose help and support I will always be grateful. James Engell, Michael Shinagel, and James Basker also read drafts of the dissertation, and each provided valuable insights and criticisms. I am especially grateful to James Basker for his continuing interest in the project. Both he and John Richetti have generously offered substantial advice, both intellectual and practical, and have helped me to sharpen and at times to reevaluate my thinking.

I wish to acknowledge the staffs of the University of Massachusetts Library, the Neilson Library at Smith College, the Widener and Houghton Libraries at Harvard, the Bodleian Library, and the British Library, for their aid in tracing, and lifting, many dusty volumes. I also thank the editors at the University of Delaware Press and Associated University Presses for all their assistance.

My colleagues at the University of Massachusetts have been unfailingly supportive. In particular, I would like to thank chairmen Robert Bagg and Vincent DiMarco, who have shown me countless professional and personal kindnesses, and Charles Moran and C. K. Smith, who read the entire penultimate draft of the manuscript and made immensely helpful suggestions, which led to important final changes.

I met my wife, Lydia Sarro, as I was beginning to write the dissertation that led to this book. As both the book and the relationship have progressed, I have been amazed and touched by her faith, her patience, and her loving support. Our daughters, Julie and Cara, provoke the laughter and the wonder that make every task easier.

A New Species
of Criticism

1

Why, How, and Whence Novels?
Congreve to Defoe

Prefaces invite skepticism. Tidy, reductive guidelines that purport to render both message and method transparent have precisely the opposite effect on all but the most naive readers. And the very placement of the preface arouses suspicion by foregrounding its problematic temporal and spatial relationship to the text. No contemporary critic has exposed the relationship more cleverly than Jacques Derrida, whose "Outwork" to *Dissemination*—a preface that appears to deconstruct itself—begins with the startling sentence, "This (therefore) will not have been a book."[1] Such an opening lays bare the contrived position of a unit that "would announce in the future tense ... the conceptual content or significance ... of what will *already* have been *written*" (7). Both anterior and posterior to the text, a preface, according to Derrida, attempts to impose interpretive strictures on a work whose very freedom, so to speak, has made the preface possible. In Derrida's words, the preface "can become a discourse on method, a treatise on poetics, a set of formal rules, only after the forging of the irruptive track of a method that is actually *put in practice* as a path that breaks ground and constructs itself as it goes along, without a predetermined itinerary" (38). In an equally provocative way, Laurence Sterne anticipated this kind of critique by placing prefaces in the middle of novels!

If the preface occupies an uncertain, ambiguous place in any text, the unique status of fictional narrative compounds the problems of interpretation. In novels, the fictionalizing that is essential to the text can be—and often is—present in the preface as well. Put more simply, the assertions of the preface may be no more true than the characters and events in the novel. Along with other manipulative strategies, prefatorial feigning can serve, often simultaneously, a variety of ends—including promoting oneself, defending oneself, parodying, and answering or obviating criticism. For the reader, the question of reliability—of how to discriminate between sincerity and ulterior motives—inevitably arises.

All of these difficulties inform those prefaces that are practically the exclusive vehicle for theorizing about fiction in the early eighteenth century. The need to defend often mediocre examples of a still nascent genre often resulted in questionable authorial practices. Some writers offered detailed, earnest-sounding discussions of purpose and technique that seem to bear no relationship to the inept or lurid narratives that follow them. Others wrapped themselves in a mantle of morality designed, among other things, to preclude critical reproach. Still others reproduced, without attribution, critical commonplaces of seventeenth-century French criticism. Why, then, bother to take these remarks seriously, let alone analyze them? Because beneath the indeterminacy and conscious duplicity lay serious grappling with the ordering of—and relationships among—three broad areas under which virtually all subsequent criticism could be subsumed: the means, ends, and sources of fiction.

More specifically, two opposed perspectives and standards of judgment emerged. A "formalist" position privileged craft over credo—emphasizing plot design, character development, and probability, often by addressing the act and consequences of reading. On the other side, moralism subordinated more technical concerns to the (preferably) virtuous and (possibly) vicious effects of reading novels. Yet neither stance could completely exclude the other, and both relied on similar rhetorical strategies to attract readers and to overcome a putative hostility to fiction. More prolific and developed commentary, especially that of Defoe, foregrounded the tensions between the two approaches and the extent to which they were complicated by a third—the claim to literal or substantive truth.

*   *   *

A witty acknowledgment of the often vestigial nature of prefaces opens a text that has been regarded as "the first important document in the criticism of fiction,"[2] Congreve's preface to *Incognita:*

> Some Authors are so fond of a Preface, that they will write one tho' there be nothing more in it than an Apology for its self. But to show thee that I am not one of those, I will make no Apology for this, but do tell thee that I think it necessary to be prefix'd to this Trifle, to

prevent thy overlooking some little pains which I have taken in the Composition of the following Story.[3]

In less than a sentence, Congreve has moved from criticizing apologies to making one—a rhetorical reversal so instantaneous that it should provoke some suspicion of his posture of diffidence and self-deprecation. His first published work may have been a "Trifle" to the youthful author, but the elaborate commentary that follows the unapologetic apology—commentary grudgingly praised by Samuel Johnson as "uncommonly judicious"[4]—suggests more ambitious claims.

Congreve begins his preface by drawing the oft-quoted distinction between romance and novel, making clear his preference for the latter:

> Romances are generally composed of the Constant Loves and invincible Courages of Hero's, Heroins, Kings and Queens, Mortals of the first Rank, and so forth; where lofty Language, miraculous Contingencies and impossible Performances, elevate and surprize the Reader into a giddy Delight, which leaves him flat upon the Ground whenever he gives of, and vexes him to think how he has suffer'd himself to be pleased and transported, concern'd and afflicted at the several passages which he has read . . . when he is forc'd to be very well convinced that 'tis all a lye. Novels are of a more familiar nature; Come near us, and represent to us Intrigues in practice, delight us with Accidents and odd Events, but not such as are wholly unusual or unpresidented [sic], such which not being distant from our Belief bring also the pleasure nearer us. Romances give more of Wonder; Novels more Delight. (A5v–A6r)

Obvious limitations qualify the distinction for contemporary readers. The attacks on romance are largely derivative, based on the polemics of Boileau and others,[5] while the "Novels" to which Congreve refers in his preface are better understood by the contemporary term *novellas*. Nor did the taxonomy bind Congreve's successors, as subsequent authors frequently used the two terms interchangeably or redefined them to suit their own needs. What remains valuable is Congreve's emphasis on the affective qualities of both genres and on reader response as the principle underlying the contrast. Comparing the difference between novel and romance to that between comedy and tragedy, he focuses squarely on the distinct psychological effects produced in the reader by the two genres—effects reduced in useful shorthand to "Wonder" and "Delight."[6] The degree to which Congreve championed verisimilitude can be debated; but whatever value the "familiar" has, derives from the psychological pleasure it provides.

Congreve's "affective stylistics" aside, the romance-novel contrast had less important consequences for the criticism of fiction than the discussion of plot that concludes Congreve's preface, in which an attempt to imitate drama in "the Design, Contexture and Result of the Plot" (A6r) implicitly endorses the Aristotelian hierarchy of plot over character, anticipating novelists like Fielding but contrary to numerous efforts by others—most notably Richardson—to center critical discussion around character. Equally consequential is the contrast with the plots of other novels, which either begin with "an unexpected accident" that proves "the only surprizing part of the Story" (A6v), or excite more suspense than the denouement ultimately satisfies. Congreve's alternative— to make the ultimate design obvious and to give the reader the pleasure both of seeing the intricate way in which that design comes to fruition, despite a series of obstacles, and of determining "whether every Obstacle does not in the progress of the Story act as subservient to that purpose, which at first it seems to oppose" (A7v)—merely echoes Aristotelian precept and common theatrical practice. But the rhetoric of opposition to inferior predecessors and the concomitant claim to originality would become a staple for countless novelists who wanted—or needed—to show that they were new and different. Another kind of difference inheres in Congreve's evocative term for his intricate relation of part to whole "Unity of Contrivance" (A7v). Substituting the word *contrivance* for *action* admits the fundamental inferiority of the upstart genre, but also implies the need for a unique critical vocabulary for prose fiction. Moreover, the term *contrivance* consciously calls attention to fiction as artifice—an impression reinforced by Congreve's self-conscious narrator, who goes so far as to digress (like the infamous hack of *A Tale of a Tub* or the more illustrious Tristram Shandy) in order to wittily defend the practice of digression (12).[7]

Congreve's formal and affective preoccupations, proceeding from a frank admission of fictionality, distinguished him from many of his contemporaries and immediate successors in two important ways. First, no discussion of morality emerged.[8] While praising the delight produced by novels, Congreve scrupulously avoided the companion term in the Horatian dictum *instruction*. Attention to plot rather than character automatically excludes a number of questions about proper models for imitation and fit guides for conduct. Second, there is no attempt in the preface—

like the narrator's unconvincing efforts in the story proper—to invoke historicity or claim that the story is true. A few years before *Incognita* appeared, the more prolific Aphra Behn advanced just such an appeal in a series of dedications and opening statements.[9] Behn's rhetorical posture has prompted significant social and epistemological questions that have been explored in invaluable recent studies of the origins of the novel,[10] but her denial of conscious artistry diminishes her significance for an emerging poetics of fiction.

Instead of Behn, the unlikely figure of Mary Delariviere Manley—scandal chronicler, Tory propagandist, and "pornographer"—serves as mother for criticism of the novel. Or, more precisely, as a somewhat wicked stepmother. John L. Sutton, Jr. has recently shown that the highly praised preface to *The Secret History of Queen Zarah* (1705)[11] is a literal translation of a portion of an essay on prose fiction contained in a courtesy book published three years earlier, namely, abbé Morvan de Bellegarde's *Lettres curieuses de littérature et de morale*. Bellegarde's book is, in turn, a paraphrase of the second part of the sieur du Plaisir's *Sentimens sur les lettres et sur l'histoire* (1683), an attack on older romances and a defense of fiction in the manner of *La Princesse de Clèves*.[12] Hence, the disparity between the coherent statement of narrative aims and the loosely structured, sensational attack on the Duchess of Marlborough that follows it. But despite the significantly altered context of the plagiarized remarks, they remain surprisingly resonant in the theoretical discourse of Manley's successors. Whether Manley saw some connection between the commentary and her experimental narrative or simply wanted to cloak a scandal-chronicle in the mantle of critical respectability, she appropriated a document as prospective as it is retrospective.

Like Congreve's, Manley's preface begins with a distinction between romance and a newer form, here called the "secret history." According to Manley, romances have faded because they induce boredom: their length, variety of subjects, and large number of ill-drawn characters have "given a Distaste to Persons of Good Sense" and have "made Romances so much cry'd down, as we find 'em at present."[13] Similarly, "Historical Novels" have failed because "they mix particular Stories with the Principal *History*," with the result that "the Curiosity of the Reader is deceiv'd by this Deviation from the Subject, which retards the Pleasure he wou'd have in seeing the End of an Event" (A3r). Secret histories, on the other hand, "are much more agreeable to the Brisk and Impetuous Humour of the *English*, who have naturally no Taste for long-winded Performances, for they have no sooner begun a Book but they desire to see the end of it" (A2v).

John Richetti has read this advocacy of unity of design, along with subsequent endorsements of probability and plainness of diction, as representing "not so much literary criticism as market analysis,"[14] since a reading public of limited capacity required simplicity of character, plot, and language. With regard to Manley's motivations—one of only two changes from the original text was the substitution of "English" for "French"[15]—Richetti's pragmatism is warranted, but it does undervalue the potent claim of a psychological affinity in certain audiences to certain literary forms. Such a claim extended and refined, consciously or not, a broader argument put forth in favor of romances by Pierre Daniel Huet in his 1670 essay *Sur l'origine des Romans*. Bishop Huet wrote that the "Inclination to Fables, which is common to all Men, is not the result of Reason, Imitation, or Custom. 'Tis natural to them, and has its Seat in the very Frame and Disposition of the Soul."[16] For support, Huet turned to the unimpeachable authority of the *Poetics:*

> As in Plenty we refuse our Bread, and our ordinary Viands, for Ragouts, so our Minds, when acquainted with the Truth, forsake the Study and Speculation of it, to be entertained with its Image, which is Fiction. This Imitation, according to *Aristotle*, is often more agreeable than the Original itself; so that two oppositely different Paths, which are Ignorance and Learning, Rudeness and Politeness, do often conduct us to the same End; which is, an Application to Fictions, Fables, and Romances.[17]

What is true of fiction in general may also be true for particular genres. In a primitive yet powerful way, Manley, in her preface, attempted to discern, or create, a psychological justification for the form—an attempt pursued with equal vigor and greater sophistication in subsequent commentary.

In her preface, Manley also echoes Huet in her insistence upon a higher standard of probability for fiction than for history:

> He that writes a True History ought to place the Accidents as they Naturally happen, without endeavouring to sweeten them for to procure a greater Credit, because he is not obliged to answer for their Probability; but he that composes a History to his Fancy, gives his Heroes, what character he pleases, and places the Accidents as he sees fit without believing he shall be contradicted by other Historians, therefore he is obliged to Write nothing that is improbable. (A4r–v)[18]

The familiar shadow of the Aristotelian preference for probable impossibilities over possible improbabilities looms large. But the definition of "the Probability of Truth" as that "which consists in saying nothing but what may *Morally* be believed" (emphasis mine, A4r) problematizes the concept. As Lennard Davis has aptly observed, such a definition links verisimilitude to a concern for moral instruction voiced later in the preface, resulting in the paradox that "if one is to write a probable work, one needs to write about the world as it is, yet such a world is not necessarily morally probable."[19] Hints of a preference for explicit moralizing, however, seem contextually inappropriate, as I will show; in fact, the insistence on probability is more closely allied to a more amply elaborated view of character development.

"One of the Things an Author ought first of all to take Care of," Manley argues in her preface, "is to keep up the Characters of the Persons he introduces" (A4v). Doing so, while maintaining probability, requires attention to the psychological traits that discriminate characters; for, despite the presence of a ruling passion—or "predominant Quality"—the "Turn of the Mind, Motion of the Heart, Affection and Interests, alter the very Nature of the Passions, which are different in all Men" (A7v). Characters, according to Manley, must therefore differ from the paragons of romance—must be neither so consistently perfect nor so perfectly consistent as to forfeit the reader's empathy. Heroes, although they "ought to have some Extraordinary Qualities, . . . ought not to have 'em in an equal degree; 'tis impossible they should not have some Imperfections seeing they are Men, but their Imperfections ought not to destroy the Character that is attributed to them; if we describe them Brave, Liberal, and Generous, we ought not attribute to them Baseness or Cowardice, because that their Actions wou'd otherwise belie their Character, and the predominant Virtues of the Heroes" (a2v–a3r). Anticipating Fielding's notion of "Conservation of Character," such a view accepts fundamentally static characterization, while allowing for—even guaranteeing—some mixture of virtue and vice—or, at least, foibles. Perhaps flexibility, both technical and moral, attracted Manley to the preface in the first place, since such flexibility permits depictions of "imperfection" and even justifies the erotic "warm scenes" with which her text abounds: "It wou'd in no wise be probable that a Young Woman fondly beloved by a Man of great Merit, and for whom she had a reciprocal Tenderness, finding herself at all Times alone with him in Places which favour'd their Loves, cou'd always resist his Addresses . . ." (A5r). More significantly, the ultimate goal of probable characterization remains sympathetic identification, a narrative analogue for Aristotelian catharsis:

> . . . Fear, and Pity in Romance as well as in Tragedies are the Two Instruments which move the Passions; for we in some Manner put our selves in the Room of Those we see in Danger; the Part we take therein, and the fear of falling into the like Misfortunes, causes us to interest our selves more in their Adventures, because that those sort of Accidents may happen to all the World; and it touches so much the more, because they are the Common Effects of Nature. (A6r)

Here, once again, the discourse centers on the audience and on the affective consequences of narrative decisions.[20]

Such an engaged audience can judge as well as feel. Maintaining, therefore, that characters' "Actions ought to plead for them," rather than "Extravagant Expressions" or "Repeated Phrases," Manley recommends a relatively detached role for the author:

> Every Historian ought to be extremely uninterested; he ought neither to Praise nor Blame those he speaks of; he ought to be contented with Exposing the Actions, leaving an entire Liberty to the Reader to judge as he pleases, without taking any Care not to blame his Heroes, or make their Apology; he is no Judge of the Merit of his Heroes, his Business is to represent them in the same Form as they are, and describe their Sentiments, Manners and Conduct. (a3v)

The plea for disinterestedness is far from absolute, since the author is obliged to offer "Descriptions, which ought to be exact and marked by Traits which express clearly the Character of the Heroe, to the end that we may not be deceived . . ." (A6v). Nevertheless, Manley largely repudiates intrusive moralizing, disdaining "Moral Reflexions, Maxims, and Sentences," which are "more proper in Discourse for Instructions than in Historical Novels,[21] whose chief end is to please," and concluding that "if we find in them some Instructions, it proceeds rather from their Descriptions than their Precepts" (a4v). While Congreve, in his preface, ignored explicit instruction, Manley, in her preface, consciously dismisses it.

Given the vehemence of the dismissal, the advocacy of moralistic conclusions with which Manley ends her preface appears highly contradictory. A conclusion must do more than satisfy the reader's curiosity, for the chief End of History is to instruct and inspire into Men the Love of Virtue, and Abhorrence of Vice, by the Examples propos'd to them; therefore the Conclusions of a Story ought to have some Tract of Morality which may engage Virtue; those People who have a more refin'd Vertue are not always the most Happy; but yet their Misfortunes excite their Reader's Pity, and affects them; although Vice be not always punish'd, yet 'tis describ'd with Reasons which shew its Deformity, and makes it enough known to be worthy of nothing but Chastisements. (a6r–v)

While the first part of Manley's statement markedly opposes the tenor of her preceding remarks, the second part, which implicitly contradicts the first, can be integrated with the rest of the preface and Manley's emphasis therein on reception. To make proper judgments, the reader requires no evaluative statement imbued with the authority of the novelist's own voice. Instead, properly discriminated and detailed descriptions will lead the reader to pity the virtuous characters (and to admire virtue) while despising the vicious ones (and, hence, vice). Affective poetic justice of this sort—whereby the reader, instead of the author, rewards virtue and punishes vice—may have provided Manley with a convenient rationale for vividly portraying vice. But more broadly, this formulation represents the most thoughtful attempt by a commentator on fiction—until Richardson's postscript to *Clarissa*—to question and refine a convention so open to questioning and refinement.

Predictably, Manley's subsequent, original remarks fall far short of the comprehensiveness and acuity of her purloined preface. In the dedication of volume 2 of her most famous scandal chronicle *The New Atalantis* (1709), Manley quotes Dryden on the efficacy of satire, offering "the scourging of Vice and the Exhortation to Virtue"[22] as justification for her attacks on thinly disguised political and social figures. Ironically enough, because the statement reveals Manley's aims and techniques much more accurately than the preface to *Queen Zarah,* her statement contributes less to theoretical discourse about fiction. Equally representative, but more significant critically, is Manley's championing of explicit portrayal—and arousal—of sexuality. She introduces the largely autobiographical *Adventures of Rivella* (1714) with a dialogue in which one speaker acknowledges that the creator of *Atalantis*

has carried the Passion farther than could be readily conceived: Her [characters] . . . are such Representatives of Nature, that must warm the coldest reader; it raises high ideas of the Dignity of Human Kind, and informs us that we have in our Composition, wherewith to taste sublime and transporting Joys: After perusing her Inchanting Descriptions, which of us have not gone in search of Raptures which she every where tells us, as happy Mortals, we are capable of tasting.[23]

An eroticization of reading, to be sure, in a text that has been characterized as "a kind of literary pimp soliciting the reader on behalf of the author."[24] But also an amoral defense of art wherein pleasurable effects on the reader represent the ultimate standard of value.

The closest analogue in tone and substance to Manley's critical agenda, both original and borrowed, appears in Mary Davys's preface to her *Works* (1725). A year earlier, she introduced *The Reform'd Coquet* with a diffidence that became standard for women novelists, calling her work a product of idleness, asking that the reader pardon the improbability of her story because improbability was the norm for the genre, and relying on the servile—if useful—apology, "But whatever my Faults may be, my Design is good."[25] While the preface to the *Works* ends with similar pleading of necessity by "a Woman left to her own Endeavours for twenty-seven Years together,"[26] in general, a more assertive posture predominates; and Davys articulates a view of her fictions as conscious artifacts designed to produce specific effects. Her preface begins with a frank admission that novels—in this context, amatory novellas—have gone out of fashion and "that the Ladies (for whose Service they were chiefly designed) have been taken up with Amusements of more Use and Improvement," namely, "Histories and Travels: with which the Relation of probable feigned Stories can by no Means stand in Competition" (iii). Granting, perhaps naively, factual status—and the advantages that accompany it—to histories and travels, Davys, nevertheless, goes on to argue that novels still have some advantages of their own but have declined largely because most have become repetitive, "flat and insipid, or offensive to Modesty and Good-manners" (iii). Significantly, the language combines ethical and artistic concerns, condemning deficiencies in either area. As Davys proceeds to detail the ways in which her works will remedy both kinds of deficiencies and retrieve a respectable place for fiction, one may once again observe a stance of uniqueness and superiority to predecessors, a rhetorical move that became reflexive as the popularity of—and critical uneasiness about—the novel continued to grow.

Davys grounds her superiority in appeals to reader response, critical authority, and public morals. According to Davys, the principal advantage of fiction over history is "Invention, which gives us Room to order Accidents better than Fortune will be at Pains to do; so to work upon the Reader's Passions, sometimes to keep him in Suspense between Fear and Hope, and at last send him satisfied away" (iv). Invention thus defined allows Davys to "order" her "Adventures" so that they are simultaneously "wonderful and probable" (v). An unconsciously Aristotelian concern with affecting the reader's passions is combined with an insistence, ultimately derived from Aristotle as well, on a unified plot: "I have in every Novel propos'd one entire Scheme or Plot, and the other Adventures are only incident or collateral to it; which is the great Rule, prescribed by the Critics, not only in Tragedy, and other heroic Poems, but in Comedy too" (v). Whoever the critics may have been—and one suspects that Davys would have been hard pressed to name them—she shrewdly professes, like Congreve, to conform to standards developed for more respectable genres. Finally, she promises not only strict adherence to poetic justice, but also stories designed "to restore the Purity and Empire of Love, and correct the vile Abuses of it" (vi). By depicting regulation of the passions, she hopes to perform "an important Service for the Public" (vii). By claiming to do so, she performed an important service for her fiction, thus maximizing its appeal.

Improvement of virtue, public and private, animates the works and critical comments of Jane Barker, Elizabeth Rowe, and Penelope Aubin, whose sincere and often strident moralizing prompted John Richetti to dub them "pious polemicists."[27] The least polemical of the three, Jane Barker, readily admits that her *Exilius; or, The Banished Roman* (1715) is a "romance"[28] of the older style; moral utility is supposed to amply compensate for fictionality or falsehood, on the one hand, and a return to a discredited genre, on the other. This particular text, according to Barker, inculcates morality in the "Young Ladies" to whom it is addressed in three distinct ways: first, by portraying "Heroick Love," (A3v) the opposite of libertinism and the necessary ingredient for a successful marriage; second, by helping "to open the Understandings of young Readers, to distinguish between real Worth and superficial Appearances" (A2v); and third, by allowing young readers to "reap many Handfulls of good Morality, and likewise gather some Gleanings of History, and Acquaintance with the Ancient Poets" (A3r). Barker thus promoted her work as a source of practical wisdom, with the expectation that her female readers would derive intellectual and moral lessons from it and apply them in their own conduct.

Discussion of two formal matters, diction and characterization, is subsumed under Barker's larger didactic program—and, therefore, closely related to her specified audience. Barker hopes that readers will accept the language "as it is, it being the familiar Stile of the Age, neither so obsolete, nor so refin'd, as to render it obstruse . . ." (A4v). The conscious adoption of middling diction, perhaps at the expense of absolute artistic achievement, argues a decidedly reader-centered creative process. And a style most accessible to Barker's young, female readership was by definition most amenable to her moral ends. In a similar vein, Barker advocates the depiction of older characters as witty rather than morose, so that young readers will not be prejudiced against or inclined to disobey their elders (A4r). Both language and character, in Barker's view, could instruct in conscious, deliberate ways.

However high-minded her purpose, Barker relied on the kind of rhetorical maneuvers adopted by more profane writers to enhance the appeal of her work. *Exilius* is supposed to be written "After the Manner of Telemachus"; and Barker refers the reader to the defenses of instructional romances offered by Fénelon and by Dryden, establishing for herself a respectable literary and critical ancestry and implicitly opposing it to current, ephemeral fashion. Rather than demonstrate that *Exilius* belongs with such distinguished company—for it is "as nauseous to praise one's own Writing as to complement [*sic*] one's own Face" (A3v)—she ventures "to use the Words of some that have read it in Manuscript" (A3v), following Manley's practice in *Rivella* and anticipating Richardson's in *Pamela*. More subtly, she dismisses her detractors as extremists, alleging that books such as hers suffer because "the Grave dislike them for treating on so Gay a Subject, and the Sparks for confining the Subject to such strict Rules of Virtue and Honour" (A2r). "Grave" and "Sparks" commonly denoted not merely extremes, but *masculine* extremes. Presumably, "Young Ladies of Quality" would see themselves as more tolerant, and respond to the book enthusiastically. And they did: the notorious publisher Edmund Curll found in Barker's work a formula—short romances, advertised as a series of novels, and reminiscent of seventeenth-century fiction—so successful that his publications continued to follow it for twenty years after Barker's death.[29]

Similar popularity greeted the works of Elizabeth Rowe, a more insistent and transparent champion of virtue and morality. In a 1756 review in *The Literary Magazine*, Samuel Johnson commended Rowe for her "attempt to employ the ornaments of romance in the decoration of religion."[30] Rowe's own remarks in the preface to *Friendship in Death* (1728) promise what Johnson commended and nothing more. While countless intellectual proofs support the doctrine that occupies the center of her book—namely, the immortality of the soul—Rowe sees a need for persuasion directed at the emotions; she hopes that her production,

> addressed to the Affections, and Imagination, will not be thought improper, either as a Doctrine, or Amusement. AMUSEMENT, for which the World makes by far the largest Demand, and which generally speaking is nothing but an act of forgetting that Immortality, the firm Belief, and advantageous Contemplation of which, *this* Amusement would recommend.[31]

Amusement, the very enemy of Rowe's sound doctrine, is enlisted in that doctrine's support. Here didacticism does not offer a protective covering that makes the fiction palatable or safe; the fiction itself exists only to lure unsuspecting readers to a religious truth. For Rowe, no other rationale was necessary or satisfactory. Her only bow—a very slight one—to aesthetic standards occurs in the dedication, where she argues that the "greatest Infidel must own, that there is at least as much Probability in this Scheme, as in that of the FAIRY TALES, which however Visionary, are some of them Moral, and Entertaining" (A2v). Presumably, only the greatest infidel would invoke probability to attack probity.

While sharing the lofty aims of Rowe and Barker, Penelope Aubin was both more prolific and more suggestive in her comments about fiction. In her prefaces, she almost uniformly promises works designed to "encourage Virtue and expose Vice"[32]— and, more specifically, "to reclaim our giddy Youth; and since Reprehensions fail, try to win them to Virtue, by Methods where Delight and Instruction go together."[33] But malleable youths do not comprise the whole audience; Aubin seeks a broader public for her instructive diversions: "It is possible that we may be glad of new Books to amuse us, and pass away the Time that must hang heavy on our Hands, and Books of Devotion being tedious, and out of Fashion, Novels and Stories will be welcome."[34] Laudable moral goals allowed for the acknowledgment of fictionality that lay behind phrases like "Novels and Stories." Even when Aubin seems to be making a claim to historicity,[35] her tone can belie the seriousness and importance of the claim, as the preface to *The Count de Vinevil* (1721) illustrates: "As to the Truth of what this Narrative contains, since *Robinson Cruso* [*sic*] has been so well receiv'd, which is more improbable, I know no reasons why this should be thought a Fiction" (6). Cleverly, she then deflects the question of truth onto the audience's moral character, hoping that "the World is not grown so abandon'd to Vice" (6) as to disbelieve her account of exemplary goodness.[36]

A chronicler of virtue would be expected to emphasize character in her critical commentary, and Aubin more than satisfies the expectation. Most of her characters are designed to "excite" the reader into imitating their "heroic Actions."[37] Imitation necessitates probability; so Aubin credits herself, at the end of *The Noble Slaves* (1722), with having created "Heroes and Heroines" who "have done Nothing . . . but what is possible."[38] Here she anticipated not only Richardson but also Johnson's chief criterion for biography in *Rambler* No. 60—that it influence conduct by drawing a subject that remains plausibly imitable.[39] Characters to be shunned rather than imitated—the negative examples—posed greater problems for the avowed moralist.[40] Aubin's only discussion of this type of character and the reader's response to it invoked both historicity and a special kind of poetic justice in order to assuage anxieties and obviate criticism. Aware that some female readers might be displeased with the wicked Henrietta's story in *The Life and Adventures of the Lady Lucy* (1726), Aubin cites an obligation "to follow Truth" and then proceeds to warn any wicked woman who might read the story that no matter what happens in her lifetime, "like Henrietta, she will be unfortunate in the End, and her Death, like hers, will be accompanied with Terrors, and a bitter Repentance shall attend her to the Grave."[41] The virtuous, on the other hand, "shall be deliver'd, even by miraculous Means; or dying with comfort, be freed from the Miseries of this Life, and go on to taste eternal Repose."[42] Aubin confidently yokes poetic justice in literature to providential justice in life. While the latter is an even more obvious fiction than the former—many evil people die wealthy and serene, and many good people die poor and miserable—it is also a reassuring one to readers seeking rewards for a character's rectitude, or for their own.[43]

* * *

Reassurance of various kinds underlies the range of commentary from Eliza Haywood, infamously immortalized in Pope's *Dunciad* as the prize of a vulgar contest between the booksellers Osborne and Curll,[44] but more recently admired as a pioneering female novelist. Within a substantial and varied corpus—from scandal chronicles to short novels of passion to so-called domestic fiction superficially similar to Fielding's[45]—Haywood seldom offered detailed or original insights into her practice; but she did amalgamate formalist appeals to method and moralistic preoccupation with goals. The latter predominates in her many novels that contain no preface at all, but begin with a respectable moral tag to be applied to the story that follows. And even the presence of an introductory discourse need not signal more substantive critical engagement: Haywood, in fact, could use a preface to deny its own importance. She opens *The Injur'd Husband; or, The Mistaken Resentment* (1723), with a self-conscious disclaimer: "Troubling the Reader with any thing of this kind, is generally so little to the Purpose, that I have often thought the Authors made use of such Introductions more to swell the Bulk of their Book, than any other Reason."[46] The expression of disdain for prefaces may seem similar to Congreve's, but it lacks Congreve's bantering tone and clever reversal. Instead, Haywood demurely follows it with an acknowledgment of her own limitations: "And how sensible soever I am of the many Faults the following Sheets are full of, I shou'd rather commit myself and them to the Good-nature of the World, than add to them by an impertinent Apology."[47] The diffidence may be emblematic of what Mary Anne Schofield has called Haywood's "double writing"—a superficial adherence to conventional forms that disguises an otherwise subversive message.[48] However intriguing the technique may be in the fiction, it is frustrating in the commentary—primarily for what it leaves unsaid.

What Haywood did say most commonly involved moral utility, literal truth, or a combination of the two. As George Whicher has noted, she usually offered readers "a warning or a hortatory example of what to avoid."[49] In the preface to *The Fair Hebrew* (1729), the author both acknowledges a reliable eyewitness as her source and avers that if "among all who shall read the following Sheets, any one Person may reap so much Advantage as to avoid the Misfortunes the SUBJECT of them fell into by his Inadvertancy, and giving a Loose to Passion; the little Pains I have been at, will be infinitely recompensed."[50] Richetti has aptly contrasted Haywood's use of ruined innocence as a warning to Aubin's use of preserved innocence as an example.[51] The negative example could appeal to the broader audience, not only by satisfying moralistic rigor but also by piquing prurient curiosity. For less obvious reasons, so could a so-called true story. Haywood did not merely claim that many of her narratives were based on fact; she actually contrasted them with fictions that were disguised as truth, as in the preface to *The Mercenary Lover:* "Of many Stories, merely the Effect of a good Invention, having been publish'd as real Facts, I think it proper to inform my Reader, that the following Pages are fill'd with a sad, but true Account."[52] Even greater vehemence, but similar prevarication, characterizes the preface to *The Fortunate Foundlings* (1744): "The many Fictions which have been lately imposed upon the World, under the specious Titles of Secret Histories, Memoirs, etc. etc. have given but too much room to question the Veracity of every Thing that has a least Tendency that way."[53] By that time, the distinction must have seemed specious; but the sanction of factuality obviously still had resonance, even if many readers were not deluded at all.[54] Haywood's posture may have increased her readership, but dwelling dishonestly on fact foreclosed the opportunity to examine fiction as artifact.

Haywood could—and did—go beyond the mask of factuality, however. In the letter to the Earl of Suffolk and Binden at the beginning of *Lasselia; or, The Self-Abandon'd* (1723), she acknowledges her authorship and offers the most revealing—if not completely candid—statement of her ends and means. While characteristically deeming the work a "Trifle," she enters into some detail to explain and justify her erotic scenes:

> My Design, in writing the little NOVEL (as well as those I have formerly publish'd) being only to remind the unthinking Part of the World, how dangerous it is to give way to Passion, will, I hope, excuse the too great Warmth, which may perhaps, appear in some particular Pages; for without the EXPRESSION being invigorated in some measure proportionate to the SUBJECT, 'twould be impossible for a Reader to be sensible how far it touches him, or how probable it is that he is falling into those Inadvertancies which the Examples I relate would caution him to avoid.[55]

However apologetic or titilating, the argument transcends Haywood's usual level of discourse by suggesting a proportionate relationship between form and content—between descriptive language and what is described—advocating, in this case, a kind of decorous indecorum. The goal: involving the reader vicariously in that which is "dangerous" in order to enhance the force of the ultimate warning against it. Haywood, however, avoided addressing the obvious difficulty with her affective approach—the possibility that the intensity of the description may actually subvert the ostensible moral. The avoidance may well have been deliberate, for the immediate context reveals that reversing a dubious reputation was uppermost in Haywood's mind. In the letter, she admits that she is trying to "clear" herself, contends that she always desired more to instruct than to please, and adroitly shifts the blame for whatever deleterious consequences her works may have had, stating, "Where I have had the Misfortune to fail, [I] must impute it either to the Obstinacy of those I wou'd persuade, or to my own Deficiency in that very Thing which they are pleased to say I too much abound in—a true Description of Nature" (vii–viii). Limiting the alternatives both places the onus of morality on the reader and begs the question of whether a true description of nature is always desirable. The rhetoric of the letter thus encourages the kind of dual pleasure that Richetti has considered as characteristic of Haywood's fiction, whereby readers gain both "the erotic sensations of the scene and the righteous superiority of being on the side of virtue."[56] Reading the letter would induce greater intellectual pleasure were its animadversions on the production and reception of fiction the norm rather than the exception for Haywood.

* * *

Defoe takes the reader much further—but in several different directions and to an uncertain destination. His prefatorial commentary has been variously characterized (a) as an attempt to assuage Puritan anxieties—his readers' and his own—about fiction,[57] (b) as a fairly accurate reflection of the moral and aesthetic views articulated in his journalistic writing,[58] and (c) as a disclaimer of authorial responsibility that invites the reader to create categories for—and confer meaning upon—the texts.[59] One critic has seen a movement toward an increased acknowledgment that the texts are fictional and an increased distinction between hero and author;[60] another has completely rejected synthetic approaches that impose a theory a posteriori upon a novelist genuinely uncertain about his goals and techniques.[61] I share this skepticism because I read Defoe in the context of his contemporaries—as a novelist raising similar questions, invoking similar standards, and exploiting similar rhetoric. Just as his novels extended and complicated conventional narrative practice, his critical comments—and the language in which he expressed them—incorporated conventional theories in a complex and ultimately enigmatic way.

Defoe's first preface, written in the persona of the so-called editor of *Robinson Crusoe* (1719), would seem the exception in its brevity and simplicity. The paucity of commentary derives more than anything else from timing: a first novel necessarily precludes

having to answer prior criticism. The danger, however, as elsewhere with Defoe, lies in underreading. For here, in pristine form,
are all of Defoe's justifications for fiction—which recur in altered
guises, proportions, and degrees of emphasis and specificity—as
well as a glimpse at the rhetorical acuity increasingly evident in
subsequent prefaces. The editor recommends the narrative on
several grounds: he believes that it describes the "Wonders" of a
life of astonishing "Variety," that it "is told with Modesty, with
Seriousness, and with a religious Application of Events to the
Uses to which wise Men always apply them (viz.) to the Instruction
of Others by this Example," and that it is "a just History of Fact"
without "any Appearance of Fiction in it."[62] An exotic, moral, and
true story told in modest language would presumably appeal to
a variety of readers in a variety of ways. Defoe's keen appreciation
of diversity of response underlies the editor's declaration that even
though the story is true, "the Improvement of it, as well to the
Diversion, as to the Instruction of the Reader, will be the same"
(1), as if it were imaginary. In a move typical of Defoe, a fiction—
disguised as a "just History of Fact"—is conceded the entertaining
qualities associated with and admired by readers of fiction. And
to complicate matters further, the editor's language substitutes a
blend of confidence and diffidence for certitude. He "thinks" that
this story he "believes" to be true will both divert and instruct—
just as he "thinks" the story eminently worth publication for the
"great Service" it does the "World" (1). Even what has been called
"a pure assertion of veracity"[63] has its nuances and subtleties—
and, one might add, sophistries.

The hedging increased in the preface to *The Farther Adventures
of Robinson Crusoe*, as Defoe responded to the numerous criticisms
engendered by his first novel and its success. Rather than directly
refute the attacks on the truthfulness of his first novel, he begins
by having the impersonal editorial persona simply dismiss the
attacks out of hand: "All the endeavours of envious people to
reproach it with being a romance, to search it for errors in geography, inconsistency in the relation, and contradictions in the fact,
have proved abortive, and as impotent as malicious."[64] Absolute
factuality crumbles in the very next paragraph, however, as the
standards of judgment are transformed: "The just application of
every incident, the religious and useful inferences drawn from
every part . . . must legitimate all the part that may be called
invention or parable in the story" (vii). Veracity and moral utility—
absolute and allied in the earlier preface—are qualified and distinguished in the second preface, with the latter justifying devia-

tions from the former. Many of Defoe's contemporaries made a similar move—but none did so in the space of a paragraph. Could Defoe have been unaware of how suspect the abrupt shift would seem? Perhaps the shift reflects what has been judged a genuine ambivalence about fiction writing on Defoe's part and an inability to find suitable language for relating fiction to moral and psychological truth.[65] It was easier to define negatively—to say that *Crusoe* was not a romance—but troubling to deny invention; therefore, the problematic term *parable* entered under the powerful sanction of morality. While the move may reveal a divided artist, the rhetorician has not disappeared. Lambasting abridgers for depriving readers of Crusoe's moral reflections, the editor complains that "they leave the work naked of its brightest ornaments; and if they would at the same time pretend that the author has supplied the story out of his invention, they take from it the improvement which alone recommends that invention to wise and good men" (viii). The curious logic reinforces the justification of invention but, as one critic has noted, seems to deny invention at the same time.[66] Moreover, it transfers the focus to the critic, to the doubter of authenticity, and to the inconsistent consequences of the doubts.

Adversaries are not the only readers Defoe explicitly mentions. In listing the virtues of the sequel, the editor again promises delight and instruction—but goes further toward uncoupling the two:

> The second part, if the Editor's opinion may pass, is (contrary to the usage of second parts) every way as entertaining as the first, contains as strange and surprising incidents, and as great a variety of them; nor is the application less serious and suitable, and doubtless will, to the sober as well as ingenious reader, be every way as profitable and diverting. (vii)

A "sober" reader seeks a "profitable" text, an "ingenious" reader a diverting one; this text was supposed to satisfy two vastly different sets of readerly expectations. Frank admission of the desire for broad appeal recurred a year later, when Defoe claimed to have designed the seriocomic introduction to *The Life of Duncan Campbell* "with the hopes of engaging many curious people of all sorts to be my readers, even from the airy nice peruser of novels and romances, neatly bound and finely gilt, to the grave philosopher, that is daily thumbing over the musty and tattered pieces of more solid antiquity."[67] The more specific language raises a question implicit in the earlier distinction: Will readers looking for diversion be instructed and vice versa? Left unanswered in the *Life of Campbell,* the question was central to several of Defoe's subsequent references to types of readers and ways of reading.

Defoe's preface as a whole provided some of the ammunition for a famous hostile reader, Charles Gildon, whose *Life of Mr. D— De F—*has been maligned with the same vehemence with which he berated *Crusoe.* It deserves derision for petty caviling and ad hominem attacks,[68] but submerged in the vitriol are some trenchant criticisms to which Defoe was sensitive. For the modern reader, Gildon suffers most for misplaced emphasis. His primary targets are the faulty view of Church and State, the impiety of Crusoe's reflections, and, most significantly, "making the Truths of the Bible of a piece with the fictitious Story of *Robinson Crusoe.*"[69] In fact, he claims that he would not have bothered to write if Defoe's faults "had extended no further than the frequent Solecisms, Looseness and Incorrectness of Stile, Improbabilities, and sometimes Impossibilities" (1). Yet, the apparently tangential catalogue of what Gildon calls "Absurdities"—such as Friday's learning a good deal of English in three weeks and then no more for twelve years (ix); Xury's speaking broken English to Crusoe, the first Englishman he has ever met (13); and Crusoe's stripping to swim to the shipwreck and, later, filling his "pockets" with biscuits (15)— remains a far more telling criticism. Gildon's repeated return to this line of attack, despite his professed reluctance, shows that he intuitively recognized its force, if not all of its implications. Although he kept citing inconsistencies in order to prove *Crusoe* fictitious,[70] Gildon unconsciously prompted more abiding questions of probability and verisimilitude, which Defoe's guise as editor kept him from answering directly.

Gildon's two most powerful criticisms can be found in the postscript to the pamphlet, where he disparaged Defoe's ripostes to unnamed detractors in the preface to *The Farther Adventures.* In his view, Defoe's claim to variety is specious, since it relies on numerous "reflections" of dubious value:

> For first, as to the Variety of the Subject, it will be a hard matter to make that good, since it's spread out into at least five and twenty Sheets, clog'd with moral Reflections, as you are pleas'd to call them, every where insipid and aukward [*sic*], and in many Places in no manner of Relation to the Occasion on which they are deliver'd, besides being much larger than necessary, and frequently impious and prophane [*sic*]; and always canting are the Reflections which you are pleas'd to call religious and useful, and *the brightest Ornaments of your*

Book, tho' in reality they were put in by you to swell the Bulk of your
Treatise up to a five Shilling Book. (30)

As one might expect, Gildon later defends the practice of abridg-
ment, particularly in the case of the vestigial reflections in both
volumes of *Crusoe,* contending that "Use and Instruction should
naturally and plainly arise from the Fable itself, in an evident and
useful Moral, either expressed or understood" (35). Based both
on a misreading of Defoe's usage of the term *variety*—which refers
primarily to *action*—and on an uncritical dismissal of all of
Crusoe's reflections, Gildon's argument nonetheless provokes consideration of unity, always related uneasily to variety and conspicuously ignored by Defoe. The secondary aesthetic point has greater
significance than the primary moral one, as it does when, in what
have become the most quoted lines in his pamphlet, Gildon casti-
gates Defoe for imprecise, ambiguous language: "What you mean
by *Legitimating, Invention,* and *Parable,* I know not, unless you
would have us think, that the Manner of your telling a Lie will
make it the Truth" (34). Even a reader entirely sympathetic to
Defoe's difficulties in classifying his art—and confident that he
did think his narrative method could make a lie the truth[71]—
cannot deny the rhetorical advantages of the suggestive, hazy terminology that still haunts Defoe's audience.

   Gildon actually contributed to the haziness with a brief and facetious remark that Defoe adapted and made the cornerstone of his
next apologia in the preface to the *Serious Reflections of Robinson
Crusoe.*[72] In the imaginary "Dialogue between Defoe, Crusoe, and
Friday," which serves as a preface to the longer remarks, Gildon's
"Defoe" asserts that the character of Crusoe is "allegorical," re-
marking, "I have been all my Life that Rambling, Inconsistent
Creature, which I have made thee" (x). The *Serious Reflections*
opens not with a distant editor's qualified defense, but with "Robinson Crusoe's Preface," in which the "real" Crusoe, armed with
the authority of personal testimony, answers doubters like Gildon
with language like Gildon's: "I, Robinson Crusoe, being at this
time in perfect and sound mind and memory, thanks be to God
therefor, do hereby declare their objection is an invention scandal-
ous in design, and false in fact; and do affirm that the story,
though allegorical, is historical."[73] Having turned the word *invention* back on his accusers, Crusoe goes on to clarify—or obscure—
the meaning of *allegorical* by identifying a "man alive, and well
known too, the actions of whose life are the just subject of these
volumes, and to whom all or most part of the story directly al-

ludes; this may be depended upon for truth, and to this I set my name" (x). Lennard Davis has traced in detail the maneuvers by which Defoe attempted to conflate the irreconcilable genres of true history and allegory.[74] In brief, confusion is piled on confusion as, on the one hand, Crusoe lists a number of "real facts" in his story, "whatever borrowed lights they may be represented by" (x), and, on the other, he suggests that life on the island "is a just allusion" to "a state of forced confinement," since it "is as reasonable to represent one kind of imprisonment by another, as it is to represent anything that really exists by that which exists not" (xii). A series of reversals like this, in which the speaking voice seems to vacillate between Crusoe's and that of the so-called real person whose story Crusoe's is supposed to represent, hopelessly confounds any valid distinction between tenor and vehicle.

A logical failure, Defoe's muddle is, nonetheless, a rhetorical success, establishing several bases of authority and appeal. As Maximillian Novak has observed, the diction—replete with words like *real, true, fact,* and *history*—reinforces an impression of literal truth, wherever else Defoe's reasoning leads.[75] Crusoe's long list of "real facts"—ultimately unnecessary if, as he insists, all of his adventures are true—serves the same purpose, contributing the persuasive power of cumulative detail. Different but equally potent traditions lay beneath the references to allegory. The word itself evokes sacred writing; and Crusoe compares his story to an earlier masterpiece, *Don Quixote,* "which, . . . to one that knows the meaning of it, was an emblematic history" (x) of a real Spanish nobleman. Turning a critic's sneer about Crusoe's quixotism into a compliment, Defoe grounds his text in a distinguished narrative line. Yet another advantage of the allegorical argument proceeded from the fact that the identity of the author of *Robinson Crusoe* and its sequels was an open secret: readers may have been tempted to read the novels as fictional autobiographies of Defoe. Whether or not Defoe intended this final possibility, it adds ironic undertones to Crusoe's explanation of the affective power of allegory:

> Had the common way of writing a man's private history been taken, and I had given you the conduct of a life of a man you knew, and whose misfortunes and infirmities perhaps you had sometimes unjustly triumphed over, all I could have said would have yielded no diversion, and perhaps scarce have obtained a reading, or at best no attention; the teacher, like a greater, having no honour in his own country. Facts that are formed to touch the mind must be done a great way off, and by somebody never heard of. (xiii)

For a reader identifying Defoe as author and subject, the passage invites disagreement, amusement, or scorn.

Commonly ignored because of the suggestive, puzzling, and retrospective discussion of *Crusoe* as history and allegory is what Defoe says about the text that follows. In the opening paragraph, Defoe champions intentionalism more emphatically than he had in his previous prefaces:

> As the design of everything is said to be first in the intention, and last in the execution, so I come now to acknowledge to my reader that the present work is not merely the product of the two first volumes, but the two first volumes may rather be called the product of this. The fable is always made for the moral, not the moral for the fable. (ix)

A conventional enough argument, but one extremely useful to Defoe in this context, allowing him to defend—indeed, exalt—a sequel limited to the kind of reflections that infuriated Gildon and merely bored others. Once again, one must wonder to what extent the critic was subsumed by the propagandist—to what extent text and genre determined and complicated prefatorial commentary.

Generic concerns certainly figured prominently in the preface to the first of Defoe's "historical"[76] novels, *Memoirs of a Cavalier* (1720). Conscious of a greater need for empirical documentation in pseudohistorical writing, Defoe uncharacteristically adopts the well-worn ruse of the newly discovered manuscript—this one being "found by great Accident, among other valuable Papers in the Closet of an eminent publick Minister."[77] Such a move eliminates the issue of factual truth by moving it elsewhere to an untraceable—and, therefore, unimpeachable—authority. Thus freed from the question that prompted so many of his logical and verbal gymnastics, Defoe could concentrate instead on the relationship between memoirs and history. By reversing the customary elevation of history over memoirs and novels,[78] the discussion anticipated many of the arguments advanced on behalf of the hybrid genre in the latter half of the century. The *Memoirs*, boasts the editor, not only meet standards of historical accuracy—with "almost all the Facts, especially those of Moment, . . . confirmed for their general Part by the Writers of those Times" (4)—but also clarify this record, offering "a confutation of many Errors in all the Writers upon the Subject of our Wars in *England*" (3). More significantly, this account transcends traditional histories through the telling details of personal testimony:

> The Actions here mentioned have a sufficient Sanction from all the histories of the Times to which they relate, with this Addition, that the admirable Manner of relating them, and the wonderful Variety of Incidents, with which they are beautified in the Course of a private Gentleman's Story, add such Delight in the reading . . . as well to the Accounts themselves, as to the Person who was the Actor; and no Story, we believe, extant in the World, ever came abroad with such Advantages" (1).

The characteristic hyperbole was possible only because Defoe continued to deny authorship, thus avoiding the more difficult issue of the relative value of invented historical memoirs.

With another historical novel, *Colonel Jack,* Defoe ignored generic questions altogether and once again refined the balance of factual truth and moral utility. It is not "of the least Moment," concludes the editor, "to enquire whether the Colonel hath told his own Story true or not; If he has made it a *History* or a *Parable,* it will be equally useful, and capable of doing Good."[79] A more extreme disregard of authenticity than Defoe had previously ventured to project is here predicated upon a more detailed consideration of precisely how a text can be useful and do good. Hence, Defoe's first reference to poetic justice—to "Virtue . . . applauded, honoured, encouraged, rewarded" and to "Vice . . . attended with Misery" (2), as well as the granting of greater weight to instruction than to delight, as in the editor's opinion that "the pleasant and delightful Part speaks for it self; the useful and instructive Part is so large, and capable of so many improvements, that it would imploy a Book, large as it self, to make Improvements suitable to the vast Variety of the Subject" (1). While such a sequel—a *Serious Reflections of Colonel Jack,* for which Defoe appears to have been clearing ground—never emerged, the preface itself offers one major improvement, with the editor providing "just and copious Observations, on the Blessing, and Advantages of a sober and well govern'd Education" (1), for which the title character serves as a negative example. Defoe may well have been sincere in his announced purpose,[80] but the extended moral observations seem an obligatory compensation for the increased flexibility about truth. When one of the principal justifications was diminished, the other was—and, perhaps, had to be—expanded.

Compensatory rhetoric did not suffice for *Moll Flanders* and *Roxana,* where the subject matter, particularly vulnerable to barbs from moralists, necessitated the most extensive prefatorial vindication—a vindication characteristically fraught with complexity and ambiguity. Literal truth resurfaces in a qualified form, through the clever use of contrast. The truth of *Moll Flanders* must ultimately be determined by its audience, given the contemporary literary milieu:

> The World is so taken up of late with Novels and Romances, that it will be hard for a private History to be taken for Genuine, where the Names and other Circumstances of the Persons are concealed, and on this Account we must be content to leave the Reader to pass his own Opinion upon the ensuing Sheets, and take it just as he pleases.[81]

According to Defoe, *Roxana* "differs from most of the Modern Performances of this Kind . . . in this Great and Essential Article, *Namely,* That the Foundation of This is laid in Truth of *Fact,* and so the Work is not a Story, but a History," in which "it was necessary to conceal Names and Persons" to avoid scandal.[82] Whether implied or stated, the claim to truth rests on a distinction between the text in question and texts with which it might naturally be identified—thus allowing Defoe to assert uniqueness and superiority, while, at the same time, coyly suggesting a certain affinity with disreputable genres. Readers who wanted scandal, readers who wanted "Truth," and readers who wanted both could all be attracted by the language.[83]

Similar benefits attended the increased distance Defoe establishes between author and text in parallel discussions of purified language. Moll Flanders's story "is put into new Words, and the Stile of the famous Lady we here speak of is a little alter'd" (1) in order to put the story "in a Dress fit to be seen, and to make it speak Language fit to be read" (1); but the author of the preface, who does not even identify himself as an editor, never directly assumes credit for the alteration but refers to it throughout with passive constructions. Deploying the same clothing metaphor in *Roxana,* the similarly unidentified preface writer speaks of a "Relator" or "Writer," distinct from himself, who must bear the blame—in case of any failure in the "Instruction"—for "dressing up the Story in worse Cloaths than the *Lady,* whose Words he speaks, prepar'd it for the World" (1). The gaps between writer, reviser, and "introducer" undoubtedly complicated the issue of authenticity, as Defoe may well have intended.[84] The gaps also allowed for a prefatorial commentator whose praise could appear more disinterested and objective than even an editor's would be. Once the position and persona were established, logic need not persist: in the final paragraph of the preface to *Moll Flanders,* Defoe explains that "pleasant things" that happened to Moll "in her last Scene" in America—presumably described by the "third Hand" who wrote her husband's story—are omitted in the text because "they are not told with the same Elegancy as those accounted for by herself" (5). Moll's unprintable language has suddenly become elegant.

Detachment adds legitimacy not only to praise but also to defense. And the defense of both novels against charges of indecency relied upon the subordination of fable to moral. While in the preface to *Moll Flanders* Defoe offers a number of often questionable justifications—from the patently false assertion, borrowed from defenders of the stage, that "there is not a wicked Action in any Part of it, but is first or last rendered Unhappy and Unfortunate" (3), to the characterization of criminal adventures as "so many warnings to honest People to beware" (4) of them— he has the principal moral argument center on Moll's penitence and its effects:

> As the best Use is made of even the worst Story, the Moral 'tis hoped will keep the Reader serious, even where the Story might incline him to be otherwise: To give the History of a wicked Life repented of, necessarily requires that the wicked Part should be made as wicked, as the real History of it will bear, to illustrate and give a Beauty to the penitent Part, which is certainly the best and brightest, if related with equal Spirit and Life. (2)[85]

And it is so related, according to the preface, which betrays Defoe's pride through references to the "agreeable Turn" given incidents "in the relating, that naturally instructs the Reader, either one way, or other" (2). Similar emphasis is placed on the remorseful conscience of Roxana at the end of her story: "The Noble Inferences that are drawn from this one Part, are worth all the rest of the Story; and abundantly justifie (as they are the profess'd Design of) the Publication" (2). Like Haywood's defense of her warm scenes, and Defoe's own continual use of contrast, these comments explicitly promise a sound moral, while implicitly highlighting the "wickedness" in the story, which in the case of *Moll*, is admittedly given "lively Description" (3). A reader could enjoy the latter under the cover of the former.

The best way of answering moralistic criticisms, however, is to place the interpretive burden squarely on the reader—and Defoe did precisely that. A reception-oriented aesthetic dominates the preface to *Moll Flanders*, with multiple references to types of readers and ways of reading. As I have already shown, Defoe, in the preface, has artfully left the question of literal truth up to the reader. He goes on to acknowledge the difficulty of purifying language thoroughly "so as not to give room, especially for vitious Readers" (1) to form corrupt impressions, only to commend the "purifier" for editing and rephrasing, so that "what is left 'tis hop'd will not offend the chastest Reader, or the modestest Hearer" (2). Setting the two extremes prepares Defoe for answering the criticism that the penitent part is not related "with equal spirit and life" as the criminal part: "If there is any Truth in that Suggestion, I must be allow'd to say, 'tis because there is not the same taste and relish in the Reading, and indeed it is too true that the difference lyes not in the real worth of the Subject so much as in the Gust and Palate of the Reader" (2).[86] And this novel "is chiefly recommended to those who know how to Read it" (2). As the still vehement disputes about the novel testify, knowing how is difficult—and Defoe's preface adds more to the difficulty than to the knowledge. Although the affective argument has some merit, the author who never claimed responsibility for his fiction used it primarily to avoid responsibility—for any number of reasons—for the moral ambiguity that continues to confound and attract readers. With equally problematic rectitude, the preface writer defends *Roxana*—a work in which "'tis hop'd you will find nothing to prompt a vicious Mind, but every-where much to discourage and expose it" (2), against accusations that it might encourage criminal activity:

> Scenes of Crime can scarce be represented in such a Manner, but some may make a Criminal Use of them; but when Vice is painted in its Low-priz'd Colours, 'tis not to make People in love with it, but to expose it; and if the Reader makes a wrong Use of the Figures, the Wickedness is his own. (2)

For the seeker of consistency, the "Wickedness" is Defoe's. Rationales or criteria for fiction that constantly change—or even disappear—signal, on one level, a supreme opportunist, who alters the rules to fit each performance and, then, judges it a success. But on a deeper level, Defoe's inconsistency represents the inevitable consequences of combining, refining, and expanding the insights of his contemporaries, whose narrower agendas yielded simpler, more unified criticism. Defoe necessarily tangled himself in contradictions—which, in turn, foreground the combination of pressures on a serious and talented practitioner of a new and unstable genre. The only way to begin to reconcile these pressures—treating the text as a conscious artifact—was foreclosed by Defoe's refusal to admit authorship—his continual, if sometimes wavering, insistence on the "truth" of his narratives. Thus, it would fall to the next generation of novelists and critics to take that next step and to combine Defoe's intriguing depth with greater range.

2

Cracking Facades of Authority:
Richardson, Fielding, and Johnson

The creators of Clarissa Harlowe, Tom Jones, and Rasselas—who also produced the most influential early commentary on the novel—could number their respective images as commentators among their most successful fictional characters. With varying degrees of self-consciousness, each fashioned a compelling persona, to which contemporaries and successors, novelists and critics, allies and adversaries could appeal to find support for their own beliefs and practices: Richardson, the staunch moralist, who subordinated artistic rules and ends to higher authority; Fielding, the witty and learned ironist—jocular, yet also serious in his efforts to anatomize the craft of fiction; Johnson, the blunt but informed conservative, for whom the genre held more dangers than advantages. Beneath the usually self-assured and sometimes self-righteous critical stances, however, lay multiple goals, often incompatible—and multiple voices, often irreconcilable. With Richardson, both the variety of contexts for his discourse and the competing moral and aesthetic demands that he tried to satisfy fostered inevitable contradictions. Fielding's suavity could not close the gaps opened largely by his problematic foregrounding of narrative theory within his texts. And Johnson remained trapped between radical critical honesty and constricting self-discipline. Entertainment and instruction, candor and caution, self-assertion and self-effacement collided to reveal the enormous difficulties in defining, defending, and controlling response to a new species of writing.

In Richardson's voluminous commentary on his three novels—he seldom discussed fiction by others in any detail—at least three different personae emerge. The most transparent—but also the most maddening—is Richardson the editor. According to the novelist himself, the pose enables him to comment assertively by providing a sort of protective coloration: he confides to Aaron Hill that he "struck a bold note" in the preface to *Pamela* because he had "the umbrage of the editor's character" to screen himself behind.[1] He never abandoned the "umbrage," which provided several distinct rhetorical advantages. It allowed him to praise *Pamela* extravagantly and with impunity, since "an *Editor* may reasonably be supposed to judge with an Impartiality which is rarely to be met with in an *Author* towards his own Works."[2] An apparently disinterested observer could also readily include commendatory letters—a practice that annoyed Fielding enough to create the devastating parodies in *Shamela*. Printing these letters served a more important end, however, than the mere self-praise that Fielding attacked. In the introduction to the second and third editions of *Pamela*, the so-called editor prefaces the letters with the humble admission that difficulties had "arisen from the different Opinions of Gentlemen, some of whom applauded the very Things that others found Fault with," thus compelling him "to submit the Whole to the Judgment of a Gentleman of the most distinguish'd Taste and Abilities."[3] In this kangaroo court of Richardson's own making, the judge, who remains anonymous, doubles as advocate, answering every objection to the text, while keeping the author above the fray. And few could be more suited to the role than Aaron Hill, Richardson's most fulsome early admirer. The troubling combination of diffidence and deviousness exhibited here would recur in other contexts.

By the time of the opening volumes of *Clarissa*, Richardson had learned that he need not rely on a partial arbiter—that disagreement alone provided sanction, or cover, for his practices. Uneasy about length—an abiding concern for Richardson—the conscientious editor claims to have sought the opinions of others, but with "no two being of the same mind as to the parts which could be omitted, it was resolved to present to the world the two first volumes by way of specimen."[4] Contradictory responses provided a rationale for leaving well enough alone. Perhaps the Richardson who solicited countless suggestions for his novels—but followed hardly any of them—justified the curious activity through similar logic. A letter to Lady Bradshaigh—source of much requested and unheeded advice—reveals his awareness of just how useful divided response could be: "Some Imperfection I intend in my best Characters, and must leave it to my Sovereign Judges the Readers, to agree as well as they can, which to blame, which to acquit. Thank Heaven, I find not often two of the same Mind, in relation to the more delicate Circumstances."[5] Richardson's habitual insistence on agreement with his own, "correct" reading of his novels gives way to support of indeterminacy when indeterminacy helps him avoid confronting a problematic issue. Then—and only then—do readers replace Richardson himself as "Sovereign Judges."

A less self-serving kind of authorial manipulation underlies Richardson's vindication of the editorial persona in a famous letter to William Warburton, whose preface to volume 3 of *Clarissa*—which Richardson had eagerly sought but later, characteristically, omitted—referred conspicuously to the novel as a fiction produced by a conscious artist:

> Will you, good Sir, allow me to mention, that I could wish that the *Air* of Genuineness had been kept up, tho' I want not the letters to be *thought* genuine; only so far kept up, I mean, as that they should not prefatically be owned *not* to be genuine: and this for fear of weakening their influence where any of them are aimed to be exemplary; as well as to avoid hurting that kind of Historical Faith which Fiction itself is generally read with, tho' we know it to be Fiction.[6]

Aptly characterized both as a recognition of the moral and artistic value of verisimilitude and as testimony to ambivalent attitudes toward fact and fiction shared by Richardson and his readers,[7] the statement also reveals a debt to dramatic theory by an author eager to appropriate dramatic practice for his fiction. The "Historical Faith" to which he refers derives from the principal of dramatic illusion. Readers gain as much by provisionally believing that the letters are genuine as audiences do by imagining themselves in Caesar's Rome or Macbeth's Scotland. Although Richardson did not draw the explicit connection—for reasons having to do, as I will show, with originality—a rare criticism of Richardson by Samuel Johnson implies one. The critic who predicated his attack of the unities of time and place in the "Preface to *Shakespeare*" on a rejection of dramatic illusion scorns Richardson's pretense of being the editor of *Sir Charles Grandison:* "What is modesty if it departs from truth? Of what use is the disguise by which nothing is concealed?"[8]

Ripe for Fielding's parody and Johnson's misgivings, the editorial pose threatened Richardson's desired univocal authority, causing him to rewrite the role and add another. As influential deconstructionist readings of *Clarissa* by William Warner and Terry Castle have pointed out, Richardson's epistolary method dispersed interpretive authority, leaving the ultimate assessment of the multiple points of view to the reader; but Richardson demanded a single, authorized reading. An editor constrained from claiming authorship occupies a weak position from which to promulgate an infallible interpretation. Yet after the "misguided" reception of the first edition of the novel, Richardson attempted to have the editor perform precisely this role by adding in the editor's name an elaborate textual apparatus of footnotes, letter summaries, and other mechanisms designed to blacken Lovelace's character and to elevate Clarissa's.[9] The urge behind these contrivances—to project a genuine authorial voice—prompted the creation of a second persona that coexists uneasily with the editor. In the two versions of the postscript to *Clarissa*, Richardson appears as the acknowledged and self-conscious author, who argues his case and defends his practice with references, however unlearned, to classical and contemporary authorities. But what may appear a more honest and reliable vehicle for communicating intentions and correcting misreadings is riddled with contradictions, leading the reader to question its honesty or its reliability.

Standing outside of the rhetorical tangle of the novels themselves is the final critical voice—that of Richardson the correspondent, as eager and prolific a correspondent as any of his characters. An audience of one might encourage greater candor, but would not guarantee it. John Carroll, the most recent editor of Richardson's letters, has seen no evidence of a conscious effort to mislead or to misrepresent; yet Carroll has noted the tone of either diffidence or self-justification that shades much of the correspondence, concluding that the "letters are proof that spontaneity and openness of heart do not ensure complete revelation."[10] The tone is characteristic of Richardson's commentary as a whole, since it tends to be retrospective and reactive, addressing specific objections and questions raised by readers. Epistolary discourse, as Richardson's novels demonstrate so well, also requires an audience of one *at a time:* a letter writer must adjust both style and content to suit a number of different individual readers. The number and variety of Richardson's correspondents ensured several adjustments. His letters therefore share with his other two modes of criticism an internal instability. Conflict within each voice and among the three voices problematize the consistency that some scholars have been eager to ascribe to Richardson's critical stance.[11]

Perhaps the most obvious example of tonal variation and critical contradiction involves the most prominent objection to Richardson's work by his contemporaries and today's distressed undergraduate alike: length. Richardson's expressed uneasiness about length in the original preface to *Clarissa*, subtly manipulative as it is, gave way in the third and in subsequent editions to the editor's more confident assertion that "it has been thought fit to restore many Passages, and several Letters, which were omitted in the former merely for shortening-sake; and which some Friends to the Work thought equally necessary and entertaining."[12] Opinions of others—the unnamed "Friends"—endure as a means of feigning humility and neutrality, but now dissension has disappeared. In the preface to *Grandison*, which intermingles diffidence and confidence, even the external authorities vanish: "The Nature of Familiar Letters, written, as it were, to the *Moment*, while the Heart is agitated by Hopes and Fears, or Events undecided, must plead an Excuse for the Bulk of a Collection of this Kind. Mere Facts and Characters might be comprised in a much smaller Compass: But, would they be equally interesting?"[13] Both statements justify the length on affective grounds, on the assumption that conveying a story is less important than immersing the reader in a particular kind of fictive experience and sustaining the reader's interest.

In the letters, however, a starkly different perspective on length surfaces, with a desperate Richardson alternately lamenting and cursing his prolixity. In reference to the early stages of the manuscript of *Clarissa*, he remarks to Edward Young, from whom he had sought advice about editing the text, "I have run into such a length!—And am such a sorry pruner, though greatly luxuriant, that I am apt to add three pages for one I take away!"[14] Complaints continued in letters to Hill;[15] and he asks Edward Moore, "Was it not time I shd. hasten to an end of my tedious Work?"[16] Even after the apparent change in attitude, a famous comment addressed to Thomas Edwards during the final stages of the composition of *Grandison* reveals still greater exasperation: "I want to reduce. I shall reduce. But this is Labor, Drudgery! I don't love it."[17] Does one dismiss the prefatorial comments as contrived defenses after the fact and accept the letters as tokens of sincere doubt and discontent? Or does the self-criticism in the letters coyly invite reassurance from friends that the length is amply justified? The impossibility of simply choosing one alternative over the other—or even of fixing some happy medium with any degree of precision—reflects an indeterminacy endemic to Richardson's multivocal method.

Complexity appears even where Richardson's position would seem to be most monolithic—in his championing of morality over entertainment. Like several less accomplished contemporaries,[18] he stridently insists that he is merely exploiting the "modest guise of a novel"[19] in order to enhance the appeal of his moral message to an audience attracted to popular fiction. The language varied, but the point persisted. In the unpublished "Hints of Prefaces to *Clarissa*," the editor proposes an attempt to see if "by an Accommodation to the light Taste of the Age a religious Novel will do Good."[20] The original postscript to *Clarissa* contains the author's description of the novel as "a work which is designed to inculcate upon the human mind, under the guise of an amusement, the great lessons of Christianity."[21] And the retrospective editor of *Grandison,* using the passive construction so characteristic of Richardsonian discussions of intention, asserts that "it may be supposed, that the present Collection is not published ultimately, nor even principally, any more than the other two, for the Sake of Entertainment only. A much nobler End is in View" (1:4).[22] Secure in his lofty purpose, Richardson can even observe that sometimes the disguise will attract but will not sustain some readers' attention, that *Clarissa* will "probably be thought tedious to all such as *dip* into it, expecting a *light Novel,* or *transitory Romance.*"[23]

Yet, this type of admission was rare: a pervasive emphasis on morality cannot mask Richardson's obvious concern about artistic means and ends—his sense of his novels as literary artifacts as well as secular homilies.[24] In the middle of a laundry list of moral goals realized in *Pamela,* the editor, as Sheldon Sacks has noted,[25] includes two formal achievements: (a) "to draw Characters *justly,* and to support them *equally*" and (b) "to raise a Distress from *natural* Causes, and to excite Compassion from *proper* Motives."[26] What "just," "equal," "natural," and "proper" mean is wisely left vague, but what is clear is a desire for approval on aesthetic terms. Although he allows that *Clarissa* will seem tedious to superficial readers who are concerned primarily with the story, the editor coyly suggests that the story is nonetheless "generally allowed" to be "interesting," and that readers can find in the letters "such Strokes of Gaiety, Fancy, and Humour, as will entertain and divert; and at the same time both warn and instruct."[27] *Grandison* has a "nobler End" than "Entertainment," but "it is hoped the Variety of Characters and Conversations necessarily introduced into so large a Correspondence, as these Volumes contain, will enliven as well as instruct: The rather, as the principal Correspondents are young Ladies of polite Education, and of lively Spirits" (1:4). On one level, entertainment is valuable only insofar as it facilitates instruction. Richardson's language qualifies the argument, however, by stressing artistic appeal to a greater degree than the argument would require.

I would suggest that a more significant cause of the conspicuous attention to entertainment and the consequent concern with form and technique lay in the Richardsonian preoccupation with originality. No reader of Richardson can ignore his self-image as a creator of something new. He coins the key phrase in a letter to Hill about *Pamela,* in which he admits thinking that he "might possibly introduce a new species of writing."[28] In the revised postscript to *Clarissa,* innovation also provides a defense for the oftencriticized ending of the novel: the author "was resolved . . . to attempt something that never yet had been done. He considered, that the Tragic poets have as seldom made their heroes true objects of pity, as the Comic theirs laudable ones of imitation: And still more rarely have made them in their deaths look forward to a *future Hope.*"[29] Even his dissatisfaction with Warburton's preface to *Clarissa* resulted less from his disdain for the French "marvellous"—with which Warburton linked the novel—than from Warburton's suggestion that Richardson was indebted to French fiction for his design.[30] The dedicatee of Young's *Conjectures on Original Composition* took obvious pride in his novelty—a pride which helps to explain many of his most substantive comments on the formal aspects of his craft.

Concern about originality shaped Richardson's divided attitude toward drama and the influence of drama on his narrative. Like his predecessors and contemporaries, he took pains to emphasize formal and thematic connections between the genres. A principal asset of the epistolary method in *Clarissa* is the presentation of conversations "written in the dialogue or dramatic Way."[31] To elaborate on the advantages of "dramatic" writing, Richardson characteristically quotes one of his own characters, Belford— whose earlier moral transgressions presumably did not foreclose critical acumen:

> *Much more* lively and affecting . . . must be the Style of those who write in the height of a *present* distress; the mind tortured by the pangs of uncertainty (the Events then hidden in the womb of Fate); *than* the dry, narrative, unanimated Style of a person relating difficulties and dangers surmounted, can be; the relator perfectly at ease; and if himself unmoved by his own Story, not likely greatly to affect the Reader.[32]

Just as the *immediate* effects of epistolary fiction, like suspense, are analogous to those of drama, so too are the *ultimate* effects. Hill, in his introductory letter to *Pamela*—which was solicited and included with evident approval—praises the author for moving his readers "with the Force of a TRAGEDY"[33]; Richardson himself explains more precisely how his next novel does the same. The manner in which Clarissa and Lovelace die lets "Pity on her Account, and Terror on his, join to complete" the author's "great End, for the sake of *Example* and *Warning*."[34] A writer who readily appropriated terms from dramatic criticism could comfortably include the language of drama in a simile: defending Clarissa's death to Lady Bradshaigh, Richardson argues that to "have given her her Reward here, as in a happy Marriage, would have been as if a Poet had placed his Catastrophe in the Third Act of his Play, when the Audience were *obliged* to expect two more."[35] All of the connections—verbal and analogical—to an established, admired genre enhance the stature of the novels and indicate that they should be judged by the same well-developed criteria and high standards as drama.

The alliance with drama proved an uneasy one, however, as Richardson, unsatisfied with parity, asserted the superiority of his productions over most dramatic writing.[36] Clarissa's death does not merely evoke pity; as he has argued, her death evokes *more* pity than the deaths of most characters in tragic drama—and promises "future Hope" in a way that their deaths do not. An almost identical contrast appears in the "Hints"—with the added comment that the vicious characters in *Clarissa* are purer than the virtuous characters of the dramatic poets (4). Most important, Richardson's principal argument in the postscript—a defense of the unhappy ending of *Clarissa*—rests largely upon a questioning of that cardinal rule of neoclassical dramatic theory and practice: poetic justice. With a diffident tone and a derivative poetics, he begins by indirectly calling forth the authority of Aristotle—as interpreted by Addison and Rapin. Addison maintains that "as the principal design of tragedy is to raise commiseration and terror in the minds of the audience, we shall defeat this great end if we always make virtue and innocence happy and successful"; while, for Rapin, "Tragedy . . . makes man *modest,* by representing the great masters of the earth humbled; and it makes him *tender* and *merciful,* by showing him the *strange accidents of life,* and the *unforseen disgraces* to which the most important persons are subject."[37] The revised postscript enhances the attack and, more prominently, the affective argument on behalf of unhappy endings, by including a monody on the death of a virtuous matron, a selection from

Psalm 53, which for the author is "of infinitely greater weight than all that has been . . . produced on this subject," and a letter to the *Spectator* (in support of Addison's position) that indirectly answers objections to Lovelace's death by observing

> that tho' the *Spectator* above-mentioned is so far against the rule of *Poetical Justice,* as to affirm, that good men may meet with an unhappy Catastrophe in Tragedy, it does not say, that ill men may go off unpunished. The reason for this distinction is very plain; namely, because the best of men . . . have faults enough to justify Providence for any misfortunes and afflictions which may befal them; but there are many men so criminal that they can have no claim or pretence to happiness. The *best* of men may deserve punishment; but the *worst* of men cannot deserve happiness.[38]

Such a scattershot combination of texts that vary greatly in stature and relevance makes Jerry Beasley's impression that Richardson's notion of tragedy was "largely improvised"[39] a charitable understatement. Whatever its weaknesses, however, this cumulative approach allowed Richardson to contrast his method favorably to much tragic drama by appealing to several loci of authority outside of himself.

Yet, after all the self-effacing reliance in the postscript on the voices of others, an assertive Richardson abruptly intervenes to demonstrate that the citations were superfluous, since "the notion of *Poetical Justice,* founded on the *modern rules,* has hardly ever been more strictly observed in works of this nature, than in the present performance."[40] Under the unique Christian system under which the text operates, the evil characters, especially Lovelace, receive the punishment due their crimes, while the virtuous heroine attains the only reward that makes moral and artistic sense—a heavenly one. A move as audacious as it was clumsy, this reversal has attracted the scorn of most critics for ensuring that Richardson could have his cake while eating it[41] and that he could both attack and embrace poetic justice from a position of moral superiority and within a respectable critical tradition. Furthermore, the sophistry reveals as divided an attitude toward authority as it does toward poetic justice. Eager, at first, to obtain authority vicariously, in much the same way as the "editor" does, Richardson then sought the self-generated authority of the innovator: he confided to Hill that he considered his broader conception of poetic justice both "noble" and "new."[42] In a curious way, theory mirrored practice both in relying upon and in improving upon precedents from drama.

Fewer complexities of tone attend Richardson's remarks on the distinct advantages of his epistolary technique over the "usual narrative way."[43] (Linear narrative serves as the inferior norm for a writer who never recognizes predecessors in the epistolary mode.) Only once, with the admission in the revised postscript that he "perhaps mistrusted his talents for the narrative way of telling,"[44] does he even slightly qualify his habitual confidence in his chosen method. More typical is a key passage in the "Hints," where the epistolary style, by which "Characters sink deeper into the Mind of the Reader, and stamp there a perfect Idea of the very turn of Thought, by which the Originals were actuated, and diversified from each other" (12), is contrasted to the

> dry Narrative; where the *Novelist* moves on, at his own dull Pace, to the End of his Chapter and Book, interweaving impertinent Digressions, for fear the Reader's Patience should be exhausted by his tedious Dwelling on one Subject, in the same Style: Which may not unfitly be compared to the dead Tolling of a single Bell, in Opposition to the wonderful Variety of Sounds, which constitute the Harmony of a Handel. (13)

Empathy and variety, mentioned here as the hallmarks of novels in letters, are repeatedly cited elsewhere by surrogates as well as the author. Hill applauds the way in which Pamela's letters give the reader access to her mind and also permit him "to feel the force in a threefold Effect—from the Motive, the Act, and the Consequence."[45] In Warburton's view, epistolary writing affords Richardson "the only natural opportunity that could be had, of representing with any grace those lively and delicate impressions which *Things present* are known to make upon the minds of those affected by them."[46] And Richardson himself not only trumpets the affective superiority of writing "in the height of a present distress" over the narrative method of recounting struggles already passed but also argues, in "Hints," that permitting characters to speak in their own voices involves the reader further by enabling him "to judge at first Sight, whether the respective Persons represented express themselves in a Style suitable to their Characters, or not" (13).

Some proclaimed strengths of epistolary writing are less convincing than others, however. To support the greater probability of epistolary fiction, Richardson quotes, in the revised postscript, from Albrecht von Haller's *A Critique of the History of Clarissa:* "Romances in general . . . are wholly improbable; because they suppose the History to be written after the series of events is closed by the catastrophe," thus requiring extraordinary memory on the part of the narrator; while a novel written in letters, once it is established that the characters "have an uncommon taste for this kind of conversation,"[47] is more probable, because characters are assumed to have related incidents immediately after they have transpired. Ian Watt has deflated the argument by observing that "the epistolary method is by no means exempt from improbability in other ways, and both methods must be accepted for what they are, literary conventions."[48] Henry Fielding did not need Watt to alert him to the parodic potential in a heroine who describes a near rape almost immediately after it occurs!

Another distinction without a difference marks Richardson's inconsistent commentary on the place and value of digressions. Ridiculing the "impertinent digressions" endemic to "dry narrative" would not exactly equip him with a ready defense for what critics saw as unnecessary, digressive material in his own extremely long narratives. His solution was to transform a potential liability into an asset. With the usual reliance on external authority, the editor of *Clarissa* cites anonymous critics who insist that "the story could not be reduced to a dramatic unity, nor thrown into the narrative way, without divesting it of its warmth and of a great part of its efficacy, as very few of the reflections and observations, which they looked upon as the most useful part of the collection, would then find a place."[49] Rhetorical sleight of hand divests the "narrative way" of digressions for which Richardson had desired to fault it, only to make epistolary digressions valuable both artistically, as a source of "warmth," and morally, as a source of instruction. Such a move not so subtly begs the real questions: Are—and how are—Richardson's "reflections and observations" superior to those found in other narratives?

Underlying questions about unity required more ample response, and Richardson obliged in equally enigmatic ways. In the initial postscript, he dismisses letters suggesting that *Clarissa* end happily as based on unavoidably insufficient knowledge: "These letters having been written on the perusal of the first four volumes only, before the complicated adjustment of the several parts to one another could be seen, or fully known, it may be thought superfluous, now the whole work is before the public, to enter upon this argument, because it is presumed that the catastrophe necessarily follows the natural progress of the story."[50] Anyone who has read correctly cannot but agree with Richardson's privileged reading. With less presumption and greater defensiveness, he uses similar language to claim that *Grandison* is also a unified text: "There is not one Episode in the Whole; nor, after SIR CHARLES GRANDISON is introduced, one Letter inserted but what tends to illustrate the principal Design. Those which precede his Introduction, will not, it is hoped, be judged unnecessary on the whole, as they tend to make the Reader better acquainted with Persons, the History of whom is closely interwoven with that of Sir Charles" (1:4). While readers have never doubted the variety for which Richardson justifiably took credit, unity has been called into question by everyone from the critics to whom Richardson responded directly to the most recent deconstructors.[51] His attempt to deal with the issue by assertion rather than demonstration, therefore, seems hollow and heavy-handed—much like the editorial apparatus designed to promote a reading in accord with the author's intentions. Complicating matters further, Richardson the correspondent threatens Richardson the novelist's insistence on unity by referring to his "No-Plan"[52] in writing *Clarissa,* and by repeatedly calling himself, during the composition of *Grandison,* "too irregular a scribbler to be able to write by a plan."[53] Yet this self-characterization has itself been seriously undermined by recent critics,[54] thus illustrating how, in certain contexts, Richardson could stretch the truth in order to maintain a desired image. And if falsehoods support the image of the spontaneous genius, one can also question the opposite image of the careful planner.

Interest in another type of unity—unity of *tone*—led to a vigorous response to criticisms of "warm scenes" for infecting avowedly moral works by deflecting the reader's attention from sound morals to prurient manners. *Pamela,* which contains more of these scenes than the other novels—despite the assertion in the preface that the story never raises "a *single Idea* throughout the Whole, that shall shock the exactest Purity, even in those tender Instances where the exactest Purity would be most apprehensive"[55]— naturally came under the greatest attack for them, as Bernard Kreissman's survey of the anti-*Pamela* literature has detailed.[56] Richardson's most significant response, which occurs in a letter to Dr. George Cheyne concerning the second part of the novel, is a divided one, with a promise to avoid warm scenes in the future, followed by a defense (once again, second hand) of his previous reliance on them:

> I will only add, that in the Two new Volumes, I shall have no Occasion for such of the deep Scenes, as I believ'd necessary to the Story in two Places in the former; and yet I have had one kind Anonymous

Gentleman, who has in a letter vindicated those very Scenes, and has pointed out in Milton (To whose *Paradise Lost* possibly they were not so necessary) Passages full as strong if not stronger, because mine were mingled wth. Horror, and Censure against the lewd Attempter of Chastity.[57]

Neither the tone, which shifts from diffidence to condescension, nor the comparison with Milton, which is invalid and irrelevant, contributes to an appealing argument.

Both, however, typify the strange contortions that this vexing issue forced Richardson to undergo. In an unpublished pamphlet justifying the fire scene in *Clarissa,* he abandons invidious comparisons, so as not "to defend myself by the Faults of Others,"[58] and relies instead on a detailed reading of the scene that stresses that the artistic propriety of using words and sentiments proper to Lovelace, the so-called author of the description, does not diminish the moral propriety of Clarissa's actions. To support his claims, he literally assumes the position of a reader reacting to the scene:

> You know, Sir, what is required of Writers, who aim at *personating* (in order to describe the more naturally) a particular Character, whether good or bad. For my Part, I must declare, that in my writing of this Scene (by some thought so inflaming) the Passion I found strongest in me, whenever I supposed myself a Reader only, and the Story real, was *Anger,* or *Indignation:* I had too great an Aversion to the intended Violator of the Honour of a CLARISSA, to suffer any-thing but alternate Admiration and Pity of her, and Resentment against him, to take place in my Mind, on the Occasion.[59]

Even Eaves and Kimpel, critics generally sympathetic to Richardson, have readily acknowledged the possibility that "he could . . . have lied or he could have failed to understand his own subconscious feelings"[60] about the sexuality in the scene. Whatever the cause, he ended up usurping the place and interpretive responsibility of the reader, in order to privilege one response and pre-empt others. Even more ingenious—and more problematic—is a distinction that he draws when replying, in the *Gentleman's Magazine,* to Haller's objection that he "has dispersed, in some parts of his book, the particulars of freedoms taken by Lovelace, which exceed the bounds of decency,"[61] in much the same way as Corneille did in *Théodore.* For Richardson, the differing contexts of reception allow for different responses: a "nice person of the [female] sex may not . . . be able to bear the scenes in action, and on the stage, in the presence of a thousand witnesses, which she may not think objectible [*sic*] in her closet."[62] Yet the converse would seem more generally valid: titillation usually occurs in private, while numbers provide something of a check to emotional response. If more developed and more eloquently expressed than the defenses of warm scenes by Manley and Haywood, Richardson's arguments are not much more convincing. They amply reflect the anxieties, conscious or not, of an author compelled to justify facets of his completed works about which he might have serious reservations in other contexts.

A different sort of double vision, no less revealing, informs Richardson's remarks on characterization, which, due both to the intimate connection between character and moral message and to the creator's own pronounced intimacy with his characters, remained his most important critical preoccupation. Challenged to mediate the competing demands of probability and exemplary morality, Richardson simply embraced both, insisting that his heroes and heroines do have flaws, which make them imitable models, while *simultaneously* implying the opposite! "It was not only natural, but it was necessary" that Clarissa have faults, maintains the editor,

> were it only to shew the Reader, how laudably she could mistrust and blame herself, and carry to her own heart, divested of self-partiality, the censure which arose from her own convictions, and that even to the acquittal of those, because revered characters, whom no one else would acquit, and to those whose much greater fault her errors were owing, and not to a weak or reprochable heart. As far as is consistent with human frailty, and as far as she could be perfect, considering the people she had to deal with, and those with whom she was inseparably connected, she *is* perfect.[63]

An admission of faults is cast in language that consciously undermines it. In the same way, in the pamphlet about the fire scene, he insists that "CLARISSA, tho' not drawn absolutely perfect, but as having something to blame herself for, tho' not in Intention, is proposed for an Example to the Sex. And her Trials are multiplied to give her so many Opportunities to shine thro' the various Stages of those Trials."[64] Finally, in the "concluding note" to *Grandison*, the editor answers the criticism that the eponymous hero "approaches too near the faultless character" (3:464) by referring both to Sir Charles's own self-reproach for "tendencies to pride and passion" (3:464) and to his proposed marriage settlement with Clementina's family, upon which "many . . . look . . . as a blot in the character" (3:464). Mere equivocation does not suffice: in the remainder of the note, the editor dwells on Grandison's noble qualities and contrasts him with "vicious" characters whose authors have made them succeed in order to show life as it is— an indirect but obvious stab at Fielding's *Tom Jones*.[65] Even were the hero's character "still more perfect than it is presumed to be, the Editor is supported" by a Tillotson sermon that recommends proposing "the brightest and most perfect Examples to our imitation" (3:466). Eaves and Kimpel have correctly located the extreme to which Richardson moved here, observing that whatever he said "in general about his characters having faults, Sir Charles is, and is meant to be, free even from foibles."[66]

The correspondence casts greater doubt on the conviction behind the advocacy of imperfect—hence, believable—protagonists. Although some of the letters imply, in the words of Alan McKillop, that Richardson "intended that [Clarissa's] half-accidental flight with Lovelace should be the tragic flaw,"[67] others suggest that he identified faults only as a gratuitous afterthought. He admits to Hill that he "struggled" to give Clarissa "Failings, that I might not seem to have aimed at drawing a perfect Character";[68] and in a more famous letter about *Grandison*, he tells Miss Mulso, "I shall want a few unpremeditated faults . . . to sprinkle into this man's character, lest I should draw a *faultless monster*."[69] Along with Richardson's expressions of satisfaction in his readers' inability to agree upon his characters' imperfections, these comments lay bare the extent to which Richardson merely nodded to probability of character—a move fully consonant with the notorious attempts in revision to eliminate shades of gray from the characters of Clarissa and Lovelace in order to ensure the exemplary moral clarity of extremes. Still, the frequency with which he offered the nod intimates an author uncomfortable with the choice that his programmatic morality compelled him to make.

Questions of verisimilitude aside, Richardson's remarks on one of his principal character types, the rake, themselves reveal striking inconsistencies. Although *Clarissa* is designed to caution against subscribing to the "dangerous but too commonly accepted notion, *that a reformed rake makes the best husband*,"[70] *Pamela* can be read as proof for the maxim; but authorial commentary on the character of Mr. B. does not clarify but obscures any distinction. In the revised postscript, Richardson refers indirectly to B. in order to denounce any sudden conversion of Lovelace, which would have enabled *Clarissa* to end with a marriage: "Nor is Reformation, as [the author] has shewn in another piece, to be secured by a fine face; by a passion that has sense for its object; nor by the goodness of a Wife's heart, or even example, if the heart of the Husband be not graciously touched by the Divine Finger."[71] But the finger remained hidden for some time, as the "Hints" describe a Pamela happy "in her implicit submission to a lordly and imperious Husband, who hardly deserved her" (2) and whose reformation was not complete until long after the marriage. Paradoxically, B.'s postnuptial reformation seems to exempt him from reproach, both here and in the preface to *Grandison,* where he is described as a "Libertine" who "from the Foundation of good Principles laid in his early years by an excellent Mother; by his Passion for a virtuous young Woman; and by her amiable Example, and unwearied Patience, when she became his Wife; is, after a Length of Time, perfectly reclaimed" (1:3). Exculpatory arguments for B. on grounds that his ineptitude as a rake signifies a fundamental simplicity and decency have some force, but Richardson avoided them in favor of the curious proposition that a reformed rake can make a good husband if he reforms after he is married!

If Richardson defended B. too obliquely, he defends Clarissa against charges of prudery too emphatically—with similar results. To those who "have censured the heroine as too cold in her love," the author of the revised postscript replies petulantly that it "was not intended that she should be *in Love,* but *in Liking* only," that she could not have been genuinely in love and simultaneously able "to shew such a command of her passions, as makes so distinguishing a part of her Character," and that he has indicated as much in the notes in order "to bespeak the *Attention* of hasty readers to what lies obviously before them."[72] Once again, assertions by the author replace persuasion by the text—or, as Eaves and Kimpel have aptly put it, "A reader might answer that it is the author's business to convey the impression that Clarissa is not cold and that logical reasoning has little to do with such an impression."[73] The primary virtue of epistolary fiction—namely, intense self-revelation by the individual characters—is thwarted here, as it is by the long defense of Hickman at the end of the postscript and the continual "clarifications" of Lovelace's "mixed" character. And tendentious corrections of hasty readings only make some readers all the more eager to join the interpretive battle—to uncover the bases of authorial manipulation, as recent readings of the novels, especially *Clarissa,* have forcefully demonstrated.

Perhaps tone poses the most formidable obstacle to appreciation of Richardson as a theorist. The contradictions that I have traced reflect an uncertain critical stance, to be sure; but that very uncertainty proceeded from a probing, acute, critical mind, sensitive to—if not successful at—resolving so many of the polarizing issues raised by his experimental genre and technique. Articulating these issues, however, is a voice—sometimes humble but usually condescending, primarily didactic and always self-justificatory—that seldom attracts the reader's sympathy. Richardson's hectoring tone undoubtedly underscored his moralistic agenda for his immediate successors and their critics; but it also discouraged—and continues to discourage—engagement with his criticism and the nuances within it. Significant recent studies that have addressed Richardson's goals and methods are only beginning to balance an inordinate modern focus on the more entertaining and more deceptively harmonious critical reflections of his principal rival Henry Fielding.

*   *   *

Drawing distinctions between Richardson and Fielding as novelists—a natural temptation to which literary historians and critics have often succumbed—often involves ignoring the many points at which their goals and methods converge.[74] It is equally tempting to contrast their critical commentary, given Fielding's superior learning and Augustan wit, the greater breadth and volume of his criticism—which addresses other novelists and other genres—and the prominence of critical remarks throughout the texts of his novels. Yet a more detailed reading of Fielding on the novel narrows the gap considerably. While William Park has exaggerated in asserting that "both Richardson and Fielding advocated the same theory of the novel,"[75] both authors did frequently begin from common premises and then moved in different—though not necessarily opposite—directions. Sharing much of Richardson's anxiety and ambivalence, Fielding masked it, at least superficially, through alternative rhetorical structures—including, most notably, the self-conscious narrator; but the structures themselves created as many complications as they removed.

Richardson's strident preaching unmistakably foregrounds moral concerns; yet Fielding, far more frequently than one might expect, also emphasized conventional didacticism. The variety of contexts in which—and voices through which—he did so, however, frustrates a simple response to his apparent orthodoxy. The explicit moralist is perhaps most evident in the dedicatory letters to Lord Lyttleton and Ralph Allen, at the beginning of Tom Jones and Amelia, respectively. Fielding hopes that the reader of Tom

Jones "will be convinced, at his very Entrance on this Work, that
he will find in the whole Course of it nothing prejudicial to the
Cause of Religion and Virtue; nothing inconsistent with the strictest Rules of Decency, nor which can offend even the chastest Eye
in the Perusal. On the contrary," he declares, "to recommend
Goodness and Innocence hath been my sincere Endeavour in this
History."[76] Likewise, *Amelia* is "sincerely designed to promote the
Cause of Virtue" and to "expose some of the most glaring Evils,
as well public as private,"[77] while avoiding harmful personal satire.
To a certain degree, the rhetoric of the dedicatory letter, addressed *in propria persona* to patrons whose exemplary character
the author had to praise, dictates such transparent righteousness,
a quality seldom characteristic of Fielding's narrators within the
texts, in whom virtuosity supercedes virtuousness.

But similar sentiments arose in other rhetorical settings as well.
In *Covent-Garden Journal* No. 10, Fielding quotes "the ingenious
Author of Clarissa" to the effect that *"Pleasantry should be made the
Vehicle of Instruction"* and concludes that by observing this maxim,
"Romances, as well as Epic Poems, may become worthy of the
Perusal of the greatest of Men."[78] Richardson's name and example
reappear in the preface to *A Voyage to Lisbon,* with an approving
reference to his position that "entertainment" is "but a secondary
consideration in a romance."[79] In the opening chapter of *Amelia,*
the narrator implicitly endorses this view by highlighting the
moral utility of the text as an instructional guide of sorts to the
"Art of Life" (1:17). Given such assumptions, the narrator quite
naturally attempts to prove that, more often than not, men themselves—and not fortune—are responsible for what happens to
them (16); this view represents a clear shift in emphasis from
the famous discussion of poetic justice in *Tom Jones,* in which the
narrator holds that active virtue often does not secure happiness—and frequently results in misery (2:783–4).

Fielding was quoting Richardson, in part, to defend the *Voyage
to Lisbon* against the charge of boredom; and *Amelia* is a very
different kind of narrative, in both purpose and performance,
from the two earlier comic novels. More typical of Fielding's tone
is the passage near the end of the preface to *Joseph Andrews* in
which a voice of apparent rectitude justifies the portrayal of un-
specified—but, presumably, serious enough—evil:

> But perhaps it may be objected to me, that I have against my own
> Rules introduced Vices, and of a very black Kind into this Work. To
> which I shall answer: First, that it is very difficult to pursue a Series

of human Actions and keep clear from them. Secondly, That the Vices to be found here, are rather the accidental Consequences of some human Frailty, or Foible, than Causes habitually existing in the Mind. Thirdly, That they are never set forth as Objects of Ridicule but Detestation. Fourthly, That they are never the principal Figure at that Time on the Scene; and lastly, they never produce the intended Evil.[80]

For Homer Goldberg, this lapse "into the pious apologetics conventional to fiction at the time" remained directed toward "the intended specific poetic effect of the work, rather than its ethical consequences."[81] In his eagerness to demonstrate the aesthetic logic behind Fielding's language, Goldberg has diminished the rhetorical importance of the convention for Fielding and his readers. Like similar apologies by Defoe and others, the apology simultaneously satisfies the reader's conscience and arouses his curiosity: while the vices are mitigated, they are still present. Two paragraphs later in the preface, the narrator continues to offer a double-edged appeal: protesting that he has no "Intention to vilify or asperse any one"—and has, therefore, taken care to avoid personal satire by completely disguising his models—he, nonetheless, hints that the reader may be able to identify some of his victims, but "only where the Failure characterized is so minute, that it is a Foible only which the Party himself may laugh at as well as any other" (10). A narrator who speaks through (at least) two mouths will inevitably have his sincerity questioned. More generally, one cannot help suspecting that because Fielding's habitual public voice—in journalism, drama, and fiction—was so ironic, he must have expected to be read ironically as often as not. If readers of Richardson find his relentless moralizing oppressive or misguided, Fielding's readers face quite a different problem: however confident of his ultimately moral aims, readers can never feel completely secure in taking his comments about the morality of his texts seriously.

Fielding's overt moralizing has received scant attention, not because it poses interpretive problems, but because it represents the most derivative commentary by a writer who, like Richardson, repeatedly underscored his originality—most notably by distinguishing his texts from contemporary or past fiction. According to the narrator, *Joseph Andrews,* an example of a "kind of Writing . . . [not] hitherto attempted in our Language" (3), differs from "the Productions of Romance Writers on one Hand, and Burlesque Writers on the other" (10). As a "Biographer," its author stands in opposition to "those Persons of surprising Genius, the

Authors of immense Romances, or the modern Novel and *Atalantis* Writers; who without any Assistance from Nature or History, record Persons who never were, or will be, and Facts which never did nor possibly can happen" (187).[82] In *Tom Jones,* Fielding returns to and develops the contrast by advocating a "classical" definition of invention as "Discovery, or finding out," or a "quick and sagacious Penetration into the true Essence of all the Objects of our Contemplation," as opposed to the vulgar sense of invention as uninhibited imaginative license—as merely "a creative Faculty; which would indeed prove most Romance-Writers to have the highest pretensions to it" (1:491). Under the more sophisticated formulation, the author's ability to "invent good Stories, and to tell them well" would be unique—and certainly not shared by those responsible for "the Romances and Novels with which the World abounds" (1:488). Fielding even invested the hoary, cliché-ridden preface form itself with a kind of novelty: as Maurice Johnson has suggested, the unapologetic, assertive tone of the preface to *Joseph Andrews,* which opens with a declaration of its necessity, contrasts sharply with the more representative diffidence of Congreve's preface to *Incognita,* in which the author pretended merely to gratify the booksellers' desire for padding.[83] The introductory chapters in *Tom Jones* also distinguish their creator from less talented writers—and, in fact, are supposed to dissuade would-be imitators "who are utterly incapable of any Degree of Reflection, and whose Learning is not equal to an Essay" (1:488).

Vigorous assertions of originality lead naturally enough to claims of authorial privilege—especially the right to deviate from established conventions and to create new ones. The narrator of *Tom Jones* need not "assign any Reasons" for the "initial Essays" to each book, "it being abundantly sufficient that we have laid it down as a Rule necessary to be observed in all Prosai-comic-epic Writing" (1:209). On similar grounds—but with more suggestive language—the narrator defends his method of selection, elaboration, and omission of detail: "For as I am, in Reality, the Founder of a new Province of Writing, so I am at Liberty to make what Laws I please therein. And these Laws, my Readers, whom I consider as my Subjects, are bound to believe in and obey; with which that they may readily and chearfully comply, I do hereby assure them that I shall principally regard their Ease and Advantage in all such Institutions" (1:77). Characteristic jocularity mitigates the seriousness behind an assertion of benevolent despotism—but, once again, complicates the reader's response. Simultaneously embracing and debunking authority, the narrator solicits both obedience and laughter but leaves the reader to balance these normally mutually exclusive reactions. Here and throughout the novels, Fielding's ironic tone puts the reader on guard and to work, requiring the reader to discern—and even to create—sense for a multileveled text. In this sense, Fielding is asking much more from his readers than is Richardson.

Coexisting almost seamlessly with declarations of literary independence are Fielding's attempts—far more elaborate than Richardson's—to invest his novels with the authority of established genres and traditions. Despite his long experience as a playwright—and its influence on his narrative technique—Fielding seldom invited comparisons between fiction and drama, relegating the stage to a broad metaphorical vehicle for human nature. Perhaps his reluctance to compare derived from a desire for readers to ignore his earlier, well-known plays and to concentrate exclusively on the novels for their own sake. In any case, Fielding turned more prominently to history. Far removed from Richardson's concerns about maintaining "historical faith"—and farther still from conventional, transparent misrepresentations of fiction as fact—Fielding reveled in artifice; thus, his continual references to his narratives as histories—and to himself as historian—necessitated a new definition of history. Michael McKeon has amply sketched Fielding's method of classifying *Joseph Andrews* through a "double negation": his *true* history differs both from romances and contemporary novels—and from history as it is commonly understood, such as collections of names, dates, and so forth—because it, like the equally "historical" works cited as models in book 3 of *Joseph Andrews* (namely, *Gil Blas, The Arabian Nights,* and *Don Quixote*), accurately portrays the fundamental characteristics of human nature.[84] Negative definition persists in *Tom Jones,* as the narrator reflects upon his apparent taxonomic quandary:

> Hence we are to derive that universal Contempt, which the World, who always denominate the Whole from the Majority, have cast on all historical Writers, who do not draw their Materials from Records. And it is the Apprehension of this Contempt, that hath made us so cautiously avoid the Term Romance, a Name with which we might otherwise have been well enough contented. Though as we have good Authority for all our Characters, no less indeed than the vast authentic Doomsday-Book of Nature, as is elsewhere hinted, our Labours have sufficient Title to the Name of History. (1:489)

In McKeon's words, Fielding sought "to distinguish between a naively empiricist and more 'imaginative' species of belief" and "to distinguish his preferred sort of belief also from the sheer creativity of romance"; hence, the significant qualifying adjectives in the terms *true* history and *comic* romance.[85]

Fielding's new historicism results in the conflation of contradictory bases of appeal. On the one hand, the negations inevitably elevate his histories over those that do rely on materials drawn from records. In the famous opening chapter of book 3 of *Joseph Andrews,* the narrator derisively refers to conventional historians as "Topographers" or "Chorographers," who do well enough describing mere geography; but "as to the Actions and Characters of Men, their Writings are not quite so authentic, of which there needs no other Proof than those eternal Contradictions, occurring between two Topographers who undertake the History of the same Country" (185). Using *biography* as a synonym for *true history,* he goes on to praise biographers (like himself) for ignoring minute details and describing "not Men, but Manners; not an Individual, but a Species" (189). Such a comparison recalls Aristotle's insistence that poetry can be truer than history; but Fielding substitutes his own prose for poetry—wittily establishing his genre as the locus of the only truth that matters. Status once again confers artistic freedom: the author of *Tom Jones* is not obliged to "imitate the painful and voluminous Historian, who, to preserve the Regularity of his Series, thinks himself obliged to fill up as much Paper with the Details of Months and Years in which nothing remarkable happened, as he employs upon those notable Aeras when the greatest Scenes have been transacted on the human Stage" (1:75). Yet, despite these logical, learned distinctions, the numerous unelaborated references to the novels as histories still prompt the reader's reflexive identification of the two genres. Maintaining the name of a genre—but altering its meaning—allowed Fielding to endow his "histories" with two kinds of authority: readers can both identify the truth of the novels with historical truth as it is commonly understood, and regard the former as superior to the latter.

A radically different attitude, tantamount to a retraction, informs the preface of the *Voyage to Lisbon,* where Fielding calls fiction "the confounder and corrupter" of true history and claims that he "should have honoured and loved Homer more had he written a true history of his own times in humble prose, than those noble poems that have so justly collected the praises of all ages" (185). While this startling reversal may reflect sincere reconsideration of the relative merits of fiction and history and of the right of fiction to lay claim to historical status—by this time, Fielding had experimented with a very different kind of novel in *Amelia*—both the autobiographical and literary contexts suggest other influences. Ill, tired, fearful of death and its consequences for his family, Fielding could hardly have been expected to strike the jocular tone so associated with his pretensions to historicity. Moreover, privileging fact over fiction makes perfect rhetorical sense in the introduction to a largely factual travel book like the *Voyage to Lisbon*. Yet, even in such circumstances, Fielding owed too much to fiction to make the condemnation absolute or absolutely convincing. He contends that some "few embellishments must be allowed to every historian," that "it is sufficient that every fact have its foundation in truth . . . and when it is so, a good critic will be so far from denying all kind of ornament of style or diction, or even of circumstances to his author" (188). Though it is wrong to "draw forth a list of stupid, senseless, incredible lies on paper, it is equally wrong to waste time and paper recording things and facts of so common a kind" (187) that only the author would bother to remember them. The embellishment and selection so essential to the historian of *Joseph Andrews* and *Tom Jones* become equally necessary for the more pedestrian recorder of a real journey. Fielding's previous conception of fiction as a unique kind of history serves once again as a source of value, even when he appears to be disowning it.

Different rhetorical tactics and different interpretive difficulties characterize Fielding's equally audacious attempt to inscribe his texts within the epic tradition. The most quoted passage—I, too, cannot resist the temptation—from the most noted early discussion of the novel as genre distinguishes *Joseph Andrews* from "those voluminous Works, commonly called *Romances*" (4) by relating it, step by Aristotelian step, not to history, but to a more self-consciously literary genre:

> Now a comic Romance is a comic Epic-Poem in Prose; differing from Comedy, as the serious Epic from Tragedy; its Action being more exalted and comprehensive; containing a much larger Circle of Incidents, and introducing a greater Variety of Characters. It differs from the serious Romance in its Fable and Action, in this; that as in the one these are grave and solemn, so in the other they are light and ridiculous: it differs in its Characters, by introducing Persons of inferiour Rank, and consequently of inferiour Manners, whereas the grave Romance, sets the highest before us; lastly in its Sentiments and Diction, by preserving the Ludicrous instead of the Sublime. (4)

By naming Homer's lost *Margites* as the exemplar of—and only precursor in—this genre, Fielding again nimbly allied tradition and originality but, in the process, provoked an apparently endless critical debate. One group of critics, beginning with Ethel Thornbury,[86] has posited genuine, substantial relationships between Fielding's novels and epic literature. Among these critics, J. Paul Hunter and Ronald Paulson have drawn comparisons between the comic novels and Fénelon's so-called modern epic *Télémaque*,[87] E. T. Palmer has traced epic conventions within the texts,[88] and Mark Spilka has read *Joseph Andrews* as "an ambivalent attack on classic literature" that adapts "the mock-epic mode to fiction."[89] On the other side, Ian Watt's seminal discussion has debunked any epic theory of the novel by citing a lack of serious adaptation of epic practice in Fielding's narratives—as well as Fielding's reluctance even to return to the phrase *comic epic in prose*. Watt has placed the emphasis on *comic* over *epic* and has concluded that Fielding used identification with the epic merely to acquire prestige for a disreputable genre among educated readers.[90] In the most detailed reading of the preface, Homer Goldberg has also supported the priority of the word *comic*, has exhumed usages contemporaneous to Fielding's to prove that *epic* could simply mean *narrative*, and has equated the phrase *epic in prose* with the word *romance*—used neutrally in this context, but pejoratively in reference to certain romances.[91] Sheridan Baker, foe of the epic and partisan of the romance as an influence on Fielding, has supported Goldberg's prosaic definition of *epic* but disputes any neutral interpretation of *romance*, arguing instead that Fielding used the word to acknowledge his most significant generic debt.[92]

More notable than the arguments themselves is the extent to which Fielding's rhetorical practice in the preface made the debate inevitable. All of the critics have tended to minimize the importance of the narrative voice behind the preface. As Wayne Booth has reminded us, the wise, urbane narrator is not Fielding himself but essentially a construct, created deliberately and with detachment by the author.[93] Such a voice differs not only from Richardson's editorial persona but also from the Fielding of the dedicatory letters—both of whom remain distinct from the created worlds of the texts. By effacing himself and investing responsibility in a playful and often ironic narrator, Fielding, in effect, licensed inconsistency—resulting, in this case, from the use of suggestive terms whose denotative and connotative significance can be at odds. Consequently, readers can view *Joseph Andrews* as either distinct from or related to either romance or epic, with any of the alternatives valorizing both text and genre.

Fundamentally similar in effect—if more transparent—is *Covent-Garden Journal* No. 8, where, at the "Court of Censorial Inquiry," the "Father" of Amelia maintains that "if her Conduct be fairly examined, she will be found to deviate very little from the strictest Observation of all [the] Rules; neither Homer nor Virgil pursued them with greater Care than myself, and the candid and learned Reader will see that the latter was the noble model, which I made use of on this Occasion."[94] Once again, critics have rushed to draw parallels, on the one hand, and to reject the comparison, on the other,[95] without due attention to the context of the remark: a contrived account of the inquisition of Amelia, laced throughout with humor and irony. While Fielding may, indeed, have borrowed from Virgil—Booth's narrative of his recent history to Miss Matthews does recall Aeneas's account to Dido—he seems less concerned with programmatic critical rigor, or absolute sincerity, than with mounting a clever defense of a tepidly received novel, within the limited, controllable confines of the periodical essay.

Less compact and discrete, the preface form offered less absolute control but greater rhetorical opportunity, which Fielding exploited in *Joseph Andrews* by immediately establishing an aura of authority for the narrator himself, however inconsistent his logic or language may appear. Whether the subject be the epic, the burlesque, or the ridiculous, the narrator embodies assurance in citing models, enumerating divisions and subdivisions, and drawing comparisons and contrasts. In the revised postscript to *Clarissa*, Richardson tended to rely upon—and even to quote—established literary and religious authorities, from Aristotle to the Bible, in order to invest his views—and, ultimately, his character—with weight and to provoke assent. More comfortable with the classics and the critical heritage, Fielding mentions Aristotle only once—and, instead, mimics the Aristotelian procedure of creating descriptive and prescriptive categories. The critical consensus on the importance, if not the meaning, of Fielding's preface and the comparative neglect of Richardson's postscript testify to Fielding's success in getting readers to take his narrator—and, thus, his commentary—seriously (even too seriously, at times).

Like authority, the issue of mimesis both allies Fielding with—and separates him from—Richardson. In an embrace of the mimetic imperative that Richardson would undoubtedly have shared, Fielding's narrator elevates *Joseph Andrews* over romances on the ground that its author is among those "contented to copy

Nature, instead of forming Originals from the confused Heap of Matter" (188) in his own brain. Yet the question of what it means to copy nature—in particular, human nature—elicited a bifurcated response from Fielding. His own narrative practice indicated a preference for generality and externality, a definition of human nature in the aggregate, and a portrayal of the species rather than the individual. Nonetheless, an undeniable attraction to a more internal, psychological rendering of character persisted. In the signed preface to his sister's *David Simple*, Fielding considers the novel's principal merit to be "a vast Penetration into human Nature, a deep and profound Discernment of all the Mazes, Windings and Labyrinths, which perplex the Heart of Man to such a degree, that he is himself often incapable of seeing them."[96] While the language of labyrinths is derived from the invocation to Genius in book 13 of *Tom Jones* (2:685), in the preface to *David Simple* it is used to refer specifically to acute psychological forces— forces that also seem to be at work in *Clarissa*—thereby provoking Fielding's engagement and empathy. In his famous letter to Richardson, Fielding praises his rival's portrayal of his heroine and the "wonderful Art" with which he had "prepared us for both Terror and Compassion" on Clarissa's account.[97] In *The Jacobite's Journal* No. 5, Fielding extends the encomium and makes it public: "Such Simplicity, such Manners, such deep Penetration into Nature; such Power to raise and alarm the Passions, few Writers, either ancient or modern, have been possessed of. My Affections are so strongly engaged, and my Fears are so raised, by what I have already read, that I cannot express my Eagerness to see the rest."[98] With no attempt to resolve—or even discuss—the conflict between generality and depth, Fielding the writer pursued the former and Fielding the reader admired the latter.

A reconciliation of conflicting ideas on the proper language for depicting human nature remained just as elusive. Defending the obvious flights of rhetoric and the ornamental style in *Tom Jones*, the narrator contrasts his practice with the plainness—and, therefore, dullness—of most contemporary *histories:*

> We have taken every Occasion of interspersing through the whole sundry Similes, Descriptions, and other kind of poetical Embellishments. These are, indeed, designed to . . . refresh the Mind, whenever those Slumbers which in a long Work are apt to invade the Reader as well as the Writer, shall begin to creep upon him. Without Interruptions of this Kind, the best Narrative of plain Matter of Fact must overpower every Reader. (1:151)

Beneath the bantering tone, Fielding implies that embellishment engages and challenges a reader in ways that an unadorned text may not. By the time of *Amelia,* Fielding had clearly revised his aesthetic; but even in *Tom Jones* itself, he signaled a change. The famous valedictory to the reader, which compares the relationship between reader and narrator to that of passengers in a stagecoach, concludes with the suggestion that just as the end of a journey provokes plain and serious talk,

> if I have now and then, in the Course of this Work, indulged any Pleasantry for thy Entertainment, I shall here lay it down. The Variety of Matter, indeed, which I shall be obliged to cram into this Book, will afford no Room for any of those ludicrous Observations which I have elsewhere made, and which may sometimes, perhaps, have prevented thee from taking a Nap when it was beginning to steal upon thee. In this last Book thou wilt find nothing (or at most very little) of that Nature. All will be plain Narrative only; and indeed, when thou hast perused the many great Events which this Book will produce, thou wilt think the Number of Pages contained in it, scarce sufficient to tell the Story. (2:912)

A phrase like "obliged to cram" captures the predicament of the architectonic novelist whose material and pace threaten his elaborate, symmetrical structure. At the same time, Fielding may have been obliquely admitting the inadequacy of an embellished style for communicating serious climactic action, or may even have been anticipating the stylistic changes evident in his final novel. All of the alternatives are possible; but Fielding, again, avoided offering definitive answers—this time, by taking refuge in an appealing simile.

Fielding's analysis of probability—an element more essential than language to any coherent mimetic theory—proves divided as well. However tongue-in-cheek, comparing Charlotte Lennox's *The Female Quixote* favorably to *Don Quixote* for its "less extravagant and incredible"[99] adventures aligns Fielding with Richardson and numerous predecessors in support of a generalized notion of verisimilitude—as does the narrator's insistence in *Tom Jones* that "private" historians should "keep within the Limits not only of Possibility, but of Probability too" (1:402). Yet, the discourse in which this statement occurs—the longest of the introductory chapters, full of learned summaries of neoclassical criticism of the marvellous—offers a more equivocal view. According to the narrator, actions "should be such as may not only be within the Compass of human Agency, and which Agents may probably be supposed to do; but they should be likely for the very Actors and Characters themselves to have performed" (1:405). Dubbed "Conservation of Character,"[100] this doctrine indeed serves probability; but as the doctrine's name implies, it extends only to character. In the words of Robert V. Wess, the "important thing to attend to in these rules is that they are all prescriptions about agents involved in events, not about relations between events."[101] Thus, the narrator can remain within the rules of his own making, can lay a claim to probability, and can still admit the marvellous into the text—as well as allow other writers the same privilege, with salutary results: "Within these few Restrictions, I think, every Writer may be permitted to deal as much in the Wonderful as he pleases; nay, if he thus keeps within the Rules of Credibility, the more he can surprize the Reader, the more he will engage his Attention, and the more he will charm him" (1:406). An additional—but only partial—qualification is added in book 17, where the narrator promises to lend Tom "none of that supernatural Assistance with which we are entrusted, upon Condition that we use it only on very important Occasions. If he doth not therefore find some natural Means of fairly extricating himself from all his Distresses, we will do no Violence to the Truth and Dignity of History for his Sake" (2:875–76). To some readers, the chain of coincidences that enables Tom eventually to gain a birthright and a wife constitute ample violence to probability—even if they do figure a providential moral order. Defining probability narrowly—and imbuing the definition with a tone of authority—may represent Fielding's attempt to preempt or deflect such criticisms, in order to justify the pursuit of often conflicting goals of verisimilitude and control.

Outside of this discussion, plot seldom drew extended commentary by Fielding—which is ironic in light of the sustained critical attention his plots have received. The few remarks he did make are striking only in their strong resemblance to Richardson's beliefs and strategies. In the preface to *David Simple,* Fielding invokes Homer both to contrast plots that depict a single action, for example, *The Iliad,* with those that show "a Series of Actions, all tending to produce one great End," for example, *The Odyssey,* and to defend the latter method, used in *David Simple* and in each of his own novels: those "who should object want of Unity of Action here, may, if they please, or if they dare, fly back with their Objection, in the Face even of the *Odyssey* itself."[102] The "one great End" remained the prominent criterion—as it did for Richardson—and provided, as in the postscript to *Clarissa* and the preface to

Grandison, a ready defense against objections to individual parts of the narrative. The narrator of *Tom Jones* warns that in the process of reading the novel, one must not "too hastily . . . condemn any of the Incidents in this our History, as impertinent and foreign to our main Design, because thou dost not immediately conceive in what Manner such Incident may conduce to that Design" (2:524). Only a slanderer, moreover, would "pass a severe Sentence upon the Whole, merely on account of some vicious Part" (2:570). In both moral and aesthetic terms, the end justifies—and subsumes—the means.

With regard to character, any similarities to Richardson's views are superficial at best. Given Fielding's advocacy of conservation of character, one could expect him to agree with Richardson both in supporting the adaptation of sentiment to character—a practice for which Fielding praised the author of *David Simple*—and in disdaining sudden conversions, by which, according to the narrator of *Tom Jones,* authors of contemporary comedy allow "a Rogue to repent in the last Act of a Play" (1:406). (Tom Jones's repentance may seem little more convincing, but at least he rejects the advances of Mrs. Hunt and Mrs. Fitzpatrick well before he is able to win Sophia at the end of the novel.) Fielding's more significant insights on characterization differ radically from Richardson's, not only in voicing a preference for the general and external but also in defining character as essentially static. Readers of *Tom Jones* are instructed that "it is a more useful Capacity to be able to foretel the Actions of Men in any Circumstance from their Characters; than to judge of their Characters from their Actions" (1:117)—a rule that presupposes considerable consistency, as does the doctrine of conservation. An apparent contradiction arises in the comparison of the world and the stage, where the narrator acknowledges that authors,

> who are admitted behind the Scenes of this great Theatre of Nature . . . can censure the Action, without conceiving any absolute Detestation of the Person, whom perhaps Nature may not have designed to act an ill Part in all her Dramas: For in this Instance, Life most exactly resembles the Stage, since it is often the same Person who represents the Villain and the Hero; and he who engages your Admiration Today, will probably attract your Contempt To-Morrow. (1:327)

Yet, although the closing metaphor implies unpredictability, the narrator in the beginning of the sentence reiterates the notion of essential, determined character—superior to and unthreatened by any single aberrant incident.

By minimizing, with questionable logic, the effect of individual actions on fundamental moral worth, Fielding paved the way for a defense of the mixed character. Although the narrator illustrates the generalization quoted above by referring to the failure of Black George to return Tom's money to him, the reader cannot help but recall Tom's own shortcomings and indiscretions and apply the reassuring remarks to Tom as well. With none of the anguish evident in Richardson's numerous notes and letters about Lovelace, Fielding went on to argue, not merely the acceptability, but the greater moral utility of mixed characters. Models of unalloyed virtue or vice are not salutary, since "from contemplating either, the Mind of Man is more likely to be overwhelmed with Sorrow and Shame, than to draw any good Uses from such Patterns" (2:527); in other words, the inimitability of utter perfection is as distressing as unenviable depravity. In a predominantly good character, on the other hand, some flaws will "raise our Compassion rather than our Abhorrence" and have positive psychological and moral effects:

> The Foibles and Vices of Men in whom there is great Mixture of Good, become more glaring Objects, from the Virtues which contrast them, and shew their Deformity; and when we find such Vices attended with their evil Consequences to our favourite Characters, we are not only taught to shun them for our own Sake, but to hate them for the Mischiefs they have already brought on those we love. (2:527)

Aside from providing a convenient defense for Tom, "this Rogue, whom we have unfortunately made our Heroe" (2:875), Fielding's comments project a more sophisticated awareness of the psychology of reading than Richardson's tenacious support and only half-hearted questioning of moral exemplars.

A similar tone of assurance and sophistication informs Fielding's attack on poetic justice, but the problematic implications of his remarks signal the danger for readers inevitably swayed by the authoritative pose. With none of Richardson's circuitous reasoning or classical quotations, the narrator of *Tom Jones* uses characteristic humor to reject the concept out of hand: "There are a Set of Religious, or rather Moral Writers, who teach that Virtue is the certain Road to Happiness, and Vice to Misery in this World. A very wholesome and comfortable Doctrine, and to which we have but one Objection, namely, That it is not True" (2:783). Elaborating more soberly, the narrator rejects any Christian basis for the doctrine, "which is indeed destructive of one of the noblest

Arguments that Reason alone can furnish for the Belief of Immortality" (2:784). Both the sarcasm and the seriousness sound convincing; yet, at the end of the novel, Fielding has conspicuously and unmistakably rewarded the virtue of his hero and punished the vice of his chief nemesis, Blifil.[103] Eager to diminish the apparent inconsistency, critics have distinguished between the comic, symbolic world of the novel and the unjust literal world of experience[104]—or have suggested that there is no inevitability to the final reckoning and that things need not have worked out as they did.[105] A less ingenious—but also less complimentary—solution derives, once again, from context. As the example to refute the validity of poetic justice, Fielding's narrator cites the "rewarding" of Tom's virtuous efforts to ensure a marriage between Nightingale and Nancy Miller with machinations that would "make him completely miserable in the Ruin of his *Sophia*" (2:784). Using a fictional character's created and easily alterable predicament as proof against a literary rule undermines the attack but, at the same time, reinforces the reader's sympathy for Tom, at a point when his affair with Lady Bellaston threatens it. Thus, the comment seems more a provisional rhetorical device than a sincere, reliable, critical judgment.

The understandable compulsion to inscribe consistency on Fielding's critical remarks—even when they are at odds with his creative practice in the texts in which they appear—offers perhaps the strongest testimony to the novelist's success at creating an authoritative and appealing persona. His eloquence, knowledge, and humor have encouraged readers to conceive of each comment as part of a premeditated and seamless critical program, in much the same way as Fielding would have had us regard individual chapters in relation to a whole novel. But under scrutiny, the analogy cannot hold; in fact, a metaphorical vehicle more apt than a series of chapters would be writing with which Fielding was equally familiar—namely, opposing legal briefs. Contrasting Fielding's criticism with Richardson's, as helpful as it may be, only obscures the more important interpretive task of contrasting it with itself—of deconstructing the very notion of a unified, integrated criticism in the first place. The same task challenges the reader of the slight—but disproportionately influential—commentary on the novel by Samuel Johnson.

* * *

As a critic of fiction, Johnson has become the captive of his acerbity and his timing. For many readers, he remains either the brusque Boswellian, whose conversational thrusts against Fielding elicit argument or apology,[106] or the more abstract, didactic critic in *Rambler* No. 4, the first in a line of earnest reactionaries who privileged morality in an excessive and reductive way.[107] Both postures—the angry antagonist and the sober moralist—have successfully projected confidence and authority; but, in truth, each facade is fractured by competing sensibilities, varying contexts, and genuine uncertainty. Johnson's attitude toward prose fiction in general, his moral argument in *Rambler* No. 4, his formalistic comparisons of Richardson and Fielding, and his odd attraction to *Amelia* reveal several contradictions, both inherent and in relation to the rest of his critical corpus. The very paucity of commentary throws the contradictions into sharper relief. Arising from the many sides of Johnson's moral and aesthetic thought, the contradictions lend ample credence to Imlac's insight, "Inconsistencies . . . cannot both be right, but, imputed to man, they may both be true."[108]

A writer and critic of his age, Johnson readily voiced the contemporary disdain for most prose fiction. In his dedication to Charlotte Lennox's *Shakespear Illustrated,* he derides most novels—in this context, the term would signify amatory novellas—and romances as products of "wit or idleness, vanity or indigence,"[109] as derivative and repetitive. One might easily expect this reaction to formulaic fiction, but elsewhere Johnson went much further. Sir John Hawkins has reported that despite Johnson's often-stated admiration for Richardson, he "could be at any time talked into a disapprobation of all fictitious relations, of which he would frequently say they took no hold on the mind."[110] Behind such sentiments lay not only Johnson's frank subordination of all fiction to truth[111] but also the manifest vapidity of much of the popular fiction published during his lifetime.

In other contexts, however, both specific texts and the novel as genre won Johnson's sanction. In the famous opening of *Rambler* No. 4, Johnson elevates contemporary fiction over earlier romances on mimetic grounds; it is superior because, in Johnson's words, it exhibits "life in its true state, diversified only by accidents that daily happen in the world, and influenced by passions and qualities which are really to be found in conversing with mankind."[112] Something more than mimesis accounts for an equally famous, apparently eccentric list: "Was there ever yet any thing written by mere man that was wished longer by its readers, excepting Don Quixote, Robinson Crusoe, and the Pilgrim's Progress?"[113] Despite several obvious differences, these works—all of which deviate in varying degrees from strict verisimilitude—share a common formal feature: a resistance to closure, which encourages sequels, both genuine and spurious, and calls attention to the text as artifice. The writer who ended *Rasselas* with a "Conclusion in which Nothing is Concluded" anticipated a modern sensibility in his preference for open endings.

If realism can give way to other formal considerations, it certainly can give way to moral dictates. Hence, Johnson's rapid movement in *Rambler* No. 4 away from an absolute preference for presenting "life in its true state" and toward an advocacy of selecting and arranging materials to serve a didactic end.[114] According to Johnson, the effect of fiction on impressionable minds[115] necessitates regulation:

> If the power of example is so great, as to take possession of the memory by a kind of violence, and produce effects almost without the intervention of the will, care ought to be taken that, when the choice is unrestrained, the best examples only should be exhibited; and that which is likely to operate so strongly, should not be mischievous or uncertain in its effects.[116]

Johnson's description of the "best" examples as characters who exhibit "virtue not angelical, nor above probability . . . but the highest and purest that humanity can reach" tacitly embraced and defended the acknowledged practice of Richardson. Conversely, his argument that vice "should always disgust; nor should the graces of gaiety, or the dignity of courage, be so united with it, as to reconcile it to the mind" implicitly attacked Fielding's "compromised" hero in *Tom Jones,* which had been published four months earlier.[117]

Elsewhere, Johnson was much more explicit about both authors and the degree to which each successfully balanced realism and morality. In *Rambler* No. 97, Johnson introduces Richardson as a writer who "has enlarged the knowledge of the human heart and taught the passions to move at the command of virtue";[118] and Miss Reynolds reported that Johnson "always spoke with the highest enthusiastic praise"[119] of *Clarissa.* More specifically, he regarded Lovelace, despite Richardson's anxieties, as the only genuinely successful mixed character, because the reader retains awareness of his faults and ultimately condemns him. In this, Lovelace was superior to his original, Rowe's Lothario, for it "was in the power of Richardson alone to teach us at once esteem and detestation; to make virtuous resentment overpower all the be-

nevolence which wit, elegance, and courage naturally excite, and
to lose at last the hero in the villain."[120] Fielding, on the other
hand, attracts memorable, blunt derision, which Johnson justifies
on the grounds of unselective realism:

> Fielding being mentioned, Johnson exclaimed, 'he was a blockhead;'
> and upon my expressing my astonishment at so strange an assertion,
> he said, 'What I mean by his being a blockhead is that he was a barren
> rascal.' BOSWELL. 'Will you not allow, Sir, that he draws very natural
> pictures of human life?' JOHNSON. 'Why, Sir, it is of very low life.
> Richardson used to say, that had he not known who Fielding was, he
> should have believed he was an ostler. Sir, there is more knowledge of
> the heart in one letter of Richardson's, than in all "Tom Jones." I,
> indeed, never read "Joseph Andrews."'[121]

Fielding, however, was in good company. Shakespeare draws
similar censure, as Johnson perceives the "great fault" of *The
Merry Wives of Windsor* to be "the frequency of expressions so
profane, that no necessity of preserving character can justify
them. There are laws of higher authority than those of criticism."[122] This higher authority compels Johnson, in a key passage
from his "Preface to *Shakespeare*," to criticize the "poet of nature"
for failing to fulfill his obligation to organize the raw material of
nature rather than to, simply, represent it:

> From his writings indeed a system of social duty may be selected, for
> he that thinks reasonably must think morally; but his precepts and
> axioms drop casually from him; he makes no just distribution of good
> and evil, nor is always careful to shew in the virtuous a disapprobation
> of the wicked; he carries his persons indifferently through right and
> wrong, and at the close he dismisses them without further care, and
> leaves their examples to operate by chance.[123]

Thus, not only conversational thrusts—which must always be
regarded as occasional and provisional—but also more authoritative published comments reinforced the apparent moralistic rigor
of *Rambler* No. 4. Does one, then (to borrow Johnson's own phras-
ing) lose, at last, the critic in the moralist? Only if one ignores the
Johnson who often forthrightly subordinated explicit moralizing
to other, openly aesthetic ends. He discounts, for example, the
myriad objections to Gay's *Beggar's Opera*. According to Johnson,
it was written "only to divert, without any moral purpose"; but
precisely because the audience must see it as no more than a
diversion, its effects are harmless: no one will "imagine that he

may rob with safety because he sees Macheath reprieved upon the stage."[124] On different—but equally significant grounds—he rejects John Dennis's criticism of Addison's *Cato* for its lack of poetic justice by arguing that if drama "be truly the *mirrour* of life, it ought to show us sometimes what we expect."[125] Both sensible audience response and the mimetic imperative could override extreme didacticism.

With hermeneutics and realism firmly in mind, Johnson could approve the mixed character in principal and in practice, in life and in letters. Boswell has reported Johnson's commendation of scripture writers for relating "the vicious as well as the virtuous actions of men; which had this moral effect, that it kept mankind from *despair*, into which they would naturally fall,"[126] given flawless, inimitable models. Far stronger than the parenthetical nod to probability offered thirty years earlier in *Rambler* No. 4, this remark weds mimesis to moral efficacy. And it was hardly isolated. Johnson praises his disreputable friend Richard Savage for possessing "all the different combinations of passions and the innumerable mixtures of vice and virtue, which distinguish one character from another,"[127] just as he admires Shakespeare for exhibiting "the real state of sublunary nature, which partakes of good and evil, joy and sorrow, mingled with endless variety of proportion and innumerable modes of combination."[128] Prince Hal, "whose virtues are obscured by negligence, and whose understanding is dissipated by levity," remains, nonetheless, a "great, original, and just character."[129] Most revealing is Johnson's extended apostrophe to the greatest mixed character in English drama: "But Falstaff unimitated, unimitable Falstaff, how shall I describe thee? Thou compound of sense and vice; of sense which may be admired but not esteemed, of vice which may be despised, but hardly detested."[130] Carey McIntosh has observed that Johnson's compulsion to conclude his treatment of Falstaff with a moral tag demonstrates his uneasiness, yet the language—"The moral to be drawn from this representation is, that no man is more dangerous than he that with a will to corrupt, hath the power to please"—is pedestrian and perfunctory, reflecting none of the enthusiasm with which Johnson celebrated Falstaff's character.[131]

In a critic so prolific—in criticism so practical and offered over such a long period of time—it requires little effort to find support for opposed positions. It is more difficult to account for the virtual absence of tension in Johnson's only extended treatment of the novel—in his apparently adamant preference for ethical probity over aesthetic pleasure, or even over honesty. Why did Johnson in *Rambler* No. 4 valorize the most narrowly didactic criteria? Johnson suggests part of the answer in his description of the readership most likely to be affected by fiction: novels "are written chiefly to the young, the ignorant, and the idle, to whom they serve as lectures of conduct, and introductions into life."[132] Accepting the Richardsonian premise that the novel should function as a conduct book for naive readers necessitated insisting that their impressions be anticipated and controlled. *The Beggar's Opera* posed little threat not simply because it was exaggerated, but because a rational adult audience would recognize the exaggeration. With more realistic plots and less experienced readers, Johnson saw a need to circumscribe interpretive freedom.

Johnson's own audience and the context for his discussion played an even larger role. While the *Rambler* includes what may be called literary criticism, it is preeminently a work of moral instruction, just as Johnson's persona is commonly that of the magisterial preacher. A moral essay concerning a popular and potentially dangerous new genre cannot proceed with the balanced method of avowedly critical writing.[133] *Rambler* No. 4 differs, moreover, from all of the other critical essays in the journal. Some tend to examine local problems of language and structure in specific texts—Milton's versification (Nos. 87–94), the use of mean expressions in Shakespeare (No. 176)—through a kind of close reading. Others do evaluate genres—pastoral poetry (Nos. 36–37), tragicomedy (No. 125)—but proceed by reference to textual examples, an approach that Johnson scrupulously avoided in *Rambler* No. 4. Specificity derives from distance: Johnson was far enough removed from these texts—and from the origins of these genres—to attempt practical criticism.[134] In the noted opening to the "Preface to *Shakespeare*," in which Johnson called "length of duration and continuance of esteem" the principal signs of artistic merit, he stresses the necessity of distance for forming comparative judgments, which are the only legitimate ones for a critic:

> As among the works of nature no man can properly call a river deep or a mountain high, without the knowledge of many mountains and many rivers; so in the productions of genius, nothing can be stiled excellent till it has been compared with other works of the same kind. Demonstration immediately displays its power, and has nothing to hope or fear from the flex of years; but works tentative and experimental must be estimated by their proportion to the general and collective ability of man, as it is discovered in a long succession of endeavours.[135]

Few works were more tentative and experimental than the novels of the 1740s; therefore, Johnson anticipated his precept by avoiding criticism of specific texts.

But one need not even look so far ahead to the "Preface to *Shakespeare*" for support for Johnson's reticence. Published just four days before *Rambler* No. 4, *Rambler* No. 3 offers an allegorical account of Criticism, in which the subject, "the eldest daughter of Labour and of Truth," either confers immortality upon or consigns to oblivion the "performances of those who professed themselves the votaries of the Muses." So many of these performances have "beauties and faults . . . so equally mingled" that Criticism is reluctant to pass final judgment, and so abdicates in favor of Time, with salutary results:

> The proceedings of Time, though very dilatory, were, some few caprices excepted, conformable to Justice: and many, who thought themselves secure by a short forbearance, have sunk under his scythe, as they were posting down with their volumes in triumph to futurity. It was observable that some were destroyed by little and little, and others crushed for ever by a single blow.[136]

The reader of *Rambler* No. 3 must come to the next number with a healthy skepticism of criticism of contemporary authors and genres. *Rambler* No. 4, then, represents a well-intentioned moral warning far more than it does a piece of candid critical writing.

A close analysis of Johnson's language, which acknowledges this distance and creates a different type, further erodes the critical authority of the text. The hesitant verb *seems* in the opening sentence—"The works of fiction, with which the present generation seems more particularly delighted, are such as exhibit life in its true state"[137]—as well as the provisional tone of the phrase "these familiar histories may perhaps be made of greater use than the solemnities of professed morality,"[138] demonstrate the difficulty of making definitive statements about so recent a genre. This uncharacteristic tentativeness extends to Johnson's advocacy of exemplary characters, where the double negative hardly indicates a ringing endorsement: "In narratives, where historical veracity has no place, I cannot discover why there should not be exhibited the most perfect idea of virtue."[139] And however confident Johnson may sound elsewhere in the essay, his remarks on readers of fiction indirectly acknowledge his inability to communicate with them. In addition to classifying most novel readers as young, ignorant, and idle, he maintains that novels "are the entertainment of minds unfurnished with ideas, and therefore easily susceptible of impressions; not fixed by principles, and therefore easily following the current of fancy; not informed by experience, and consequently open to every false suggestion and partial account."[140] The penultimate sentence of the essay goes further, shifting the indictment from ignorance to misplaced pride: "The Roman tyrant was content to be hated, if he was but feared; and there are thousands of readers of romances waiting to be thought wicked, if they may be allowed to be wits."[141] Such unflattering descriptions would naturally result from an assumption that none of these readers would be likely to read or be guided by the *Rambler*. Like later periodical reviewers of fiction, Johnson created hierarchies among the reading public and condescended to novel readers—a tactic presumably satisfying to his own implied audience but, at the same time, signaling the powerlessness of the critic.

For specific and openly aesthetic commentary free of some of the rhetorical constraints of *Rambler* No. 4, one must turn to Johnson's conversation, however compromised its status may be.[142] Speaking to Boswell, Johnson develops the contrast repeated by virtually every critic and teacher who has ever analyzed the relative merits of Richardson and Fielding:

> Sir, . . . there is all the difference in the world between characters of nature and characters of manners; and *there* is the difference between the characters of Fielding and those of Richardson. Characters of manners are very entertaining; but they are to be understood, by a more superficial observer, than characters of nature, where a man must dive into the recesses of the human heart.

Moving from argument to metaphor, he compares the difference between Richardson and Fielding to that "between a man who knew how a watch was made, and a man who could tell the hour by looking on the dial-plate."[143]

Predictably, response has been partisan. Defenders of Fielding have accused Johnson of slighting the novel of manners and ignoring Fielding's conspicuous efforts to "show what goes on beneath the dial-plate."[144] Conversely, the simile actually structures Ian Watt's entire critique of *Tom Jones* in *The Rise of the Novel*, although Watt has faulted Johnson for not appreciating Fielding's unique artistic aims.[145] Watt's attraction to the simile is appropriate and his criticism of Johnson ironic, since his own theory of "formal realism" privileges the Richardsonian approach in much the same way. Still, he has accurately traced the comment to Johnson's admiration of the dramatic mode of characterization resulting from Richardson's epistolary method, in which characters reveal themselves without the obtrusive and limiting intervention of an external narrative voice. More recently, Mark Kinkead-Weekes has persuasively linked Johnson's stated preference for "characters of nature" to his immersion in Shakespeare during the preparation of his edition.[146] But perhaps the most basic source for Johnson's sentiments lies in one of the principal tenets of his moral writing: each of us is inevitably attracted to talents that he does not possess. While he may not have recognized his affinities with Fielding— which later critics have dutifully enumerated[147]—Johnson must have been aware that he himself was an intrusive storyteller, for whom dialogue was not a strength.[148] *Rasselas*, the narratives in the *Rambler* and the *Idler*, and even *Irene* subordinate developed characters to an overarching narrative voice. Richardson had presumably found a better way, winning Johnson's conscious praise— and, perhaps, his unconscious envy.

Several critics have noted the apparent inconsistency of Johnson's preference for psychologically complex and highly individualized characters, given his repeated insistence on the ethical and aesthetic superiority of generality.[149] Johnson's language, however—his often idiosyncratic use of the terms *nature* and *manners*— clearly represents an attempt to conflate complexity and universality, on the one side, and shallowness and specificity, on the other. He faults Warburton, for instance, for judging Polonius "a character only of manners, discriminated by properties superficial, accidental, and acquired," and concludes that only "part of his character is accidental, the rest is natural." More specifically, while the sententious courtier may be a character of manners, the embodiment of "dotage encroaching upon wisdom"[150] is a character of nature. From the same perspective, Johnson elsewhere relegated "manners" to signifying transitory customs: Shakespeare errs in *Cymbeline* by comingling the "manners of distant ages"[151] and in *Julius Caesar* "his adherence to the real story, and to Roman manners, seems to have impeded the natural vigour of his genius."[152] The most famous comparison of nature and manners differs only in the emphasis provided by Johnson's adjectives:

> Nothing can please many, and please long, but just representations of general nature. Particular manners can be known to few, and therefore few only can judge how nearly they are copied. The irregular combinations of fanciful invention may delight a-while, by that novelty of which the common satiety of life sends us all in quest; but the

pleasures of sudden wonder are soon exhausted, and the mind can only repose on the stability of truth.[153]

Although nature need not—and does not—always mean *general* nature, it does so in the context of opposition to manners. Unfortunately, Johnson reconciled depth and generality by fiat rather than by argument. In other words, he seems to have wanted it both ways—for "characters of nature" to signify both dramatically rendered personality and generalized normative code.[154]

However troubling the terminology and its implications, Johnson's attraction to dramatic characterization—both grounded in and combined with a reader-centered desire for pathos—contributed significantly toward his unlikely admiration for *Amelia*. According to Johnson, characters of nature elicit a complex emotional, psychological, and moral response precisely because the audience can empathize with them. And empathy increases with familiarity. Hence, Johnson's extravagant and often-questioned praise of the scene of Queen Catherine's preparations for death in *Henry VIII:* "This scene is above any other part of Shakespeare's tragedies, and perhaps above any scene of any other poet, tender and pathetick, without gods, or furies, or poisons, or precipices, without the help of romantick circumstances, without improbable sallies of poetical lamentation, and without any throes of tumultuous misery."[155] Similar enthusiasm greets domestic tragedies such as *Timon of Athens,* which "strongly fastens on the attention of the reader,"[156] and *The Fair Penitent,* which is "easily received by the imagination and assimilated to common life."[157] Thus, Amelia, like Clarissa, emerges as a character primarily through dialogue in dramatic scenes, many of which evoke deep pathos; the author of *Amelia,* like the author of *Clarissa,* exploited the affective power of domestic tragedy,[158] though he ultimately undercut this power with a problematic happy ending. Little wonder that Johnson would find both the character and the novel congenial.

More wonder, given his pronounced antipathy to Fielding, that Johnson indicated a preference for Fielding's final novel over Richardson's masterpiece. Disputing Mrs. Thrale's enshrinement of Clarissa as the perfect character, Johnson observes that "there is always something which she prefers to truth. Fielding's Amelia was the most pleasing heroine of all the romances."[159] Here the rigorous moralism of *Rambler* No. 4, with Johnson's insistence upon icons of unalloyed virtue, drives a judgment that jars with the modern reader's appreciation of the greater complexity of

Clarissa's character. Equally surprising—but nonetheless compatible with Johnson's affective bias—is his expression of respect for Fielding's superior ability to sustain the reader's attention. Boswell has recounted Johnson's arguing that "'what we read with inclination makes a much stronger impression. If we read without inclination, half the mind is employed in fixing the attention; so there is but one half to be employed on what we read.' He told us, he read Fielding's 'Amelia' through without stopping."[160] To Richardson, however, Johnson pays the double-edged compliment that "Clarissa is not a performance to be read with eagerness and laid aside for ever, but will be occasionally consulted by the busy, the aged, and the studious."[161] The remark may seem, in assuming such a serious audience for Richardson, a commendation from one moralist to another; but the adjectives chosen to characterize Richardson's readership were the exact opposites of those used a year earlier in *Rambler* No. 4 to depict the intended audience of prose fiction. The language implies—and, I would argue, consciously—that Richardson was not reaching the readers whom both he and Johnson most desired to instruct.[162] Elsewhere, Johnson embraces Richardson's subordination of story to doctrine but slights the story in a way that would certainly have offended a writer as sensitive as Richardson: "Why, Sir, if you were to read Richardson for the story, your impatience would be so much fretted that you would hang yourself. But you must read him for the sentiment, and consider the story as only giving occasion to the sentiment."[163] *Amelia,* on the other hand, both satisfied Johnson's moral demands for fiction and accomplished what he claimed few books could: it interested him enough to finish it.

What makes Johnson's discourse on the novel especially interesting is its impressionistic nature: his tendency to examine isolated features of individual texts in different contexts necessarily resulted in provocative but unorganized insights. Yet, I doubt that a more systematic critical effort would have yielded any greater coherence, given the fundamental conflict within Johnson between absolutely candid responses and a superimposed, moralistic self-discipline. In this conflict, however, lies Johnson's greatest contribution to criticism of the novel. Like Richardson and Fielding, he was a critic in dialogue with himself—even at odds with himself—and has, thus, bequeathed, not limits, but possibilities—a multiplicity of interpretive stances and strategies. Ironically enough, all three writers—Johnson, Richardson, and Fielding— strove mightily to mask a dialogic tendency that today's readers would wish to celebrate.

3

Respect, Readers, or Both?
The Later Novelists

By the middle of the eighteenth century, the novel had attained
a certain status but not lasting security. The success of Richardson
and Fielding, in both theory and practice, helped to institutional-
ize the genre—so much so that the writers of the fledgling literary
reviews felt obliged to devote regular, if grudging, attention to
prose fiction. Given a wide, diverse audience, it was no longer
necessary to include elaborate prefatory definitions or defenses
to convince readers that novels should not be dismissed out of
hand; therefore, internal commentary predictably diminished.
Yet, broader acceptance of the genre often complicated the task
of individual novelists—especially those eager for both a large
and a serious readership—thereby producing a different kind of
critical discourse. With the deluge of inferior fiction, many writers
attempted either to establish their credentials as legitimate heirs
to the already canonized masters or to foreground the uniqueness
that distinguished their work from both the inhibiting example of
these masters and the consistently similar—as well as consistently
poor—productions of the hacks, against which sober critics railed.

Much of the commentary offered by a wide variety of novelists
in the latter half of the century, then, serves less as sophisticated
formal analysis than as a revealing barometer of the shifting place
of the novel in literary culture and in important interpretive sub-
cultures. Searching for both critical acceptance and commercial
success, many novelists self-consciously exploited the open-ended
form of the preface in order to attract distinct audiences—often
several at once. As a result, broad issues of general interest—such
as morality, probability, and originality—predominated over more
minute formal concerns. Yet, a search for readers or respect could
not—and did not—eliminate risk-taking and innovation: although
several safe commentators were content to repeat conventional

formulae, others attempted to alter, extend, or complicate the conventions in provocative ways.

* * *

No prefaces were more blatantly self-conscious than those that demeaned or parodied the form itself, thus enabling authors to attack the posturing—and the dullness—of their contemporaries. Henry Brooke begins *The Fool of Quality* (1766) with the blunt complaint, "I hate prefaces. I never read them, and why should I write them."[1] In *Eden Vale* (1784), Catherine Parry less histrionically compares prefaces unfavorably to dramatic prologues, since the former usually consist of "a few dull prosaic lines, which seldom say any thing but what has been better expressed, and more to the purpose, before."[2] Several novelists furnished a possible explanation for this deficiency by repeating Fielding's lament that the difficulty of writing a preface was seldom rewarded with the reader's attention to the result.[3] The most common charge leveled against the preface, however, involved its use as a forum for diffident and pandering apologiae. Harriet Lee archly observes that "it should seem as if little remained for [an author] to say in his own person," since the days of false modesty are over.[4] Richard Graves goes further, ironically cataloguing various prefatorial excuses in the transparent persona of the editor of *The Spiritual Quixote* (1773). Having informed the reader that the original author probably committed suicide, Graves as editor concludes, "I cannot but think, that instead of an Editor's informing the world, that a work was produced, either amidst an hurry of business, or in retirement; in a fit of sickness, or on a journey; by a youth under twenty, or by a Lady; or the like interesting circumstances; it would be more likely to rouze the curiosity of mankind, to assure them, that it was written by a man that had either hanged or drowned himself."[5] In a similar vein, Robert Bage includes a preface to *Mount Henneth* (1782) solely "to soften the severity of . . . criticism, by information of the reasons, which drew me in to write," namely, new silk gowns for his daughters![6] Sarcastic and parodic metaprefaces like these are grounded in self-contradiction—having been created, in effect, to deny the value of their own existence. Inviting—but ignoring—ontological complications, the authors attempted to establish themselves as superior wits in order to win readers; yet, their use of the preface as a rhetorical tool differed only in degree from that of the inferiors whom they derided and who were pursuing the same goal.

"Pleading prefaces"[7]—like those parodied by Graves and

Bage—in fact, represent the most conspicuous attempt to identify and satisfy a particular audience. The vast majority were written by women seeking indulgence or candour from readers and critics—due to unique hardships, laudable moral aims, or simply the inadequacies of their gender. Despite contempt or indifference from reviewers, prefaces like that of the aptly titled *Memoirs of Harriot and Charlotte Meanwell* (1757), in which the novelists diffidently "forego all claims to the reputation of Authors" in the hope that the critics will disregard "inaccuracies, which the disadvantages of the sex at once excuse or amend,"[8] pleas like those of the Gothic novelist Eliza Parsons that admitted artistic deficiencies be weighed against poverty and widowhood,[9] and the omnipresent phrase "By a Lady" flourished into the nineteenth century. If the rhetoric was conventional—a gesture recognized as such by the critics—why did it persist? Patricia Meyer Spacks has inferred female writers' reluctance to assert themselves—a reluctance embodied in their narratives; but a more obvious reason is implicit in her acknowledgment that women were writing primarily for other women.[10] A tone of humility would presumably attract the kind of female readers who ignored the reviews; it would signal that the ensuing narrative might appeal to them. No different from the suggestive titles and cover illustrations of today's popular romances, female diffidence shrewdly targeted a specific reading public. Countless minor novelists moved a step further and consciously promised women edification and entertainment.[11] Even Frances Burney, in the important preface to *Evelina*, amusingly acknowledges the dependence of novelists of either sex on patronesses of the circulating libraries:

> Perhaps were it possible to effect the total extirpation of novels, our young ladies in general, and boarding-school damsels in particular, might profit from their annihilation; but since the distemper they have spread seems incurable, since their contagion bids defiance to the medicine of advice or reprehension, and since they are found to baffle all the mental art of physic, save what is prescribed by the slow regimen of Time, and bitter diet of Experience, surely all attempts to contribute to the number of those which may be read, if not with advantage, at least without injury, ought rather to be encouraged than contemned.[12]

Significantly, these remarks—and the novel they help to introduce—were published anonymously and sound as though they might have been written by a man. Like other ambitious female novelists, Burney commonly avoided associating herself and her texts exclusively with female readers of limited tastes. In addition to anonymity, strategies for eschewing the dubious benefits of gender included avoiding prefaces altogether—Radcliffe is a prominent example—or, like Burney, devoting them, as I will show, to more substantial issues, which engaged reviewers and more discriminating readers. The double burden of being a novelist and a woman necessitated emphasizing authorship over gender. And when talented female writers appeared to seek indulgence, they did so in conscious, clever, and often subversive ways. Elizabeth Inchbald might appear to be an exception, since in the preface to *A Simple Story* (1791) she baldly invokes necessity as her only muse, despite the fact that her dramatic writing had left her far from impoverished. But the fulsome paean to necessity with which she concludes the preface can hardly be taken entirely seriously:

> Welcome, then, thou all-powerful principle, NECESSITY!—THOU, who art the instigator of so many bad authors and actors—but, to their shame, not of all:—THOU, who from my infancy seldom hast forsaken me, still abide with me.—I will not complain of any hardships thy commands require, so thou doest not urge my pen to prostitution.—In all thy rigour, oh! do not force my toils to libels—or, what is equally pernicious—panegyric on the unworthy![13]

On a different level, one recent critic has read resentment and protest behind Inchbald's prefatory complaint that she had been compelled to write despite a narrow female education.[14] Whether the preface was frivolous, sarcastic, or both, Inchbald dropped it after the second edition—by which time the critics had warmly applauded her novel.

Harriet Lee, who is more explicit about requesting lenience toward *The Errors of Innocence,* is also more explicit about the double-edged effect of gender identification:

> That the author of the following sheets is a woman, is a truth that she has omitted in the title page, simply thro' the fear that those puerile compositions which have occasionally appeared under that sanction, might rather render it a disadvantage, than a recommendation, in the eyes of the judicious. Should the avowal of her sex and youth, however, contribute to silence malevolence, or blunt the arrows of criticism, she is but too sensible of the imperfections of her work, not to aim at entitling it to every possible indulgence.[15]

Lee desired indulgent readers—but also "judicious" ones.

A similar double appeal emerges from Burney's dedication of

Evelina "to the Authors of the Monthly and Critical Reviews." Promising not to invoke "the language of adulation, and the incense of flattery"—the customary resources of the dedicator—the author claims to crave simple justice, unlike the majority of novelists. In the next breath, however, she reminds the critics that they "were all young writers once"—and should therefore pardon her anxiety—quotes Shakespeare's Portia on the value of mercy, dubs the reviewers "Magistrates of the press, and Censors for the Public", and concludes with an apparently craven compliment: "In addressing you jointly, I mean but to mark the generous sentiments by which liberal criticism, to the utter annihilation of envy, jealousy, and all selfish views, ought to be distinguished."[16] Is the language sincere or parodic? The rhetoric admits both readings and appeals to both the sentimental and the cynical reader. No reader claims to be more cynical than a reviewer, but even a reviewer can succumb to flattery. Burney thus covered every affective base except the most obvious. In what I read as a deliberate omission, the anonymous author never mentions gender.

But certainly the most insistent—and probably the most intriguing—pleading occurred in the prefaces of Charlotte Smith. In addition to commenting seriously on the art and craft of fiction, Smith continually reminded the critics that she wrote only from necessity, in order to augment her meager income and to support her many children. In Smith's case, however, the object was less critical indulgence than it was legal justice. As Anne Ehrenpreis has noted, Smith was separated from a reprobate husband in 1788; and although her father-in-law, who had died in 1776, provided for the children, the will was not settled until twenty-two years later.[17] Hence, Smith's particular disdain for lawyers. In the preface to *Marchmont* (1796), she cites the precedent of the "great master of novel-writing, Fielding," who "attacked this legal pestilence before inferior writers ever touched upon it,"[18] and despairs of having any more tangible effect than he did. The villainous lawyer in the novel is drawn from real life, but actually softened, just as the evil characters in *The Young Philosopher* are made "a *little* like people of the sort" Smith had seen, because nothing she "could *imagine* would be so correct, when legal collusion and professional oppression were to be represented."[19] Criticized by the reviewers for including too many of these allusions to her personal affairs in her novels, Smith responds, in the preface to *The Banished Man* (1794), in both aesthetic and personal terms. She compares a novelist to a history painter or a landscape painter who transmutes observation and experience into art, but she also

threatens to be even more explicit about the identity of her perse-
cutors.[20] In short, she exploited the only medium available to her
for venting outrage and seeking redress (not to mention making
money) but also demonstrated through her critical commentary
an awareness that fiction in general—and her fiction, in particular—did much more than this. Like her accomplished sisters,
Smith sent mixed messages as she sought both serious critical
attention and substantial popular support.

A related strategy for attracting a particular audience involved
establishing strata of readers and appealing to the highest level.
Both the anonymous author of *The History of Lord Clayton and Miss
Meredith* (1769) and Sophia Lee in *The Life of a Lover* (1804) justify
the presentation of "uncommon characters"[21] by arguing that
more worldly readers, who "take a wider range in life,"[22] will
recognize the fidelity to nature. More generally, Helenus Scott
maintains that *The Adventures of a Rupee* (1782) can be judged
only by those "who have natural taste with acquired knowledge."[23]
Pursuing the same end negatively, novelists frequently voiced disdain for the tasteless and ignorant majority of readers—a majority
of whom, as the preface to *Evelina* suggests, were assumed to be
women. Elizabeth Griffith, for instance, has modest hopes for *The
Delicate Distress* (1769), since the "generality of NOVEL READERS
may . . . probably, be disappointed in not meeting with any extraordinary adventure, or uncommon situation, in the following
pages,"[24] while George Hadley anticipates female readers' dissatisfaction with *Argal* (1793) because its author avoids persecuted
maidens, love at first sight, improbable recoveries, and convenient
deaths![25] Such an attitude also underlies Bage's sarcastic self-
mockery in claiming that "if my pretty country women will read
nonsense, I am not a man to bar them so reasonable a liberty."[26]
The search for intelligent, sophisticated readers of both sexes—
or those who wished to consider themselves as such—made deni-
gration of women a common rhetorical move, even for female
writers.

Disrespect for the consumers predictably extended to the producers and the products. No single statement anatomizes the objections better than Thomas Holcroft's lament in the preface to
Alwyn (1780):

> Novels have fallen into disrepute. Lovesick girls and boys are supposed
> to be the only persons capable of being amused by them: and while
> poverty of stile, a want of knowledge of the human heart, of men and
> manners; while a puny tale of love and misfortune, cross fathers, and

unhappy children, unnatural rigour, and unaccountable reconciliation, without discrimination of character, without variety of incident,
but with one set of phrases, one languid, inanimate description, with
scarce a single ray of imagination to comfort the disconsolate reader,
are their great characteristics; Novels shall continue to want admirers:
but Tom Jones shall never want admirers.[27]

The concluding reference evokes an extinct golden age—albeit
only thirty years earlier—and implies that a restoration will commence with the novel at hand. However apt his judgment, Holcroft
also carried to an extreme the tendency to separate oneself from
inferior contemporaries—common to many novelists in the period and to anyone working in a suspect genre. Today, producers
of so-called quality television programs ritualistically condemn the
state of their medium for the same reasons. In both cases, self-
interest must qualify absolute sincerity.

*   *   *

Few television producers, however, would frame their objections
on moral grounds or reflect more broadly on the moral uses and
abuses of their genre, as many novelists seemed compelled to do.
Insistent, recurring moralizing prefaces reflected a genuine shift
in sensibility from the days of the rogue-hero but still remained
fraught with rhetorical posturing and ironic possibilities. Given
the plethora of treatises attacking the immorality of fiction,[28]
moral rationales furnished a preemptive defense aimed at placat-
ing the attackers and, more importantly, at comforting readers
guilty at their own pleasure. Small wonder, then, that many novelists made explicit either the specific message (from "the danger
arising from the uncontrolled indulgence of strong affections"[29]
to the "virtue of fortitude"[30]) or the more general moral goals
(from increasing knowledge and faith[31] to combating prejudice
and exhibiting the truth[32]) informing their texts. The clumsiness
and condescension behind such explicit didacticism is cleverly
ridiculed in the "Advertisement" to Thomas Leland's seminal historical novel, *Longsword, Earl of Salisbury* (1762):

It is generally expected that pieces of this kind should convey some
one useful moral: which moral . . . is sometimes made to float on the
surface of the narrative; or is plucked up at proper intervals, and
presented to the view of the reader, with great solemnity. But the
author of these sheets hath too high an opinion of the judgment and
penetration of his readers, to pursue this method. Although he cannot
pretend to be very *deep*, yet he hopes he is *clear*. And if any thing

lies at bottom, worth the picking up, it will be discovered without his direction.[33]

A simpler—but equally suspect—tactic, used even more commonly, was the broad promise of pleasing instruction. As Harriet Lee recognizes, the frequency with which the gilded pill was invoked rendered it merely formulaic: "The wish of conveying instruction under the veil of amusement, has been so often, and so fruitlessly professed, that a repetition of it will be rather apt to excite the smile of incredulity, than to awaken any sanguine hopes of success"; yet, she then proceeds to offer just such a repetition, hoping that "the goodness of the intention" will "plead in excuse for its vanity."[34] While Lee, along with many other novelists, may have been perfectly candid, her practice tends to suggest that novelists found the formula, however empty, as irresistible as politicians find tired patriotic slogans.

Novelists' defensive uses of moralistic disclaimers in strikingly different contexts amply illustrate the versatility of the device. Creators of potentially corrupting characters embraced the aging doctrine of the negative example to present their texts as not merely innocent but also instructive. Smollett argues the affective superiority of the eponymous hero of *Ferdinand Count Fathom* over any paragon of virtue on the ground that "impulses of fear, which is the most violent and interesting of all the passions, remain longer than any other upon the memory";[35] and almost thirty years later, Charles Johnstone relies on a legal analogy in support of the proposition that "example is two-fold, to prevent as well as to excite" imitation: "Now that the former is no less useful than the latter, requires no better proof than the principle of our most excellent laws, which punish crime, but take no notice of virtue."[36] Even Fanny Hill offers her memoirs as a cautionary tale and an acceptable exemplum; but her reference to the conclusion as a "tail piece of morality"—a double entendre that has not eluded recent readers[37]—points to a satiric, subversive motive on Cleland's part. More frequently, novelists positioned instruction as a cover for artistic deficiency, pleading that good intentions—much like personal hardship—should outweigh errors in execution.[38] The editor's advertisement of Edward Bancroft's *History of Charles Wentworth* (1770) carries such reasoning to an absurd extreme:

> Novels that merely entertain, merit no encouragement, because they divert the mind from more useful objects: but to make them a vehicle of instruction, under the mask of amusement, it is necessary that they

be not too interesting. Wherever curiosity is greatly excited, the mind becomes impatient to know the final event, and every moral or instructive reflection, that may be interposed, suspends the gratification of its curiosity; and is, on that account, either read with disgust, or intirely passed over.[39]

The editor goes on to praise characters who are "diversified by few striking peculiarities" and letters which are not "distinguished by the peculiarities of stile"[40] as conducive to—even necessary for—the primacy of the moral message! As transparent and ridiculous as the argument sounds, it resonates uncomfortably in attempts in our own era to identify art with propaganda and to subordinate aesthetic pleasure to political correctness. Bancroft's make-believe editor, therefore, may well have found readers that agreed with him—at least, enough to buy the novel.

Jacobin novelists—who did, in fact, view fiction as propaganda—adapted the explicitly didactic stance of conservative moralists for their own radical purposes. William Godwin's desire for a gradual enlightenment of the masses is reflected in the abstract but inflammatory preface to *Caleb Williams* (1794). Attempting to demonstrate "that the spirit and character of the government intrudes itself into every rank of society," the author records "the modes of domestic and unrecorded despotism by which man becomes the destroyer of man" in the form of a novel in order to influence "persons whom books of philosophy and science are never likely to reach."[41] Thomas Holcroft prefaces the *Memoirs of Bryan Perdue* (1805) with a more elaborate—if reductive—summary of the intentions behind his entire *corpus* of fiction:

> Whenever I have undertaken to write a novel, I have proposed to myself a specific moral purpose. This purpose, in Anna St. Ives, was to teach fortitude to females: in Hugh Trevor, to induce youth (or their parents) carefully to inquire into the profession which each might intend for himself: and, in the present work, to induce all humane and thinking men, such as legislators ought to be and often are, to consider the general and the adventitious value of human life, and the moral tendency of our penal laws.[42]

Neither writer—Godwin or Holcroft—could afford to take for granted his audience's comprehension of the "proper" moral; but both could safely imagine readers accustomed to—and, thus, unoffended by—ex cathedra authorial pronouncements.

Surprisingly, a few novelists swam against the tide and questioned the reflexive high seriousness common to sincere moralists, opportunistic hacks, and radical reformers alike—hinting at a more openly aesthetic discourse. Clara Reeve moves tentatively in this direction in her preface to *The Old English Baron* (1778), suggesting that the "business of Romance is, first, to excite the attention; and, secondly, to direct it to some useful, or at least innocent, end; Happy the writer who attains both these points, like Richardson! and not unfortunate, or undeserving praise, he who gains only the latter, and furnishes out an entertainment for the reader!"[43] With perhaps deliberately confused syntax, Reeve seems to have been asserting the priority of entertainment over instruction. Less equivocally, Charles Jenner, in his Fieldingesque introductory chapters of *The Placid Man* (1770), admits the validity of didactic justifications for fiction, but adds that "this is a more serious light than I find it necessary to view these productions in: I would rather look upon them in that of pleasing and innocent amusements."[44] Elaborating on the salutary powers of illusion, he concludes that the "kind of ideal happiness which arises from the contemplation of imaginary objects is in the power of everyone and is frequently no mean relief from the real evils of life."[45] Rather than grounding his work on a foundation of artistic merit, Jenner justified by trivializing—by reducing fiction strictly to diversion—perhaps the safest course when venturing outside the umbrella of moral utility. But even a slight venture was rare in an age of pronounced opposition to light reading by the cultural establishment.[46] Far simpler to don the preacher's robes, however ill-fitting a disguise they might be.

* * *

Probability, invoked with the same insistence and regularity as morality, raises similar questions of context and conventionality. According to most novelists, rectitude actually required verisimilitude, which could be advanced in two different ways. The first involved continuing the charade of historicity common to earlier novelists, thus aligning moral with factual truth. As late as 1800, Maria Edgeworth assumes the role of detective in order to ensure the reader's assimilation of the moral of the supposedly historical *Castle Rackrent*:

> We are surely justified in this eager desire to collect the most minute facts relative to the domestic lives, not only of the great and good, but even of the worthless and insignificant, since it is only by a comparison of their actual happiness or misery in the privacy of domestic life, that we can form a just estimate of the real reward of virtue, or the real punishment of vice.[47]

Edgeworth conveniently yokes factuality and poetic justice; but in the relentlessly pessimistic *Sidney Biddulph* (1761), Frances Sheridan has her make-believe editor reject such artificial constructs as antithetical to the moral imperative of presenting unvarnished truth: readers should not "condemn what is drawn from real life.—We may wish to see nature copied from her more pleasing works, but a martyr expiring in tortures, is as just, though not as agreeable, a representation of her, as a hero rewarded with the brightest honours."[48] Flexible enough both to admit and to reject poetic justice, the claim to historicity also neatly sidestepped the author's responsibility for a probable narrative, a stance rebuked by the anonymous author of *Sophia* (1788), who unabashedly declares that "the Story of the following is entirely imagined; the Characters I own are borrowed; I own this, as I do not see the great Merit of writing *upon Facts,* and as the only Merit I can claim, is the Fable."[49] Novelists who wished to advance stronger claims for their own abilities rejected the pretense of transcribing facts—and even of basing their characters on real people. Burney, for example, professes in *Evelina* to "draw characters from nature, though not from life."[50] The unspoken but widely shared assumption was that either a transcription of true facts or effective mimetic realism would ensure a reader's sympathetic identification and, thus, his or her apprehension of the moral.[51] Smollett keeps a foot in both traditions, not only admitting that *Roderick Random* was based on real experiences, with the circumstances altered and disguised to avoid personal satire, but also supporting invented, natural narratives over romances, and therefore faulting *Gil Blas,* an important model for *Random,* for "uncommon" or "extravagant" situations and sudden "transitions from distress to happiness," both of which deviated from probability.[52]

As Smollett's language indicates, supporting the probable inevitably involves disparaging the "marvellous"—which, in turn, often presumes an unsophisticated audience. Even at the height of the Gothic vogue in the 1790s, certain novelists questioned the predilection of readers toward "the productions of a wild, romantic, creative fancy"[53] or "the wild, the terrible, and the supernatural"[54]—adjectives that would shortly be enshrined in Romantic criticism and practice. Two decades earlier, Jenner had specified the bases, both moral and aesthetic, for objections to less supernatural—but equally fantastic—fiction:

> Extraordinary events and surprising incidents happen to so few people, that they have, in general, no effect upon the minds of common

readers, and serve only to fill the heads of young people with romantic notions and wild ideas, which either are never met with in real life, or if they are—the more is the pity. The life of an honest man, or even some years of it, tolerably conversant in the world, may afford incidents sufficient, with the natural remarks upon them, to furnish amusing and even instructive memoirs, without having recourse to elopements, kidnappings, duels, disguises, exchanges of children in the cradle, and various other extraordinary matters which are calculated only to make the reader stare, and rarely exist but in novels.[55]

Jenner may well have been urging "common readers" and "young people" to renounce such fare in favor of his more realistic fiction, but he may have been even more eager to reinforce in his current readers a feeling of cultural superiority over consumers of escapist adventures.

The potential for banality in Jenner's preferred subject matter hints at the way in which disdain for the marvellous could be used to excuse lack of creativity. Along these lines, Jane West's *A Gossip's Story* (1796) reveals perhaps more than she intended about her earlier novel, *The Advantages of Education* (1793):

It had no splendour of language, no local description, nothing of the marvellous, or the enigmatical, no sudden elevation, and no astonishing depression. It merely spoke of human life as it is, and so simple was the story, that at the outset an attentive reader must have foreboded the catastrophe. Indeed it required some attention from the reader, which in works of this kind is also a fault: for not ambitious of dazzling the imagination, and of inflaming the passions, it uniformly pursued its aim of ameliorating the temper and the affections.[56]

Much like morality, probability can make a virtue of necessity. Recognizing this, Richard Cumberland, in one of his introductory chapters to *Henry* (1795), ruminates on the competing pressures facing novelists who aspire beyond the mundane:

To represent scenes of familiar life in an elegant and interesting manner, is one of the most difficult tasks an author can take in hand; for of these every man is a critic: Nature is in the first place to be attended to, and probability is not to be lost sight of; but it must be nature strongly featured, and probability closely bordered on the marvellous; the one must touch upon extravagance, and the other be highly seasoned with adventures—for who will thank us for a dull and lifeless journal of insipid facts? Now every peculiarity of humour in the human character is a strain upon nature, and every surprising incident is a degree of violence to probability: How far shall we go then for

our reader's amusement, how soon shall we stop in consideration of
ourselves? There is undoubtedly a land-mark in the fields of fancy,
sunt certi denique fines, but it requires a nice discernment to find them
out, and a cautious temper not to step beyond them.[57]

Exacerbating the dilemma for a novelist in the 1790s was over a
half-century's worth of novel writing, which led readers and
writers to crave innovation—a desire that naturally resulted in
strained probability. Thus, Cumberland shrewdly begged the
question of where or how the line he discussed could be drawn.

Cumberland may, in fact, have been recalling the more detailed
and famous remarks in Horace Walpole's 1765 preface to *The
Castle of Otranto,* where Walpole abandoned the earlier facade of
a translator of an Italian manuscript and explained his procedure
as "an attempt to blend the two kinds of romance, the ancient
and the modern."[58] To avoid both the "unnatural" machinery of
the former and the "cramped imagination" of the latter, Walpole
proposes "to conduct the mortal agents in his drama according
to the rules of probability; in short, to make them think, speak,
and act, as it might be supposed mere men and women would do
in extraordinary positions."[59] Walpole's synthetic theory appealed
to a prominent successor in the Gothic mode, Clara Reeve, who
baptized *The Old English Baron* (1778) "the literary offspring of
the Castle of Otranto,"[60] but found the practice of her mentor
deficient in carrying the marvellous to an unhealthy extreme. According to Reeve, in *Otranto,* "the machinery is so violent, that it
destroys the effect it is intended to excite. Had the story been
kept within the utmost *verge* of probability, the effect had been
preserved, without losing the least circumstance that excites or
detains the attention."[61] Devendra P. Varma has detailed Walpole's
bitter rejoinder—his characterization of Reeve's novel as "a professed imitation of mine, only stripped of the marvellous, and so
entirely stripped, except in one awkward attempt at a ghost or
two, that it is the most insipid dull nothing you ever saw" and as
"so probable, that any trial for murder at the Old Bailey would
make a more interesting story."[62] The controversy illustrates the
seriousness with which these formal innovators sought a workable
natural supernaturalism and the degree to which a mimetic
framework remained for them a basic, necessary condition of narrative. The comparative silence of their successors on the issue
signals not a resolution but rather a lack of incentive for specula-
tion—given popular and, at least initially, critical approval of
Gothic fiction.

If Walpole and Reeve demurred from questioning assumptions regarding adherence to nature, the earliest experimenters in so-called historical fiction were even more diffident about encroaching on the domain of history. The advertisement to *Longsword, Earl of Salisbury* mentions—but avoids justifying—embellishment of facts, relying instead on indulgent or apathetic responses from different classes of readers: "The out-lines of the following story, and some of the incidents and more minute circumstances, are to be found in the antient English historians. If too great liberties have been taken in altering or enlarging their accounts, the reader who looks only for amusement will probably forgive it: the learned and critical (if this work should be honoured by such readers) will deem it a matter of too little consequence to call for the severity of their censure."[63] Sophia Lee more boldly elevates works like *The Recess* (1785) over conventional historical writing, explaining that history, like painting, only perpetuates "the most striking characteristics of the soul"; whereas "too often the best and worst actions of princes proceed from partialities and prejudices, which live in their hearts, and are buried with them."[64] Yet Lee's implicit defense of a new subgenre remained shrouded under the persistent pretense of a manuscript source—this one dating from the Elizabethan era. For many of the same reasons as probability, history retained a preeminence that made it dangerous for novelists to challenge openly in the name of fictional integrity.

* * *

Such reticence seldom extended to the often-related issue of originality, where the influence of an already recognized canon placed novelists in defensive postures. Just as Richardson and Fielding both reflected and encouraged the growing tendency of eighteenth-century authors to stress the novelty of their achievement, their successors sought to distinguish themselves from the predictable norm by promising uniqueness, even when the commonplace narratives that they offered did not satisfy the expectations that their prefaces raised.[65] But as the very promises—however valid—accumulated, they themselves appeared derivative, thus accentuating the difficulties faced by writers who grew up with an awareness of an earlier generation's eminence and who already sensed a "burden of the past."[66] In the preface to her first novel, Burney articulates—and, then, enacts—the inhibitions felt by those who attempt to succeed distinguished forefathers without transgressing the dictates of probability:

To avoid what is uncommon, without adopting what is unnatural, must limit the ambition of the vulgar herd of authors; however zealous, therefore, my veneration of the great writers I have mentioned, however I may feel myself enlightened by the knowledge of Johnson, charmed with the eloquence of Rousseau, softened by the pathetic powers of Richardson, and exhilarated by the wit of Fielding, and humour of Smollett; I yet presume not to attempt pursuing the same ground which they have tracked; whence, though they may have cleared the weeds, they have also culled the flowers, and though they have rendered the path plain, they have left it barren.[67]

Immediately following her cogent analysis, Burney retreats from assertiveness by entreating that her remarks "not be imputed to an opinion of my own originality, which I have not the vanity, the folly, or the blindness, to entertain."[68] Even some novelists who openly embraced experimentation at the expense of probability, as a means of breaking from an intimidating past and a mediocre present, retained some of this uneasiness. As early as 1754, Sarah Fielding and Jane Collier cast *The Cry* in the form of a "Dramatic Fable," in which individuals relate their pasts to an allegorical assembly, not only because the portrayal of the "labyrinths of the human mind" requires "a certain freedom in writing, not strictly perhaps within the limits prescribed by rules," but also because the authors cannot hope to equal the best novelists and do not wish to add to the worst.[69] Nearly a half century later, Godwin, who in his miscellany *The Enquirer* (1797) elevated present over past by insisting that Fielding and Smollett both "fall below the ordinary standard of elegant composition at the present day,"[70] craves pardon for the "boldness and irregularity" of his design of mixing "human feelings and passions with incredible situations"[71] in the Gothic novel *St. Leon* (1799). His excuse: writers "who bring up the rear of our illustrious predecessors, must be contented to arrive at novelty in whatever mode we are able."[72] In a genre with a past that was contrasted nostalgically with a deficient present, formal innovators could not escape looking over their shoulders, as Fielding's and Collier's seriousness and Godwin's jocularity both attest.

The very urge for distinction that led many novelists to foreground their originality led others to ridicule a pursuit of novelty that merely pandered to the most fickle, transient tastes. Relying on the familiar topos of disrespect for novel readers, Albinia Gwynn, in her preface to *The Rencontre* (1784), comically extends the appetite for novelty to its absurd—but, apparently, common—extreme, with devastating consequences for any reputation:

Alas! writing novels is *not* the path to fame; even Richardson, the divine Richardson! is neglected, if not almost forgotten, stands unheeded on the shelf, with Fielding and Smollett, whilst every new piece of nonsense is read before them; bubbles that burst, and are lost for ever, almost as soon as the breath of vanity blows them into being— but they are *read* first—NEW!—there is magic in the word—well then, at least I have *this* advantage, I shall be new, shall be read of course, and then—alas, my dear friend! will you not, by *your* plaudit, endeavour to keep me from sinking a little while—Alas! perhaps I shall be forgotten—Heigh-ho!—I really am so melancholy I can add no more.[73]

More soberly, Jenner, who consciously attempted to imitate Fielding, defends imitation in theory by exhuming the classical definition of the term, which had been cited by Fielding. Invention consists of discovering something "of the manners of mankind, by the help of . . . observation and reflection." Jenner would advise "a moderate genius" not to be "too much ashamed of a guide; a good imitation is often not inferior to a tolerable original, and always superior to a bad one."[74] For Jenner, the degree of "genius" determined the latitude a novelist may have: he lauds the "eccentric" Sterne for a "natural and inexhaustible fund of humour" that permitted Sterne to make "his readers laugh, by some trick or other, which, in another man, would have been insupportable."[75] Sterne, however, serves primarily as the exception that proves the rule; according to Jenner, the multitude should refrain from indulging an uncritical desire for something new.

Still, the dubious security of mediocre, predictable imitations attracted contempt, given the preponderance of depressingly similar love stories in the publishing market.[76] This depressing situation provided the radical novelists with a useful pretext for promoting new subject matter. In *The Banished Man* (1794), Charlotte Smith promises to try "the experiment that has often been talked of, but has never yet been hazarded . . . to make a novel without love in it."[77] Even without mentioning it, the Jacobins could assume some impatience with the unnervingly familiar— and, thus, at least the potential for sympathy toward their openly political interests. In this light, Smith could defend both a woman's right to advance political opinions and her flattering portrait of the French Revolution in *Desmond* (1792).[78] And Godwin's flippancy about novelty in *St. Leon* could not mask his genuine concern—especially in *Caleb Williams*—to make political theory accessible through fiction.[79] For these writers, the convention of emphasizing originality—born of defensiveness and a desire to set one's work apart—supported their openness about serious attempts to "revolutionize" the genre.

Whatever the underlying motives, originality also conveniently permitted declarations of independence from established rules—expressed with varying degrees of confidence. Sarah Fielding and Godwin might apologize for deviating from the norm, but they considered the results ample recompense. Walpole, who actually professes to have followed the rules of drama and to have imitated Shakespeare by mixing scenes of "buffoonery and solemnity," still lays claim to the innovator's license, in language that recalls Richardson and Fielding: "I might have pleaded that, having created a new species of romance, I was at liberty to lay down what rules I thought fit for the conduct of it."[80] Far more forthright, Tristram Shandy defends his digressions as "the life, the soul of reading," repeatedly underscores his freedom of temporal and spatial movement, and poses the provocative rhetorical question, "Is a man to follow rules, or rules to follow him?"[81] The advertisement to Mary Wollstonecraft's loosely structured *Mary* (1788) puts the matter more lyrically, maintaining that those "compositions only have power to delight, and carry us willing captives, where the soul of the author is exhibited, and animates the hidden springs. Lost in a pleasing enthusiasm, they live in the scenes they represent; and do not measure their steps in a beaten track, solicitous to gather expected flowers, and bind them in a wreath, according to the prescribed rules of art."[82] Rules, in other words, are not broken as much as they are superceded and rendered irrelevant by the author's immersion into the characters and events of the narrative. Whatever their differences, each of these novelists seemed compelled to refer to a set of generally accepted rules, perhaps as a sign of knowledge and competence that, in effect, licensed worthwhile innovation in the eyes of sophisticated readers.

Writers of lesser ambition, on the other hand, could find security in the lack of strictly codified canons for prose fiction. The critically semiliterate Herbert Lawrence, author of *The Contemplative Man* (1771), fulsomely rejoices in the comparative freedom of his chosen form: "How fortunate it is for us Historians, or, to take it a Peg lower, for us Life-writers, that no modern *Aristotle* has stept forth, and laid down Rules for the Conduct of History, like the Unities of Action, Time, and Place, prescribed by the Ancients to all dramatic Writers. I hug myself when I think of it."[83] Beneath the sarcasm lay the fact—so comforting for novelists of questionable talent—that the fluidity of the genre allowed them, not simply to write as they would, but to write at all. Uncertainty, moreover, undermined authoritative assessment by allowing novelists to question any criteria used by the assessors, as Elizabeth Griffith does in *The Delicate Distress* (1769):

> I know not whether novel [*sic*], like the *epopée*, has any rules, peculiar to itself.—If it has, I may have innocently erred against them all, and drawn upon myself the envenomed rage of that tremendous body, the *minor critics*.—But if I have spread a table for them, they shall be welcome to the treat, and let them feed upon it, heartily.—Sensibility is, in my mind, as necessary, as taste, to intitle us to judge of a work, like this; and a cold criticism, formed upon *rules for writing*, can, therefore, be of no manner of use, but to enable the stupid to speak, with a seeming intelligence, of what they neither feel, nor understand.[84]

Privileging feeling over debatable rules—in much the same way as many popular contemporary novels, films, and television series do implicitly—legitimized the responses of a large undiscriminating audience—then, as now, the source of commercial success.

The vogue for sentimental novels like Griffith's—ignited, to a great degree, by Sterne—virtually guaranteed commentary that relied more on catchwords than on criticism. A profusion of novels of varying degrees of sophistication purported to be "delicate in sentiments . . . skilled in the human heart,"[85] to exhibit "the strongest sensibility, and the warmest imagination,"[86] to call forth "the tear of Sensibility,"[87] to encourage in the reader the "sympathy of friendship, or the tenderness of compassion,"[88] or to illustrate "passions" instead of "manners."[89] Similar language surfaces in Sophia Lee's defense of the publication of the jejune and long-shelved *Life of a Lover* (1804). A novel "planned and written at the early age when imagination takes the lead of reason, and the heart occasionally over-rules both, will necessarily want the harmony and style which alone secures the approbation of the judicious"; but Lee, nonetheless, concludes that "we can be young only once in our life, and all the impressions of that season will have a lasting influence over the hearts of sensibility."[90] Attempts to define terms like *sentiment* and *sensibility* (terms that remain polysemous even now[91]) would unnecessarily complicate the work of novelists searching for a wide—but not necessarily deep—audience, which needs only read the magic words. In *The School for Widows* (1791), an exasperated Clara Reeve attacks this flexibility, specifically in regard to the word *sentiment:*

> This word, like many others, seems to have degenerated from its original meaning: and, under this flimsy disguise, it has given rise to a

great number of whining, maudlin stories, full of false sentiment and false delicacy, calculated to excite a kind of morbid sensibility, which is to faint under every ideal distress, and every fantastical trial; which has a tendency to weaken the mind, and to deprive it of those resources which nature intended it should find within itself.[92]

Concurring with Reeve, a critic for the *Monthly Review* then turns the tables on her by proceeding "to illustrate her opinion by an instance taken from her own pen."[93] But the theory deserved as much criticism as the practice for leaving the original meaning unspoken and, thereby, drawing a distinction without specifying a difference. Even an apparent defense of regulative standards may have amounted to little more than a rhetorical evasion of them.

Amorphous discussions of sensibility typified the novelists' relative neglect of generic considerations, from the variations among subgenres to the relation of the genre as a whole to other kinds of writing. Smollett, to be sure, consciously located his earlier novels within the tradition of satire, opening *Roderick Random* with the statement that "of all kinds of satire, there is none so entertaining, and universally improving, as that which is introduced, as it were, occasionally, in the course of an interesting story, which brings every incident home to life"[94] and attacking, in *Ferdinand Count Fathom,* the hypocritical tendency to approve classical satire—or even satire a generation removed—while dismissing contemporary efforts.[95] In his 1764 preface to *The Castle of Otranto,* Walpole renews the more traditional generic link with drama and includes the editor's assurances that the "rules of drama are almost observed throughout the conduct of the piece. The characters are well-drawn, and still better maintained. Terror, the author's principal engine, prevents the story from ever languishing; and it is so often contrasted by pity, that the mind is kept up in a constant vicissitude of interesting passions."[96] A year later, as I have shown, increased confidence led both to the abandonment of the editorial facade and to the more pronounced assertions of originality.[97] In this respect, Walpole's shift epitomized a general transformation among novelists: assured of wide acceptance of the novel as a distinct genre, they had less of a need to support their work by drawing connections to more established literary forms. Mention of dramatic theory and practice naturally diminished as a canon of fiction emerged as an alternate point of reference. Moreover, as originality superceded imitation as a mark of merit, few novelists could be expected to make the conventions of other genres touchstones for their own texts.

* * *

Generic self-sufficiency contributed to relative critical neglect of plot, an area where dramatic precedent would naturally have exerted the greatest influence. Smollett's famous definition of a novel—in the dedication to *Ferdinand Count Fathom*—as a "large, diffused picture, comprehending the characters of life, disposed in different groupes, and exhibited in various attitudes, for the purpose of an uniform plan, and general occurrence, to which every individual figure is subservient,"[98] reflects an Aristotelian conception of the primacy of plot. Seldom, however, did Smollett's contemporaries or successors endorse this primacy by focusing their commentary on structural concerns. The few significant remarks tended to reiterate, in conventional terms, the importance of unity. In the preface to *Alwyn* (1780), for example, Holcroft's variation on the novel/romance contrast, which involves an explicit comparison to drama, makes unity of design the distinguishing characteristic of the novel:

> In a Romance, if the incidents be well marked and related with spirit, the intention is answered; and adventures pass before the view for no other purpose than to amuse by their peculiarity, without, perhaps, affecting the main story, if there should be one. But in a Novel, a combination of incidents, entertaining in themselves, are made to form a whole; and an unnecessary circumstance becomes a blemish, by detaching from the simplicity which is requisite to exhibit that whole to advantage.[99]

Cumberland also advocated integration, criticizing even his idol Fielding for the ostensibly irrelevant episode of the Man of the Hill in *Tom Jones*.[100] And in his odd, suspiciously dispassionate account of the composition of *Caleb Williams*—which in many ways resembles Poe's *Philosophy of Composition*—Godwin professes to have outlined the novel by beginning at the end and working his way backward, thus preserving "unity of plot" and "unity of spirit and interest."[101]

However authoritative these precepts may sound, they were consistently undermined by discursive practices prevalent among novelists, including some of the "preceptors." Cumberland could be faulted for digression since he interrupted his narrative with theoretical introductory chapters; and although Smollett had attacked "some celebrated writers" (read Fielding) in *Peregrine Pickle* (1751) for resorting to observations by the narrator and other "such paultry shifts, in order to eke out the volume,"[102] he violated his own standard by including an extended discussion of satire at the beginning of *Fathom*, his next novel. The presence of a narrator, arguably the most obvious departure from drama, offered artistic opportunities that compensated for breaching a criterion derived from dramatic theory—as Sterne, along with his numerous imitators and admirers, perceived and illustrated. Hence, Tristram's famous chapter on the progressive nature of his digressions,[103] and Herbert Lawrence's Shandean belief that digression is absolutely necessary "when you have a crooked Subject."[104] This perspective implied that a different genre required a different poetics, but adherents postponed the difficult task of developing one in favor of ridiculing or simply ignoring older standards.

Character, on the other hand, provided more fertile ground for suggesting the uniqueness of the genre and, not surprisingly, received greater emphasis in commentary, lending support to Francis Coventry's assertion, in the dedication to *Pompey the Little* (1751), that "the characters of a novel principally determine its merit."[105] Many novelists, to be sure, examined character less for its own sake than as it impinged upon broader concerns like morality and probability. Smollett, Bancroft, Cumberland, and Melmoth, for example, all addressed the importance of sustaining contrast of character for greater moral efficacy;[106] while Jenner, Hadley, and Mary Hays championed the more probable mixed character over the virtuous paragon or the monster of depravity.[107] Wollstonecraft offers the most interesting variation on this largely conventional discourse in the preface to her unfinished novel, *The Wrongs of Woman* (1798), where she derides the gender bias that results in static characterization of women: "In many works of this species, the hero is allowed to be mortal, and to become wise and virtuous as well as happy, by a train of events and circumstances. The heroines, on the contrary, are to be born immaculate; and to act like goddesses of wisdom, just come forth highly finished Minervas from the head of Jove."[108] With some important exceptions in novels by women, Wollstonecraft's assessment was usually—unfortunately—correct.

More significant in the longer term was an abiding concern for psychology and the inner life, which, as Richardson's example had demonstrated, the novel could display and examine in new ways. Fielding and Collier's introduction to *The Cry* endorses Richardsonian practice in promising "not to amuse [the reader] with a number of surprising incidents and adventures, but rather to paint the inward mind" and in acknowledging the difficulty of uncovering the "intricate and unopened recesses in the heart of man."[109] Writing four decades later, Burney concurs, as she concedes at the beginning of *Camilla* (1796) that the "historian of human life finds less of difficulty and of intricacy to develop, in its accidents and adventures, than the investigator of the human heart in its feelings and its changes."[110] Between the two lay the most influential attempt at looking inward: Tristram Shandy's "Opinions" matter far more, of course, than his "Life." With action subordinated to thought and emotion, Lee could argue for the superiority of *The Recess* over history that was confined to names and dates; and Godwin could support his decision to alter the narration of *Caleb Williams* from third to first person on the ground that the latter was better suited for "the analysis of the private and internal operations of the mind, employing my metaphysical dissecting knife in tracing and laying bare the involutions of motive."[111] Finally, novelists of sensibility regularly urged upon readers a sympathy—a literal feeling with characters—inevitably encouraging further attention to the workings of the mind and heart. Although the promise frequently outstripped the performance, all of these attitudes contributed to a movement toward more complex psychological fiction,[112] which penetrated character as only the length and breadth of the novel form would allow.

* * *

The novelists' desire to elevate their texts and their genre—the subtext for so much of this commentary—required dialogue, not merely with readers, but with an increasingly prominent critical profession—at the head of which stood the review journals. Not only did reviewers serve as an implied audience—as was apparent in women novelists' remarks on gender, for instance; reviewers and their activity actually became a prominent focus in many introductory discourses. Burney's dedication of *Evelina* to the reviewers—with its disingenuous flattery—represented one approach, which could vary in tone from ostensible sincerity to manifest satire. On the one hand, the prolific Courtney Melmoth dedicates the first volume of *Family Secrets* (1797) to the critics, with no comment other than a denial of any intention to pander and with intimations of eagerness for critical response to his work.[113] On the other hand, Thomas Amory facetiously raises the customary obsequious language of the dedicator to the highest pitch at the end of the preface to *John Buncle* (1756): "I have only to add, that I wish you all happiness; that your heads may lack no ointment, and your garments be always white and odiferous: but especially, may you press on, like true critics, towards perfection; and may bliss, glory, and honour be your reward and your Portion."[114] Other dedicators proceeded to lampoon the critics more directly. Reeve dedicates *The Exiles* (1788) to one "Peter-Pertinax Puff, Esq.";[115] and Richard Graves commends *The Spiritual Quixote* (1773) to Monsieur Pattypan, the king's pastry cook, and underscores terms equally applicable to criticism and baking:

> Though a stranger to your person, I am no stranger to your ingenuity and your profound skill in your profession. I have often amused myself with some of those elegant *compositions* with which you daily *entertain* the publick. I have long been acquainted with the *virtues* of your diet-bread; am a great friend to your *wigs;* and think myself under great obligations to your admirable *puffs*.
>
> As I am convinced therefore you will make a *proper* use of my works; will do justice to their merit, and *cover* their defects: that, by the well-known goodness of your *taste,* you will *preserve* them from the attacks of the *sourest* criticks; and, by the *sweetness* of your disposition, defend them against their *bitterest* enemies: if you are not over-stocked with waste-paper by my brethren of the quill, I beg leave to dedicate these few sheets to your service.[116]

Bage chooses still another form of mockery, preempting the reviewers by offering a harsh review of his own *Mount Henneth* (1782): "If readers expect to find, in these volumes, any thing like wit, humour, plot, character, or keeping, they will be much disappointed. The work puts us in mind of Doctor Johnson's sarcasm on Macklin's conversation;—a perpetual renovation of hope, with perpetual disappointment. To say the least we can of it, it is bad in the beginning, worse and worse in its progress, but the end is Heaven."[117]

At the same time that he sarcastically mimics the critics, Bage also celebrates their impotence, consoling fellow novelists with the thought that the books of "this class, are printed, published, bought, read, and deposited in the lumber-garret, three months before the reviewers say a syllable of the matter."[118] Despite the exaggeration—there is evidence both that the reviews had some influence on readers' choices and that books had a shelf life longer than Bage would allow—the statement contains a kernel of truth: the power of fads, word of mouth, and the circulating libraries ensured many novels a substantial audience regardless of the critics' response. Authors, therefore, could—and did—consciously bypass the critics and appeal directly to a generalized common reader. Reeve's mock-dedication to Peter-Pertinax Puff concludes with the promise to "throw myself upon the favour of the public, and depend upon its candour and generosity, in defiance of thee and all thy family, and I will not call myself thy client, nor friend, nor humble servant."[119] Even Burney, who publicly courted the reviewers, could privately, in a letter to her father, take solace in the ultimate power of quantity over self-styled quality:

> Miss Cambridge asked me, early, if I should not take some care about the Reviews? No, I said, none. There are two species of Composition which may nearly brave them; Politics and Novels: for these will be sought and will be judged by the various Multitude, not the fastidious few. With the latter, indeed, they may be Aided, or injured, by Criticism; but it will not stop their being read, though it may prejudice their Readers.[120]

Context, however, belies Burney's cavalier facade. She was responding reassuringly to Dr. Burney's indignant disapproval of negative criticisms leveled at *Camilla*—in spite of his efforts, unknown to his daughter, to fix the reviews.[121] Elsewhere, she openly admitted to anger,[122] which is evident even in this letter when she reveals that Miss Cambridge "laughed at my composure; but though I am a good deal chagrined, it is not broken."[123] Chagrin at criticism implies at least some respect for the critic. Burney's divided attitude emblematizes the situation of the genre in the latter half of the century—and of popular genres today. Some novelists—like today's producers of endless, mindless film sequels—reached no higher than mass approval and financial success. Others, including Burney, used critical discourse to stake out respectability on a number of fronts. For them, it could be conferred only by the newly emerging literary establishment embodied by the reviewers, however much they might have resented institutional power or individual judgments. Even when unaddressed, the reviewers, therefore, served as a primary implied audience for novelists' numerous critical insights—many of which they supported and many of which their systematic processes and institutionalized structure allowed them to improve upon.

4

Hierarchies of Fiction for a Cultural Elite:
Periodical Reviewers (I)

In chapter 5 of *Northanger Abbey,* the narrator, having noted Catherine's penchant for novel reading, feels obliged to defend both heroine and genre:

> Alas! if the heroine of one novel be not patronized by the heroine of another, from whom can she expect protection and regard? I cannot approve of it. Let us leave it to the Reviewers to abuse such effusions of fancy at their leisure, and over every new novel to talk in threadbare strains of the trash with which the press now groans. Let us not desert one another; we are an injured body. Although our productions have afforded more extensive and unaffected pleasure than those of any other literary corporation in the world, no species of composition has been so much decried.[1]

Deliberate hyperbole allowed Austen to balance what she must have viewed as the prejudiced, redundant, and extreme opinions of the periodical reviewers in the latter half of the eighteenth century. Even a cursory glance through *The Monthly Review* and *The Critical Review* would have given Austen's readers ample evidence to support her indictment. For the reviewers seem to have relished making disparaging—even devastating—comments on novels and novelists. One critic for the *Monthly* compares the drudgery of reading novels to the fate of "Druso's debtors, who were driven to the sad alternative, of hearing him read his wretched histories, or paying him what they owed him."[2] Another sarcastically observes that "the very Printer's Devils, and Errand-boys to the Circulating-Libraries, are now become Authors, to save their masters the *heavy article* of copy-money!"[3] In the *Critical* one reviewer recommends *Emma; or, The Unfortunate Attachment* "to those who are in want of a soporific, and we do it very confidently, as we have experienced its effects";[4] and another claims to have discovered the source for all contemporary fiction in the curious machine observed by Gulliver at the academy of projectors at Lagado, "by means of which the most ignorant person, at a reasonable charge, and with very little bodily labour, might write books . . . without the least assistance from genius or from study."[5] With a more extended mechanistic analogy, a reviewer for the *Monthly* offers a convenient "Recipe for Dressing Up Novels *ad libitum*":

> Go to Middle Row, Holborn; where, since mankind have discovered that their own hair is sufficiently capable of distortion, the sellers of old cast-off wigs have given place to the dealers in cast-off books; there on the bulks, from among the classes of a groat or sixpence *per* volume, buy any old forgotten novel, the older the better; give new names to the personages and places, reform the dates, modernize such circumstances as may happen to be antiquated, and, if necessary, touch up the style a little with a few of those polite cant words and phrases that may be in fashion at the time. All this may be done with a pen, in the margin of the printed book, without the trouble of transcribing the whole, unless it is to be carried to a bookseller for sale; for then you must shew a manuscript. In either case, it may be boldly sent to the printer; for printers, like surgeons and lawyers, are bound to keep the secrets of their employers.[6]

Behind the satire lay obvious conclusions: novels were too numerous, too similar, and too dull.

But if the state of the genre left much to be desired, the genre itself sometimes attracted conspicuous praise, expressed in language that anticipated Austen's. As early as 1751, Cleland's seminal review of *Peregrine Pickle* for the *Monthly* makes high claims for the novel, primarily on the ground of the public utility that results from communicating moral principles to readers "who are profitably decoyed into the perusal of these writings by the pleasure they expect to be paid with for their attention."[7] Near the end of the century—after forty years of morally and artistically inferior fiction—in the *Monthly*, a reviewer of Charlotte Smith's *Celestina* echoes and amplifies Cleland's enthusiasm; the reviewer compares the genre, in Aristotelian terms, to poetry and concludes that the

> modern Novel, well executed, possessing the essential characters of poetry, perhaps even more precisely than the ancient Romance, certainly deserves a place among the works of genius:—nor ought the multiplicity of insignificant or contemptible pieces, which are poured

forth under this title, to preclude from notice such as possess superior merit. This circumstance rather furnishes a reason for taking some pains to bring them forward out of the promiscuous crowd, in which they first appear, and give them that distinction, to which, in every walk of literature, genius is entitled.[8]

Two years later, Smith's finest novel, *The Old Manor House*, provokes a similar testimonial from a reviewer for the *Critical:* "Among the various productions of literary genius, there is, perhaps, none that has a more legitimate claim to an ascendancy over the human mind than a well-written novel."[9]

The gap between possibility and performance—between the theoretical potential of the genre and the practical failure of countless individual texts—was only the most visible difference articulated and exploited by the critics; a similar pattern of opposition informed the treatment of significant and significantly charged issues like gender, morality, and originality. However apparently distinct, all of the contradictions derived from a common source: a self-conscious attempt on the part of the reviewers to stratify the genre and its audience, in order to establish and maintain authority over an elite class of readers.

* * *

In a business of words, quantity most amply marks stature. The preface to the third series of the *Critical* (1772) affirms that it "is our duty . . . to treat each performance with no more than that proportion of regard to which it is justly entitled."[10] The editors go on to offer considerable latitude to writers of promise: "When we discover latent marks of genius, we suffer many imperfections to pass unnoticed by; and as we wish to afford all encouragement to rising talents, we attend with patience for happier effusions from the same pen."[11] Novelists with potential, therefore, merited candour—or liberality—along with suggestions for improvement. As a corollary, accomplished authors received constructive criticism as a testimony to their abilities. Faced with numerous letters protesting its mixed assessment of *The Mysteries of Udolpho,* a reviewer for the *Critical* contends that "while we cheerfully give to literary excellence its full tribute of praise, we must be allowed to point out whatever appears faulty in the most unexceptionable productions; and the more eminent the writer, the more pressing is our duty to guard against those faults which are concealed from common eyes under an accumulation of beauties."[12] Naturally enough, novelists who appeared to follow the reviewers' advice earned the reviewers' approbation.[13]

Consideration of this kind was reserved for only the best novels and novelists. There was an important difference between *noticing* a novel in a paragraph in the "Monthly Catalogue" and subjecting a work to the exacting demands of authentic criticism in a major article. Length of treatment thus served as a reliable barometer for seriousness of treatment, and most novels languished beneath the rigor of critical attention. A critic for the *Monthly* writes that Elizabeth Blower's *George Bateman* is "much superior to the usual furniture of a circulating library; and though it will not bear the severity of criticism, yet it sometimes affects the heart without offending the judgment."[14] A reviewer for the *Critical* dismisses a less competent work, *The Man of Failing*, less charitably, judging it "too insignificant to draw on it the vengeance of criticism for its faults, and too trifling to demand praise when no faults can be discovered."[15] Conveniently enough for themselves, the reviewers never defined the term *criticism* precisely; but their implication was sufficiently clear. If even reputable novels did not merit criticism, the vast majority lay as far below it as possible. From this perspective arose the numerous complaints about the burden of reading novels, like the metaphor of Druso's debtors. The unpleasantness of the task provided a ready excuse for cursory reviews—even a justification for the frequently leveled and half-acknowledged charge that the critics did not read all of the novels that they reviewed. In the *Critical,* a reviewer professes to "have taken the pains" to review an execrable novel from the infamous Noble only to silence the accusers; but he adds that this is "a trouble which they must not expect we shall take for the future."[16] Thirteen years later, the response to *Cuckoldom Triumphant* is similarly indignant and similarly ambiguous: "We have been charged with reviewing books which we never read. We are certainly ashamed to say that we have read the volumes before us."[17] Still more candidly, the reviewer of *The Happy Orphans* remarks, "We were willing to suspend our account of this production, till we had leisure to read it; an honour, not due to many of the novels of these our romancing days."[18] Even the most minimal effort became insufferable with repetition—leading one exasperated critic to complain, "We are tired of giving general descriptions and characters of novel-writing."[19]

As these comments suggest, a novel did not need to be dreadful to be unworthy of serious attention. Countless formulaic narratives drew censure—or relative neglect—on account of their mediocrity. In a review of *Hartlebourn Castle* near the end of the century, a reviewer in the *Critical* regretfully observes that mediocrity "has become so general a characteristic of novels, that it must be our plea for dismissing them with a very brief notice. When a work, like the present, is so nicely balanced, that to find fault is as difficult as to bestow commendation, what is left for the reviewer?"[20] What was left was to compliment slightly—and, thus, slightingly—novels that substituted "regularity and decency of conduct" for "variety or splendour of invention,"[21] to bemoan harmless but insipid efforts—"Water-gruel may be a very wholesome beverage, but it will never be eagerly devoured"[22]—and to encourage fledgling authors not to content themselves with "that moderate share of literary reputation which a tolerable facility in the art of epistolary writing may have obtained among the circle of their friends, but by conversing intimately with the best models of good writing, acquire that elegance and refinement of taste, which will neither be capable of being pleased with, nor expect to be pleased by, *mediocrity.*"[23] Such advice had to be repeated regularly since "in novel-writing, like poetry, to fall short of excellence is to fail in the only object worth attempting: mediocrity is attainable by most, but it is only that rare combination of fancy with judgment and general information, that can save a work of pure fiction from neglect."[24]

Or at least from the neglect of readers that mattered. Vituperative and satiric commentary on undiscriminating readers, more emphatic than grudging, brief notices and the reflections on mediocrity that prompted them, served not as an end in itself but rather as an initial step in the generation of a critical hierarchy. The primary audience for fiction was usually described by critics as young, middle-class, and female—or, in the less neutral language of one annoyed reviewer, "idle templars, raw prentices, and green girls."[25] Unoriginal adventures and insipid love stories found a ready readership among what Samuel Johnson termed "the young, the ignorant, and the idle."[26] These "idle and trifling beings, who glean the chief of their sentiments from . . . [novels], and never think higher than romances and novels enable them to do,"[27] remained content with "a train of love adventures, with elopements, duels, and all the various *et cetera* thereunto belonging, and not for any thing like rational investigation, or philosophical truth."[28] Their motivation for reading—"to fill up the vacancies of time"[29]—was as pitiful as their reading material. Young women received the harshest treatment, typified by a comparison of their appetite for novels to a taste for unripe fruit: "Surely the youthful part of the fair sex have as keen a relish for novels, as they have for green apples, green gooseberries, or other such kind of crude trash, otherwise it would not be found worth while to cultivate these literary weeds, which spring up so plenteously, every month, even under the scythe of criticism!"[30] Vulgar readers, untalented writers, and unscrupulous publishers formed a miserable—but unbreakable—circle of dependence.

With rhetoric like that of a critic's response to *Miss Melmoth; or, the New Clarissa* in the *Monthly*, the reviewers continually distanced their responses from those of common novel addicts:

> The good-natured and benevolent Reader will receive more pleasure from the perusal of this work, than the critic. The former, whose *heart* must be *rent* by the cruel fate of the first Clarissa, will be delighted with the better fortune of her amiable name-sake; while the latter will be less benignly employed in marking the inferiority of the new production.[31]

In the *Critical*, a reviewer evaluates *The Embarrassed Lovers* in a similar manner:

> The embarrassments which Henry Carey, Esq. and the honourable Miss Cecilia Neville met with may be highly interesting to many of those readers who spend, or rather mispend, their time in the perusal of such kinds of writing. Such readers may enter into the spirit of these embarrassments, and eagerly pursue the thread of the narration. For our part, we can seldom get through a score pages of performances of this sort, without being heartily tired, and we generally drudge through the remainder with aching heads.[32]

Attacking debased standards, however, amounted to an admission of critical impotence: authors were guaranteed readers—and sales—if they pandered to the popular tastes. A critic for the *Monthly* says as much, under the protective cover of sarcasm, in his review of *The Libertine Husband Reclaimed:* "Whatever defects . . . may be found in the characters, incidents or style of a novel, if the story be tender, and tenderly told, it is sufficient to secure the Author's reputation: while he has such a powerful advocate in the hearts of his fair Readers, he may bid defiance to the critic's frown."[33] As is true today, a popular novelist—an eighteenth-century Sidney Sheldon or Judith Krantz—could blithely brave critical severity.

But even voices in a wilderness were occasionally heard. Again using comparative language, the critics claimed kinship with a small group of readers who shared their greater discernment and who indulged rarely, not habitually, in fiction. In the *Monthly*, a reviewer's response to *The Inquisition* aptly illustrates the distinction: "To those who make a general practice of novel reading, we may recommend these volumes, for they might easily have worse of the kind. Those, however, who occasionally pursue works of fiction as a recreation from severer studies, will be but little satisfied with this."[34] More humorously, the *Critical* employs a familiar Baconian metaphor in refraining from recommending *Female Friendship* "to readers of sentiment or taste. Those who devour books of this kind, without digesting them, may possibly be of another opinion: they may fall to with a good appetite to dishes which would turn our stomachs."[35] The sophisticated reader looks beyond simple amusement for more useful instruction: while the majority may applaud the paucity of reflections in Charlotte Clarke's *History of Henry Dumont,* because, as a *Monthly* reviewer says, "the story stands still, and their [the readers'] curiosity remains suspended," a reader "of tolerable taste and judgment," according to the reviewer, "will dismiss one of these *merely narrative* volumes, before he has read half a dozen pages of it."[36] But even reading solely for amusement would presumably be permissible for discriminating readers: since they turned to novels only for relaxation—and so infrequently—they were unlikely to develop an unhealthy addiction.

The favorable references to this type of reader were not at all disinterested. For the privileged, tasteful few were none other than the implied readers of *The Critical Review* and *The Monthly Review.* In fact, the structure of each number—which normally confined novel reviews to the "Monthly Catalogue" at the end—as a "recreation from severer studies," both presumed and shaped such an audience's reading habits. W. Denham Sutcliffe, an early scholar of the review journals, claimed that they were addressed to the "common" reader, who would find it easier to read reviews than to read books.[37] Within his own frame of reference, he was correct; but he used the term *common* relatively. These readers were not, by and large, the literati—but nor were they presumed to be among the hordes who were drawn to the popular novel. In a more recent study, Thomas Treadwell has come closer to the mark in concluding that "the Reviews catered to an audience whose interests lay chiefly in history, theology, science, and current affairs and for whom novel reviews were of use chiefly as a guide to the reading matter of their wives and children."[38] The significance of the assumed audience cannot be exaggerated. It shaded every negative comment on novels, novelists, and novel readers.[39] Even when the critics explicitly addressed the clientele of circulating libraries and the authors who stocked their shelves, they were actually speaking to their own readers and to writers who wanted the attention of these readers. Given a broad public that ignored them, the reviewers took what satisfaction they could in narrowing the circle and preaching to the converted within it.

* * *

Nowhere is this appeal to an elite more apparent than in the reviewers' bifurcated response toward female novelists. Condescension informed most of the reviews, which professed to treat women—especially the many who pleaded unique hardships or laudable moral ends—with special consideration. Some commentary appears genuinely indulgent; a reviewer for the *Monthly,* for instance, hesitates "to criticize the production of a *Lady's* pen; especially as, whatever its defects, it is friendly to the cause of virtue and morality, which is more than can be said in favour of many of the romances of this age and country."[40] Elsewhere, attack predominates: "We cannot compliment the authoress on her success in these volumes. The story is incoherent and improbable; and the actors are always inconsistent, and at variance with themselves: but we must not be too severe with a lady, whose intentions appear to be good, whatever her book may be."[41]

Less often—but often enough—the critics tired even of this posture, opting instead to attack openly female writers' exemption from genuine criticism.[42] As early as 1762, a *Monthly* reviewer regrets the excessive tenderness shown to female authors:

> It seems high time . . . to deal plainly with the sex, in order, as far as the influence of the Review may extend, to prevent them from growing equally ridiculous with those pitiful male-Scribblers, who have so plentifully stacked the Circulating Libraries with Adventures, Familiar Letters, and Novels:—and, if possible, to convince them that every woman who has learnt to spell, is not a Cockburn, a Jones, a Carter, or a Lennox.[43]

A cogent appeal, but hardly successful, for thirty years later, a *Monthly* reviewer still feels compelled to lambast plaintive novelists and pliant critics:

> It has of late become a policy to elude, as may be supposed, critical strictures, by an appeal to the humanity of the reader; and by pleading personal circumstances as the motive for having recourse to the pen. When such a plea is offered in a female character, we scarcely know how to receive it, until repetition familiarizes us to it; and then

we cannot but recollect, that the public opinion of literary merit has no connection with, and will very seldom be influenced in favor of, the private motives of the writer.[44]

Disregarding gender made especially good sense in light of numerous female impersonators from Grub Street. Reviewers for both the *Monthly* and the *Critical* use *The School for Husbands* as a pretext for condemning the practice; I quote from the latter:

> We are not without suspicion that in anonymous publications, the words *written by a Lady* are sometimes made use of to preclude the severity of criticism; but as the Reviewers are generally chuck and greybeards, this piece of *finesse* seldom answers the purpose intended.—Whether or nor the work before us be really written by a Lady, is neither known to us, nor of the least consequence. Had it been destitute of merit, justice to our readers would have prevented our suffering it to pass unnoticed.[45]

All of these approaches served the same important end. The focus on gender replaced and precluded any detailed commentary on the individual texts in question. In this respect, attention to gender resembled the rhetorical tactics, discussed by Edward Bloom and others,[46] commonly used to dismiss any poor or mediocre novel: punning on titles, bemoaning the state of the art, attacking disreputable publishers, and so forth. Attention to the so-called privileges of female authorship, then, was primarily a code that enabled the reviewers to communicate disdain—and, therefore, discrimination—to their regular implied audience. And as Treadwell has noted, the emphasis given to history, science, and politics in the longer articles suggests that the editors regarded their readership—correctly or not—as overwhelmingly male. To men who presumably read fiction infrequently, liberality toward a female novelist—or almost any mention of gender—signaled a forgettable novel. Female readers remained mired in the stereotype illustrated by the following imaginary dialogue, taken from a review of *Generosity* in the *Critical:*

> Young lady. You have read Generosity, I find: what do you think of it?
> Reviewer. It is one of the most trite, trifling, improbable, and absurd stories that I ever saw.
> Y. L. I would not give a pin for your opinion: you never like what the rest of the world are pleased with. I found it delightful:—what charming love-scenes! How many weddings!
> R. Pray, my dear girl, do you think the characters—

Y. L. Hang the characters: it is a charming book—the dear Lord Walton—[47]

As readers or writers, most women were noticed to remind men that they were beneath notice.

Other kinds of references to gender reinforced the stereotype of inferiority. Reflecting the assumption that women should confine their subjects to feelings and emotions and write in a delicate style,[48] a reviewer for the *Critical* can say, with complete sincerity, of Charlotte Lennox's *Sophia,* "A woman only can enter justly into all the scruples and refinements of female manners."[49] With such a bias, reviewers routinely postulated female authorship for anonymous novels that possessed feminine qualities—some less desirable than others. "From the ease of the language, the vivacity of spirit, the delicacy of sentiment, and the abundance of love and tenderness" in *The History of Miss Delia Stanhope,* a *Monthly* critic does not hesitate "to pronounce, that a Lady wrote it."[50] Similar characteristics reveal the sex of the author of *Laura and Augustus;* but a *Critical* reviewer adds that the novelist "would betray herself, by a few inaccuracies in language, and a little improbability in some of the incidents."[51] Other notices, like that of *The History of Miss Dorinda Catsby and Miss Emilia Faulkner,* are less oblique: "Some romance-writing female (as we guess from the style) with her head full of love scenes,—shady groves, and purling streams, honourable passions and wicked purposes,—has here put together a flimsy series of such adventures and descriptions as we usually meet with in the amorous trash of the times."[52] Even greater censure was reserved for female writers who crossed their allotted boundaries. "The productions of a lady ought not to be condemned with asperity," intones a superficially charitable *Critical* reviewer in 1770, "unless they transgress against that delicacy and decorum by which the fair sex should always distinguish themselves."[53] The lesser latitude permitted to women inevitably increased the critics' opportunities for attack.

With the better female pens—especially toward the end of the century—the critical response was vastly different. Novels by Fanny Burney, Charlotte Smith, Elizabeth Inchbald, Clara Reeve, Ann Radcliffe and others received serious and lengthy attention and were judged within the same categories and by the same criteria as novels written by men—plot, character, diction, probability, pathos, and sentiment, to name a few. In his review of *A Simple Story,* for instance, a *Critical* commentator applauds Inchbald for accuracy and preservation of character, excitement of the proper emotions, adherence to probability, unflagging invention, and the artful fusion of two plots. The principal flaw: abruptness, especially in the ending and in an unelaborated-upon gap of seventeen years between two volumes—a fault that the reviewer hopes Inchbald will remedy through revision.[54] But in the review of the second edition a few months later, the *Critical* reviewer admits that "what at first appeared to us as a blemish, has been approved of by many critics as a new and artful way of conducting a story."[55] Here the commentator is actively engaged in responding, criticizing, advising, revising—and treating Inchbald as a novelist who was a woman, rather than the other way around.

Gender-based judgments did persist in the tendency—noted long ago by J. M. S. Tompkins and recently examined by Jane Spencer—to group the best female novelists and to discuss their merits in relative terms, reinforcing the sense of a uniquely feminine—and inferior—mode of writing.[56] Occasionally, a critic would go so far as to compare the merits of a female novelist to those of her male counterparts. Burney's *Cecilia*, according to a reviewer for the *Monthly*, has "much of the dignity and pathos of Richardson; and much of the acuteness and ingenuity of Fielding."[57] More broadly, a retrospective *Critical* reviewer maintains that the "prosaic epic, which . . . arose to its meridian in the hands of Fielding and Smollett . . . has continued with a milder, but not less captivating splendour, in those of Miss Burney, Mrs. Smith, and Mrs. Lennox."[58] According to a *Critical* reviewer, Mary Hays's *Victim of Prejudice* contains "many passages which, for warmth and vigour of pathos and composition, are scarcely inferior to the effusions of Rousseau."[59] Finally, another *Critical* reviewer implies—with questionable judgment—that, in one respect at least, Inchbald is superior to Fielding and Smollett: while the men, "excellently as their novels were written, were indifferent dramatists,"[60] Inchbald has succeeded in both genres. Complimentary assessments like these, however, commonly implied that a truly superior female writer would transcend her inherent femininity—an implication made explicit in a *Monthly* critic's enthusiastic response to Smith's *Desmond:*

Among the various proofs which the present age affords, that the female character is advancing in cultivation, and rising in dignity, may be justly reckoned the improvements that are making in the kind of writing which is more immediately adapted to the amusement of female readers. Novels, which were formerly little more than simple tales of love, are gradually taking a higher and more masculine tone, and are becoming the vehicles of useful instruction.[61]

Hardly protofeminists, the reviewers, nonetheless, could—and did—recognize female writers of superior talent, and encourage in them a professionalism equal to their own. Such an attitude underlies a *Monthly* reviewer's commendation of Burney for eschewing the dubious benefits of gender: "The author of Cecilia asks no undue lenity: she doth not plead any privilege of her sex: she stands on firmer ground; and with a spirit superior to solicitation or fear, may meet the decision of impartial criticism."[62] And her novel may meet the eyes of the critical elite influenced by such impartial criticism.

* * *

Like gender, the criterion of morality was applied differently in different contexts. Condemnation of moral impropriety conveniently dispensed with inferior and pedestrian novels. Even the best novelists, though, were not immune to censure on moral grounds. Impressed with the first two volumes of *Tristram Shandy,* the *Monthly* altered its opinion with the publication of the more salacious volumes 3 and 4—and with the revelation of the author's identity and occupation. The reviewer Owen Ruffhead argues that a clergyman ought to observe greater discretion, calls the work indecent and dull, and encourages the author, with "friendly admonitions," to stop writing if he cannot do better.[63] John Langhorne is kinder to the more sentimental fifth and sixth volumes— which "are not so much interlarded with obscenity as the former"—but he begins his review with a long moralistic preamble that gives primacy to the critic's duty as moral censor: "In reviewing the works of the learned, we are not only to observe their literary excellencies or defects, not merely to point out their faults or beauties, but to consider their moral tendency; and this more particularly, as it is of greater consequence to society that the heart be mended, than that the mind be entertained."[64] Over thirty years later, Samuel Taylor Coleridge's disapproving review of *The Monk,* which begins with an excellent critique of the affective deficiency of supernatural romance, ultimately returns to and reiterates the priority of morality over artistic merit:

A more grievous fault remains,—a fault for which no literary excellence can atone,—a fault for which all other excellence does but aggravate, as adding subtlety to a poison by the elegance of its preparation.

Mildness of censure here would be criminally misplaced, and silence would make us accomplices. Not without reluctance, then, but in full conviction that we are performing a duty, we declare it to be our opinion, that the Monk is a romance, which if a parent saw in the hand of a son or daughter, he might reasonably turn pale. The temptations of Ambrosio are described with a libidinous minuteness, which, we sincerely hope, will receive its best and only adequate censure from the offended conscience of the author himself.[65]

Conversely, critics in both *The Monthly Review* and *The Critical Review* regularly commended those works in which the story was subservient to—and a vehicle for—sound moral principles.[66]

Even novels that promised laudable instruction received careful scrutiny as reviewers searched for moral integrity. Aware that a negative example could overwhelm a positive precept, critics objected to a too vivid portrayal of vice, as a *Monthly* reviewer's criticism of *The Modern Fine Gentleman* illustrates:

The only apology that can be made by the Author, is, that the Fine Gentlemen, the worthless heroes of the piece, are not exhibited for the Reader's *approbation;* that, on the contrary, as they act like scoundrels, exemplary justice takes place, and they are punished as they ought to be. This is admitted; but, still, we contend, that *such* characters form but a very improper sort of acquaintance for the young, and unguarded, of either sex.[67]

Virtue, on the other hand, had to be conspicuously rewarded. *The History of Miss Indiana Danby* displeases a *Monthly* critic because the "*punishment of virtue,* however countenanced by the practice of our tragic writers, is an unhappy reverse of that moral tendency of which our novelists ought never to lose sight; viz. the just discouragement and exemplary chastisement of vice."[68] Unrewarded or compromised virtue would, of course, fail to encourage virtuous conduct among impressionable readers. Consequently, *A Lesson for Lovers,* in which one small error dooms an otherwise noble heroine, is judged dangerous—the example of *Clarissa* notwithstanding—because "the painter of fictitious life should take care how he mixes his *shades,* lest what was designed for instruction should only produce melancholy; and despair of reaching the rewards of virtue should quell all nervous exertions."[69] For similar reasons, the affective consequences of novels of sensibility left the critics uneasy. Whereas one *Monthly* critic doubts if "tender and pathetic moral tales ever do, in fact, contribute to promote virtue and morality in the world" since they communicate "false and romantic notions of life,"[70] two years later another critic disapproves of novelists like the author of *The Count de Hoensdern* who "move us to pity instead of exciting us to action. They teach us to consider every failure of our wishes as an insupportable misfortune, instead of convincing us that misfortunes are often the creatures of our own fancy; in short, to weep and wail is the morality that such writers teach!"[71]

Modern readers may weep and wail at a preoccupation with moral rectitude that seems excessive—and, perhaps, affected—especially in light of its manifest, admitted failure to influence the literary marketplace. Complaints that most novels failed to meet appropriate standards—and that most novel readers preferred titillation or mere amusement to solid instruction—begat nothing but further complaints. Attacking Charlotte Smith for attempting "to pour *herself* upon the Public" in *The Banished Man* in order to sustain its attention, a *Critical* reviewer ruefully acknowledges that the "public, careless of the future, and little grateful for the past, reads a novel only to be amused, and if amusement is wanting, quickly abandons the most favorite author, little enquiring to what cause the defect may be imputed."[72] To account for perseverance in the face of apparent futility, the audience, once again, was central. The critics assumed readers who, like themselves, enjoyed feeling morally as well as intellectually superior—and who would, therefore, welcome reminders of the general public's deficiency in both respects. Criticizing immorality or amorality with oppressive regularity may certainly have reflected a sincere sense of social duty, but it also betrayed a disconcerting smugness.

But an attitude of superiority, however smug, did have its advantages for criticism. While moral probity may have been necessary for approved fiction, it was seldom sufficient. Some reviewers, like the *Critical* reviewer who responded to the aptly titled *The Triumph of Benevolence,* did allow good intentions to compensate for a haphazard performance: "The pleasure which the author of these volumes evidently takes in recommending benevolence, will not suffer us to examine them with critical severity. We cannot say that his history is a masterly performance; but as we applaud the design, we will not condemn the execution of it."[73] More often, though, professional integrity required the critic to insist that a worthy message be communicated through an agreeable and artistically correct medium. A *Monthly* critic observes that if "a novel . . . contains good instructions without being conveyed in an entertaining form, the work has no real claim to commendation,"[74] and a *Critical* reviewer agrees with the preface to Thomas Day's widely read children's book *Sandford and Merton* that this type of work cannot be useful if it is not entertaining.[75] While novelists invoked the image of the gilded pill to *justify* their gilding, critics recalled the image to *require* it. Thus, the reviewers frequently insisted that the familiar justification by *negative merit*—that a novel may not be good but at least it was harmless—was not good enough.[76]

The moral novelist, therefore, had to exploit those narrative devices that were conducive to aesthetic pleasure. In a review of *The Amicable Quixote,* a *Monthly* critic grants the artist considerable creative latitude. The writer may use both his observation and imagination, personify virtues, introduce a variety of characters, or unite virtues in a single character. "Sometimes his observation will furnish him with the power of giving instruction; sometimes his imagination will furnish entertainment to the mind";[77] but both genius and judgment must be apparent in a novel of any distinction. Perhaps no one makes the point more emphatically than the *Critical* reviewer of *Juliet Grenville:* "Utility, . . . though the principal, is not the sole consquence derived from writings of this sort. For if they be the work of a masterly hand, of a hand that is guided by a regular and lively fancy combined with just reflexion, and accomplished in the art of elegant composition, they present us with the most agreeable entertainment that the mind can receive."[78]

Since overt didacticism disrupted this equilibrium—and, thus, threatened the interest and involvement of the reader (especially the type of reader who most needed instruction)—it drew repeated critical fire. The reviewers for both journals respond negatively to Johnson's *Rasselas* because they find the moral reflections intrusive and distracting. A reviewer for the *Monthly* holds that the "diversity of characters, and variety of incidents, in a romance, keeps attention alive; and moral sentiments find access to the mind imperceptibly, when led by amusement: whereas dry, didactic precepts, delivered under a sameness of character, soon grow tiresome to the generality of readers."[79] In the opinion of a *Critical* reviewer, *Rasselas* can be recommended heartily to philosophers, but not to novel readers, since "the laws of history . . . prohibit tedious reflections, long dissertations, and balanced disquisitions either in morals or politicks; such only are permitted as rise easily from the subject, and illustrate, without breaking the thread of the narrative."[80] Heavy-handed reflections do not instruct precisely because they do not entertain. Thus, a *Monthly* reviewer applauds Thomas Holcroft's *Hugh Trevor* for treating the fundamentally moral question of a career choice not through extended discussion but by portraying characters in action.[81]

Effective moralizing involves the reader in action as well. The preceding criticisms suggest that more than sustaining the reader's attention, novels with *implied* moral applications require the reader's participation and cooperation. In a critique of unusual psychological insight, a *Monthly* reviewer faults *The Exemplary Mother* and other novels of the "admonitory class" for repelling readers that they need to attract, concluding that

> narratives are more welcome, and not less instructive, when the events and catastrophe are so calculated as obviously to suggest profitable inferences, which are left to the operation of the reader's mind; than where the writer furnishes all the deductions and documents himself: for the reader in the latter case being merely passive, rather tires than improves, and is more inclined to pass with rapidity from incident to incident, than to afford that regular attention which the Author merits and requires.[82]

The reader's deduction—rather than the author's dictation—allows for successful moral communication.

Given these attitudes, it is not surprising that irony and sarcasm suffused critical responses to morally pure, but artistically flawed, novels—the kind of novels likely to win support from naive and sentimental readers. A *Monthly* reviewer writes that "the benevolent and virtuous sentiments" of *The Tutor* soften his "severe brow"; but while these sentiments induce him "to respect the heart of its Author, they excite in him a regret that he cannot express the highest admiration of his [the author's] genius."[83] Less obliquely, *The History of Mr. Cecil and Miss Grey* is characterized as "very sober, very innocent, but, we are sorry to add, when speaking of a moral production, very dull."[84] *The Memoirs of the Marchioness de Louvoi* serves primarily to deliver morals agreeably to young girls. "Considering the piece in this light, rather than in that of a mere novel, whatever triteness may be observed in the sentiment, or irregularity in the method, will scarcely need an apology."[85] With tongue similarly planted in cheek, the reviewer of *Female Sensibility* maintains that as "a composition it is defective; and as a picture of real life it is erroneous. It is in its morality alone that it is unexceptionable."[86] A *Critical* reviewer could be equally biting, as this comment on *The Reclaimed Libertine* illustrates: "If any thing can save these volumes from critical damnation, it must be the avowed design with which they are written: they are manufactured in so slovenly a manner, that they deserve no praise as literary productions."[87] As for *The Daughters of Coquetry,* a reviewer observes: "The moral to be drawn from this work is so good, that we are blind to the dulness, the insipidity, and the improbability of the narrative."[88] In a good reviewer, the moral censor and literary arbiter had to coexist, so that he could balance the competing claims of morality and entertainment both along with and for the benefit of sophisticated readers, however unbalanced the broader reading public remained.

* * *

A final area of dispute with the popular audience centered on the issue of originality. Most novel readers received sneering condescension for having an indiscriminate thirst for novelty at all costs. To a reviewer for the *Critical,* the adventures in *A Friend to Virtue* are not admirable; they "are, however, something new, and that is the cry constantly heard in the circulating library."[89] According to another reviewer, *The Offspring of Fancy* "discovers neither much regularity of design, nor attention to embellishment, as is necessary to give the stamp of genius to a literary production. It may however serve in some degree to amuse those readers whose taste is chiefly for what is new, and who prefer variety to excellence."[90] With similar disdain, a reviewer in the *Monthly* paraphrases Pope's *Art of Sinking* to characterize *The Unfortunate Beauty:* "This novel, in which we have met with nothing, either greatly to disgust or to please, ends tragically; which is uncommon in this species of writing:—*but, any thing for a surprize,* as the author of the treatise on the Bathos has it."[91]

On the other hand, the reviewers themselves appear to have prized originality; as Tompkins has observed, they welcomed "the smallest departure from the beaten track of love and roguery" with obvious relief.[92] A *Critical* commentator even ventures to commend the Gothic romances for gratifying the "love of novelty, which arises out of the constitution of our nature."[93] However inbred the love may have been, critics certainly scorned "the threadbare patterns of modern novels"[94] and the multitude of unimaginative and safe novelists, as a *Monthly* reviewer's comment on *The Benevolent Man* amply demonstrates:

> Many of our modern novel-writers endeavour to persuade themselves and their Readers, that a natural story, and a good moral, are the only ingredients essential to this species of writing. To search for new characters, to invent uncommon incidents, to explore the hidden recesses of the heart, and to uphold and display the endless varieties

of taste, humours, and passions, which appear among mankind,—these are Herculean labours, too vast for their feeble powers to sustain. They therefore satisfy themselves with conducting a number of common and well-known characters, through a series of incidents, such as daily occur in life; interspersing a few trite moral sentences through the work; and bringing the tale at last to a happy issue, for the encouragement of virtue.[95]

Earlier in the century, a natural story would inevitably have won some respect; by the time of this review, however, it was the refuge of the untalented. To be natural was not enough, but to be novel was not easy. As the reviewer of *The Fashionable Friend* admits, "Since almost every track is become beaten, authors are obliged to make the most of what is left them; for this reason most of our later novels are very barren of incidents, and the writers seem to aim less at diversifying their tales, than at working up a single circumstance in the most striking manner."[96]

Under these circumstances, novelists who found various means to breathe some life into shopworn narrative conventions earned significant praise. The author of *Charles and Charlotte* "has the merit of giving, in some degree, . . . originality to a tale which has been told in a thousand different forms, by making choice of incidents and situations not commonly introduced in works of this kind."[97] Both Elizabeth Griffith's *History of Lady Barton* and Charlotte Lennox's *Euphemia* are credited with deviating profitably from the customary pattern by beginning where novels usually ended—namely, with a marriage.[98] Most notably, a *Critical* commentator's predictably laudatory review, which begins with an expression of regret about the tendency for the otherwise admirable imitation of nature and of one's predecessors to deprive a work of variety and novelty, accords Smollett's *Humphry Clinker* the ultimate accolade:

> The celebrated author of this production is one of those few writers who have discovered an original genius. His novels are not more distinguished for the natural management of the fable, and a fertility of interesting incidents, than for a strong, lively, and picturesque description of characters; in which he is almost unrivalled. The same vigour of imagination that animates his other works, is conspicuous in the present, where we are entertained with a variety of scenes and characters almost unanticipated.[99]

However hyperbolic, this comment suggests the principal distinction between the learned reviewer and the ignorant reader in regard to originality, a distinction captured even better in John-son's famous definition of the highest form of wit as that "which is at once natural and new, that which though not obvious is, upon its first production, acknowledged to be just; . . . that, which he that never found it, wonders how he missed."[100] In fact, a reviewer in the *Critical* uses exactly the same terms to commend *A Simple Story*, concluding that "the incidents are natural; and, what is more extraordinary in the present state of novel-writing, they are new."[101] Like *Humphry Clinker*, Inchbald's novel maintains the deli-cate balance between probability and originality forsaken in texts that gratified an uncritical taste for novelty. While the reviewers—and, by deliberate implication, their acute readers—commonly in-sisted upon realism as the proper—and properly elevated—plane for fiction, the masses sought fantasy and escape. Thus, a *Critical* reviewer faults an author who, "by endeavouring to render his work uncommon, has made it unnatural";[102] another asks that novelists generally "avoid what is only uncommon, if destitute of probability or the resemblance of nature";[103] and yet another ar-gues that "uncommon and unexpected incidents please by their novelty and the surprize which they occasion; but when what is uncommon is absurd, and what is unexpected is highly improb-able, disgust takes the place of pleasure."[104] Critics for the *Monthly* often agree, complaining that Robert Bage's *Barham Downs* has "a novelty in the manner" that "will be judged too deficient in na-ture"[105] and offering a satiric analysis of the burden of originality placed upon every novelist: "As the common occurrences in life are too insipid to bear reading, the composers of novels, regard-less of probability, describe remarkable accidents, calculated to entertain and surprize; every novel that appears, therefore, ren-ders the task of this species of writing more arduous, and requires invention to be racked for new situations and adventures, more extraordinary than have yet been conceived."[106]

A similarly refined response emerged in discussions of imita-tion. Reviewers commonly dismissed the numerous and often popular imitators of Richardson, Fielding, Sterne—and, later, Radcliffe—with asperity. A *Monthly* reviewer, for instance, is driven to ask, "Can the admirers of Richardson *equal* him in nothing but his faults?";[107] and in response to "Doctor Kunastrokius's" *Explanatory Remarks on Tristram Shandy*, another *Monthly* reviewer suggests with arch simplicity that "it must be an excellent joke that will bear repeating."[108] For a *Critical* commentator, *The Life and Opinions of Bertram Montfichet* is nothing more than a "spurious bantling" of *Tristram Shandy*—a "dead letter without the spirit."[109]

This last phrase epitomizes the reviewers' nuanced posture: they did not object to imitations and sequels per se but rather to inferior and all-too-predictable copies of the letter that were devoid of the spirit. Although some of the imitators of the best novelists received modest approval,[110] more frequently the critics lamented the fact that "the manes of Richardson, Fielding, and Smollett" had been "tonsured"[111] by unqualified mimics, who helped bring the genre into disrepute. Praising the comic style of Fielding and Smollett, a *Monthly* reviewer comes to the unhappy conclusion that the "many ineffectual attempts at humour that have been made will . . . shew, that it is not so easy to succeed in it as, from the seeming *facility* and apparent *negligence* in some applauded compositions," authors "may have promised themselves they should be able to do."[112]

Beneath such attitudes lay the growing sense, as time went on, of having declined from a golden age in fiction. In one of the fullest statements of this position—a statement that also implies, once again, a hierarchy of readers—a *Critical* reviewer faults the otherwise commendable *George Bateman* for a too laborious, even servile, imitation of the

> two great novellists [*sic*], Richardson and Fielding: that frequent exhibition of scenes in low life so distinguishable in the former, and that bias towards the serious and the melancholy, so observable in the latter, are studiously copied in George Bateman, but are not always properly united. Fielding's wit and humour supported him in all his vulgar characters; Richardson's intimate knowledge of, and acquaintance with human nature, rendered his minute investigation of little incidents and circumstances interesting and pathetic. In inferior writers they have too often a different effect; to those, however, who can lose sight of these great originals, this novel, though it be rather too long, will afford entertainment.[113]

From the same perspective, reviewers for both journals reject John Raithby's *Delineations of the Heart* because it imitates Fielding's manner but not his wit, humor, and knowledge of human nature.[114] On the other hand, that rare imitator won approval who captured the spirit without mechanically parroting the manner of a successful predecessor. A reviewer for the *Critical* credits the author of *Dinarbas*—a sequel to *Rasselas*—for not attempting to imitate Johnson's style;[115] and another *Critical* reviewer finds Jane West's *A Gossip's Story* a better imitation of Fielding's humor than any *professed* one—presumably referring to Cumberland's more workmanlike *Henry*, published two years earlier.[116] No less than

Young, the critics recognized that he who imitates the *Iliad* does not imitate Homer.

A worthy imitator required abilities not far inferior to those of his model, and the best imitator implicitly acknowledged his debt by trying to overreach his predecessor.[117] Reviewers for both the *Monthly* and the *Critical* so characterize Rousseau for *La nouvelle Héloïse,* modeled to some degree on *Clarissa.* At the beginning of a long *ars/ingenio* comparison between Richardson and Rousseau, a reviewer for the *Critical* considers it "the highest encomium on Mr. Richardson, that he has been deemed worthy the imitation of a writer of Rousseau's eminence, and that he still remains unrivalled in copying nature, though he may perhaps be greatly excel [*sic*] in deep reflection, the finer tints that discriminate genius, and certain magic powers peculiar to Rousseau, of conjuring into a single expression the substance of volumes."[118] Without entering into an elaborate comparison, a *Monthly* reviewer concludes that "though Mr. Rousseau falls short in many respects of Mr. Richardson, whose manner he has imitated, yet in others he so far excels him, as to appear himself an inimitable original."[119] Not quite so paradoxical as it might seem, the finest imitations are necessarily original.

The best could be recognized and appreciated only by the best. In regard to originality—and every other mark of literary value—the reviewers' position assumed a community of privileged readers. I analyze the phenomenon readily—but criticize it reluctantly—since I am implicated in a similar process, like any other player in the games of criticism. In the eighteenth century, fiction was, by definition, popular—and, therefore, unsettling to the critics. We modern critics have simply defined our community—and the objects that it deems worth considering—more narrowly. Only recently, while engaged in often acrimonious debate over what constitutes literature and literary study, have we begun to realize that elitism may be necessary but problematic—and that we may be in danger of narrowing ourselves into irrelevance. Therefore, I dare not condescend to these early judges, as they did to novelists and readers, under the lofty but flimsy sanction of culture.

5

The Balanced Critical Practices of Practical Critics: Periodical Reviewers (II)

Extratextual, ideological concerns surfaced prominently and repeatedly in novel reviews not only because of their intrinsic importance and their utility in cultural politics but also because of the difficulties surrounding generic and formal analysis. The novelty of novels argued against a systematic critical vocabulary and carefully defined evaluative criteria, as did the general disrepute of the genre, which discouraged sustained attention to individual texts. Prohibitive circumstances could not, however, entirely prevent the emergence both of a rudimentary genre theory—which differentiated and, to some degree, established hierarchies of the various subgenres of fiction—and of commentary centered around the constituent elements of narrative craft. On the microcosmic and macrocosmic levels, the most significant feature of the critical discourse in both areas was balance. Influenced by the beauties/faults approach of their neoclassical predecessors, many reviewers weighed the advantages derived from a novelist's technical and generic choices against shortcomings resulting from those decisions, just as they commonly balanced aesthetic effects and moral or psychological consequences. A similar process extended to the treatment by reviewers in the aggregate of each subgenre and each formal characteristic: no kind of fiction or narrative device attracted unequivocal praise or blame.

Balance of the latter type was sometimes consciously imposed in the pages of the review journals themselves but more often can be discerned only from a reader's active synthesis of contending—and often contradictory—voices of individual critics. Balance may appear inevitable and unremarkable, given the autonomy conferred upon reviewers by editorial restraint and anonymity, the fundamentally inductive nature of their task, and changes in perspective over two generations. One can detect, however, a less random dynamic of opposition that ensured a continually unstable critical consensus. Again and again, once a significant number of reviewers sanctioned a particular characteristic—as often by citing its breach as its observance—critics had to confront inferior or problematic texts that embodied the trait and praiseworthy texts that lacked or rejected it, leading them to question its value. Instead of a conservative golden mean intolerant of eccentric genius—a mean that sometimes devalued individual reviews—this larger pattern of oscillation encouraged imaginative, prospective, and confrontational judgments.

* * *

The extent to which an awareness of genre developed in the periodicals is evident in William Enfield's 1796 review of *Camilla* for the *Monthly,* in which he posits three rough categories of fiction:

> Perhaps all novels, which have character enough to be brought into any classification, may be divided under three heads; romantic, pathetic, and humorous: the first describing scenes and characters which are beyond nature, in order to excite curiosity and to amuse the fancy; the second, touching the heart by an interesting development of sentiment and passion; the third, delineating amusing and instructive portraits of characters as they exist in real life, with that particular cast of thought and expression by which individual manners are distinguished. Though few novels fall exclusively within any one of these classes, every good novel has a prominent character, from which its proper place in this arrangement may be easily discovered.[1]

Deliberately broad so as to foreground essential differences, Enfield's classification provides a useful paradigm for grouping the various subgenres that reviewers routinely distinguished more minutely. "Romantic" fiction could include Eastern tales, Gothic romances, and historical novels, which often, ironically, rested on the border of realism. Novels of sentiment or sensibility clearly fell under the heading of "pathetic"—to many reviewers, in more ways than one! And to be considered "humorous" a novel did not necessarily need to be comic, as long as it observed probability and nature. Treated with differing degrees of critical enthusiasm, each of the subgenres nonetheless attracted a similar pattern of balanced and dynamic reception.

Early, positive reactions to Oriental tales emphasized the moral efficacy of well-contrived romance, even at the expense of valued aesthetic criteria. Reviewers for both the *Monthly* and the *Critical,* for instance, applaud John Hawkesworth's *Almoran and Hamet* for conveying moral lessons in a form that not only delights but also leaves a forceful impression on the mind,[2] to which end the reviewer for the *Monthly* grants the author liberty to "adorn the probable . . . with every incident to make it agreeable, and to charm and surprize the reader."[3] Equally magnanimous, the *Critical*'s reviewer of *Oriental Anecdotes* supports the blending of history and romance, since it provides "enough of real incidents to afford the pleasure of instruction, and of the seasoning of fiction, to save the perusal from the tediousness of merely dry historical matter of fact," thereby imparting a moral "to those who read for the sake of entertainment, or relaxation from graver studies or employment."[4] Entertainment may, in fact, have exercised more influence than the reviewers cared to admit: sound principles could not save *Rasselas* from criticism for dull overt moralizing; yet, more fantastic narratives were readily exempted from censure, with a *Monthly* reviewer going so far as to "shade" the defects of John Langhorne's *Solyman and Almena* "for the sake of the useful instruction it conveys."[5]

Whatever enthusiasm or tolerance the genre generated could not overpower distaste for its mannerism and tumidity, its excesses in style and subject matter. As early as 1759, a critic for the *Monthly* berates an English translation of the French *Abassai: An Eastern Novel* for "affectation of sentimental refinement, unnatural representation of the passions, and high-sounding pretences to virtue and heroism."[6] Ten years later, a *Critical* reviewer opines that Longinus himself would have disapproved of this type of sublimity as "the tawdry daubing of art, not the vivid depiction of nature," concluding that the "unaffected productions of true poetic genius animate and transport the mind with rapture, while insipid dulness and extravagant ostentation inspire us only with frigidity and disgust."[7] Even the praiseworthy moral tendency of the genre cannot prevent one of the *Critical* reviewers from complaining that he is "weary of Eastern imitation; of bombast without sublimity; and of inflated pomp without true majesty."[8] One amateur psychologist among the reviewers attributes this dissatisfaction to the temperamental unsuitability of the English for the genre, maintaining that "the cool, reasoning, northern reader is more apt to be disgusted than charmed with the perpetual glare of brilliant images, the eternal round of laboured allegories and metaphors, and the crowd of incredible events, enchantments, and prodigies"[9]—a complimentary assessment of readers' tastes, to be sure, but more wish fulfillment than diagnosis, given the genre's continued popularity[10] (or perhaps a clever attempt to shape tastes to conform to the flattering stereotype).

Other attacks rested on more familiar and secure foundations. A *Monthly* critic notes with asperity in a 1792 review of *Solyman and Fatima* that "an Eastern tale ought at least be a tolerable representation of Eastern manners, sentiments, and language."[11] Failure in this respect extended to many other novels, including most notably *The History of Rhedi,* which combined Oriental settings and characters with Scottish idioms![12] Even more damning—because more inclusive—was the criticism exemplified in a line from the *Monthly's* primarily positive review of *Solyman and Almena:* "In truth, few of the Oriental Novels differ any essentially from each other."[13] No genre could completely escape the problematic but potent demands of probability and originality.

Not even Gothic fiction, with its far greater success and its undeniable appeal to reviewers and readers alike. Epitomizing critical opinion on the strengths of the genre are the reviews of what contemporary critics still consider the exemplary Gothic novel, *The Mysteries of Udolpho.* With an emphasis centered on the reader, a *Monthly* reviewer judges the novel to be "distinguished by a rich vein of invention, which supplies an endless variety of incidents to fill the imagination of the reader; by an admirable ingenuity of contrivance to awaken his curiosity, and to bind him in the chains of suspence; and by a vigour of conception and a delicacy of feeling which are capable of producing the strongest sympathetic emotions, whether of pity or terror."[14] Less enthusiastic, one of the *Critical* reviewers nonetheless believes that Radcliffe consistently succeeds in sustaining the reader's curiosity through continuous invention;[15] and in the next number the *Critical* reviewer calls *Udolpho* "the most interesting novel in the English language."[16] Especially appealing to both journals was Radcliffe's technique of the explained supernatural, whereby "mysterious terrors . . . are ingeniously explained by familiar causes,"[17] as a means of yoking the probable and the marvellous. Invention, affective power, and verisimilitude—all long-standing critical desiderata—happily coalesced, leaving little room for serious dispute.

When faced with less unequivocally successful texts and forced to rank literary merits, the stoutest defenders of the genre predictably extolled innovation. For the *Critical* reviewer of *The Contrast,* works of fiction "may be rendered interesting, when evincing, by striking coincidences, a fertility of invention, or displaying the glowing imagery of a rich imagination."[18] Although he lists depiction of the working of the human mind and moral utility as other valid goals, his ordering and language make his priorities clear. With remarkably similar generalizing language, a reviewer for the *Monthly* commends *Count Roderic's Castle: or Gothic Times:* "In works of fiction, fertility of invention is unquestionably the first excellence; and this excellence the author of the romantic tale before us certainly possesses."[19] Here, as elsewhere, the formerly derogatory term *romantic* became a compliment because of its association with invention, which was privileged over other values. Yet, invention represented a highly ambiguous and unstable standard as applied to Gothic fiction. A perceptive critic like the reviewer of *The Castle of Hardayne* can, on one level, endorse the revaluation of *novel* and *romance* and, on another, can question how genuinely novel—or unique—romances may necessarily be:

> When the title-page announces a *novel,* we expect to find . . . tender stories, of which the beginning, the middle, and the end, is *love*— sometimes degenerating into intrigue,—as others, drawn out into an insipid routine of affected sentiments—lip-deep—unimpassioned, and therefore harmless—playing round the fancy—but little calculated to touch or penetrate the heart—made of 'such stuff as dreams are'. By the *romance* our attention is somewhat more awakened: and to those who are not obliged by their occupation to follow succeeding tales of mystery and horror till repetition destroys the effect, it may afford entertainment, by gratifying that curiosity, or love of novelty, which arises out of the constitution of our nature.[20]

Romances, in other words, may merely have the advantage of recency. If invention is, at least in part, in the eye of the beholder, experienced eyes will inevitably grow jaundiced, as the opening of the review of *The Italian* in the *Critical* illustrates:

> It was not difficult to foresee that the *modern romance,* even supported by the skill of the most ingenious of its votaries, would soon experience the fate of every attempt to please by what is unnatural, and by a departure from . . . observance of real life. . . . In reviewing the Mysteries of Udolpho, we hazarded an opinion, that, if a better production could appear, it must come only from the pen of Mrs. Radcliffe; but we were not totally blind to the difficulties which even she would have to encounter, in order to keep up the interest she had created in that work, . . . and the present publication confirms our suspicions.[21]

Radcliffe suffered—unfairly, in my view—because novelty, for which she was once praised, remained the preeminent and unyielding criterion for judgment.

Positing an inbred love of novelty, however, moves in the direction of a more durable explanation of the power of Gothic novels: an irresistible psychological attraction to the supernatural and the horrific. For the *Critical* reviewer of *Vathek*, to "admire marvellous occurrences, and to follow, with an eager attention, the author who . . . employs spirits of the air, or the earth, to attain his purposes, by means the most extraordinary and astonishing" amounts to "a passion so deeply implanted, that, from the cradle, it is discovered in the imperfect lispings of the infant, and still adheres to us in spite of reason, judgment, and philosophy."[22] Assumptions like this—so favorable to the genre—may have been simplistic but were also irrefutable. Complementing these assumptions was an aesthetics of terror initiated as early as 1757 with Burke's linking of sublimity to terror—amplified and disseminated to such a degree that few readers would have been surprised by an end-of-the-century reviewer's observation, "Scenes that impress with terror have at all times been eagerly received."[23] Such attitudes facilitate the accepting—and even the embracing—of what reviewers of the first Gothic novel, *The Castle of Otranto*, derided as "monstrosities" and "absurdities."[24]

Fertile imagination and psychological penetration implied a considerable degree of what critics of the period called genius but did not guarantee the necessary complement of genius—namely, judgment. Hence, the frequent practice of applauding scintillating parts of Gothic novels, while faulting the whole for poor development and structure. Even in a work like *Udolpho*, argues a reviewer for the *Critical*, "four volumes cannot depend entirely on terrific incidents and intricacy of story. They require character, unity of design, a delineation of the scenes of real life, and the variety of well-supported contrast."[25] From a comparable standpoint, a reviewer for the *Monthly* admits that he "could point out many parts" of *Hubert de Sevrac*—a novel that he thinks will "be perused by many with pleasure"—that are "delineated with strength and spirit"; but he concludes that "as a whole, the composition rather fails in effect, owing to the multiplicity of characters and incidents, and to the frequent change of scenes."[26] More negative notices simply reversed the order—discussing the inferior whole before the superior part. In the same number of the *Monthly*, the reviewer of *The Genius* maintains that scenes "of supernatural horror, ill-connected, in frightful succession agitate the reader: but they furnish some situations not unworthy of selection by future writers, who possess a less disorderly imagination."[27] Two numbers later, *The Count de Santerre* receives similar treatment: the novel offers "no true delineation of character; and the events, so far from being probable, are scarcely within the verge of possibility, yet the fancy is captivated by some incidents of an unexpected and extraordinary nature, and above all by those gloomy and horrid scenes, on which the authoress exerts all her powers of description."[28] Either posture reveals critics reluctant to dismiss the most attractive features of the genre but equally reluctant to ignore conventional formal expectations.

Among these expectations, the nexus between probability and morality—and often the condescension associated with a discussion of it—surfaced prominently in indictments of the genre. Although some critics became reconciled for a time to supernatural machinery, others stigmatized it for its unsalutary effects on unsophisticated readers. A *Monthly* reviewer, for instance, judges *The Cavern of Death* "interesting and impressive" but cannot approve of "this mode of impression, which fills the mind of the juvenile reader with horrid ideas of supernatural agency, and makes him fancy, like Macbeth, that he sees bloody spectres flitting before his eyes, and ensanguined daggers streaming in the air."[29] Credulity, moreover, appears to have known no age limit, as a scathing attack on *The Castle of St. Vallery* articulates vividly:

> Of all the resources of invention, this, perhaps, is the most puerile, as it is certainly among the most unphilosophic. It contributes to keep alive that superstition which debilitates the mind, that ignorance which propagates error, and that dread of invisible agency which makes inquiry criminal. . . . The labours of the poet, of the historian, and of the sage, ought to have one common end, that of strengthening and improving man, not of continuing him in error, and, which is always the consequence of error, in vice. The most essential feature of every work is its moral tendency. The good writer teaches the child to become a man; the bad and the indifferent best understand the reverse art of making a man a child.[30]

The unlikely assumption that readers confirm their superstitions through Gothic novels and do not turn to them primarily for escapist entertainment reinforces the stereotype of the ignorant novel reader—implicitly opposed to the knowing critic.

Moving beyond such crude polemics, Coleridge's fascinating review of *The Monk* draws a much more sophisticated connection between supernatural fiction and moral action. According to Coleridge, the suspension of natural law in the novel renders natural human agency impotent—thus offering the reader no convincing model, either exemplary or cautionary:

No proud man, for instance, will be made less proud by being told that Lucifer once seduced a presumptuous monk. *Incredulus odit.* Or even if, believing the story, he should deem his virtue less secure, he would yet acquire no lessons of prudence, no feelings of humility. Human prudence can oppose no sufficient shield to the power and cunning of supernatural beings; and the privilege of being proud might be fairly conceded to him who could rise superior to all earthly temptations, and whom the strength of the spiritual world alone would be adequate to overwhelm.[31]

Replacing the superstitious dolt with a more thoughtful implied reader raises not only the level of discourse but also the moral stakes. A more believable moral threat casts the deficiencies of the novel—and, by extension, of the genre—in a harsher light.

Yet, the exclusively aesthetic commentary later in the review would seem to obviate any moral concerns for a reader of any sophistication, since it implies the forfeiture of such a reader's interest through excess in frequency and intensity of horror:

The merit of a novellist is in direct proportion (not simply to the effect, but) to the *pleasurable* effect which he produces. Situations of torment, and images of naked horror, are easily conceived; and a writer in whose works they abound, deserves our gratitude equally with him who should drag us by way of sport through a military hospital, or force us to sit at the dissecting-table of a natural philosopher. To trace the nice boundaries, beyond which terror and sympathy are deserted by the pleasurable emotions,—to reach those limits, yet never to pass them,—*hic labor, hoc opus est.* Figures that shock the imagination, and narratives that mangle the feelings, rarely discover *genius,* and always betray a low and vulgar *taste.*[32]

Coleridge was hardly the only critic to draw such a conclusion. For the *Critical* reviewer of *The Neapolitan,* "Pity and terror are the powerful engines by which the poet melts the soul to tears, or harrows it almost to phrensy. . . . But then it is by observing a due medium,—not by 'over-stepping the modesty of nature.'"[33] A negative response to Eliza Parsons's *The Voluntary Exile* holds that our feelings "are more interested when the heart is softened rather than shocked: descriptions of misery may be aggravated and multiplied until they excite disgust."[34] And the catastrophe of the German novel *The Sorcerer* "harrows up the soul with emotions too shockingly vivid to be gratifying; they exceed in a great degree all the limits of pleasure which critics point out as the sources of satisfaction we receive from perusal of works of this nature."[35] Imposition of limits only reinforced the fragility of invention as a source of praise. What novelists might have viewed as stretching the Gothic imagination to its boundaries, critics recoiled against as excess for the sake of novelty and for the sake of pleasing a bloodthirsty readership.

Indeed, even Coleridge's assumption of an acute implied reader could not mask the disdain for most actual readers that he shared with others who rejected the taste for Gothic fiction. Maintaining, with characteristic British chauvinism, that superstition and horror commonly achieve popularity "at the rise and decline of literature"—and, thus, that an enthusiastic response to the Gothic is a positive sign in Germany but a negative one in England—he hopes that "satiety will banish what good sense should have prevented; and that the public will learn, by the multitude of the manufacturers, with how little expense of thought or imagination this species of composition is manufactured."[36] Enfield conveys a similar hortatory tone in his review of *Camilla*, praising Burney for avoiding "the infection of that taste for the marvellous and terrible which . . . has, with some writers, become the fashion of the day,"[37] just as the *Monthly* reviewer of *The Abbey of St. Asaph* criticizes that work for its "compliance with the present rage for the terrible."[38] While occasionally a reviewer would commend "the cultivated literary taste of the present period,"[39] the detractors of Gothic fiction commonly adopted the elitist rhetoric of their predecessors—placing themselves and their audience above the material, either directly or with the sarcasm of sentences like the opening of a review of *The Countess of Hardayne:* "To those who are fond of ruined castles, of mysteries, and of banditti, these volumes will afford considerable pleasure."[40] Any extension of the ridicule to other reviewers, however, threatened the critical enterprise as a whole; therefore, mere dismissive gestures could not always suffice. Early and in a few cases continuing critical enthusiasm for the genre identified numerous merits; conscientious reviewers of those texts that possessed these merits felt obliged to acknowledge them, even as the reviewers subordinated these merits to other values. Thus, with the kind of candor that ensured balance, Coleridge himself admitted that *The Monk* represented "the offspring of no common genius."[41]

So-called historical fiction often overlapped in reviewers' minds with the generic category of the Gothic[42] but generated different evaluative criteria, which led to generally more severe judgments. Yet, a similar pattern of initial support is evident in responses to the earliest attempts at the form. In 1762, Leland's *Longsword, Earl of Salisbury,* the first self-styled historical romance, wins lavish

praise from a *Critical* reviewer for an adroit combination of fiction
and history:

> We are indebted to the author of this work for the introduction of a
> new and agreeable species of writing, in which the beauties of poetry,
> and the advantages of history are happily united. The story of this
> *romance* (as he modestly entitles it) is founded on real facts, and with-
> out doing any great violence to truth, pleases the imagination, at the
> same time that it improves the heart.[43]

Over twenty years later, the next significant historical novel, Sophia Lee's *The Recess*—which was far more influential than
Longsword—occasions equal admiration from a *Critical* commentator. While rejecting as unnecessary Lee's return to the familiar
subterfuge of the discovered manuscript, the reviewer concludes
of the opening volume: "It is new; it is instructive; it is highly
interesting; and we wish that this mode of writing were more
frequent."[44] Even "the neglect of the peculiar manners of the
age"[45]—which came to be known as "costume"—does not vitiate
the power of the novel; although three years later, a reviewer for
the *Critical* does commend Lee further for remedying the defect.
Her work, the reviewer adds, "may be styled familiar history, for
it fills up the vacant chasms with those little incidents not unsuit-
able to the greater incidents, or the temper of the actors."[46] A
critic for the *Monthly* calls it "a very ingenious and pathetic novel"
by an author who possesses "a copious fund of imagination." The
critic writes that Lee's "powers of description are very great, and
there is a richness in her style which shows that her genius is
ardent and vigorous."[47]

For the *Monthly* critic, however, Lee succeeds in spite of—rather
than because of—her chosen form. In *The Recess*, according to the
critic, "fiction is indeed too lavishly employed to heighten and
embellish some well-known and distinguished facts in the English
history; we say *too lavishly*, because the mind is ever distracted
when the fact so little accords with the fiction, and Romance and
History are at perpetual variance with each other."[48] This open-
ended criticism anticipated several strains of objections—all of
which stressed the deleterious effects of most historical fiction on
youthful, ignorant readers.[49] At the most basic level, casting the
educative power of the genre as its most redeeming feature—
condescending enough in itself—gave way to despair at inept
practice, as a *Critical* commentator's review of *The Countess de Hen-
nebon* demonstrates: "We have owned our predilection for histori-

cal novels, chiefly because the idle readers of these works might, in this way, have some remote chance of information. But, where history and geography are repeatedly violated; where probability can scarcely be found; where names and titles are constantly mutilated and disfigured, the whole must be pronounced contemptible."[50] From a related point of view comes the conclusion that "the mixture of ancient and modern customs, which cannot be discriminated by general readers, will mislead."[51] Mere superficial accuracy would not satisfy more trenchant critics of the genre, who regarded any hybrid as intellectually dishonest and morally suspect. For the *Monthly* reviewer of *Earl Strongbow*, "History and fable have distinct merits"—namely, imparting information and inculcating "wholesome principles by fictitious machinery, to illustrate them." To combine the two "is to poison the sources of information to young readers, who, after feasting on history embellished with these meretricious ornaments, will not easily relish the dry details of truth."[52] If education was the only admissible goal, historical novels could not escape being considered either flawed vehicles or dangerous obstacles.

Only by altering the terms of analysis can a critic alter the conclusions, as the reviewer of *Cicely* gamely attempts, first by arguing that readers seldom credit the historicity of historical fiction and, second, by questioning whether "the writer who, by deviating into the regions of fancy, awakens and calls into exercise the more exalted energies of the human mind,—does not really benefit his species more than the plain narrator of those sordid and disgusting facts which so frequently stain the page of history."[53] The latter argument, while undeniably true in many cases, is rendered irrelevant by its generality: grounded on assumptions about the relative merits of history and fiction at least as old as Sidney's *Apology for Poetry,* it carries no special brief for historical novels but merely opposes any kind of interesting imaginative writing to dull historical writing. Nor does it account for the possibility that readers might be more entertained without pseudohistorical machinery—or, as one reviewer puts it, that "lovers of romance" might "deem such stories not sufficiently amusing," just as "adherents to historical accuracy" might sneer at "inconsistency and falsehood."[54] As for the former argument, our experiences with novels and films like *Gone With the Wind*—or with so-called reality-based programming or television docudramas—support the notion of a credulous public, easily confused and more apt to believe glamorous theatrical history than unadorned—but more accurate—accounts. Suspicions of ignorant readers that may seem quaintly reactionary when viewed retrospectively still resonate strongly in the jeremiads of our own intellectual elites, testifying to the strength of a popular culture in which genres like historical fiction continue to play a significant role.

* * *

Another staple of popular literature, the sentimental novel, actually succeeded at altering the critical lexicon—for a time. As William Park has demonstrated, the influence of sentimental fiction by Sterne and others led to a foregrounding of pathos as a criterion of value in fiction, with the result that reviews of the late 1760s were replete with terms like *affecting, passions, delicacy, distresses, tears,* and *sensibility,* used approvingly, while words like *natural, just, easy,* and *probable* began to lose their prominence.[55] Rather than denounce mimetic conventions, advocates for sensibility, like the reviewer of Brooke's *The Fool of Quality,* could simply argue that a novel of sentiment transcended such conventions:

> To criticize in the terms of art upon this novel would be as absurd as to condemn a Chinese landscape for not being drawn according to the principles of architecture and perspective. There is a freedom and goodness of heart discernible through the whole, which, to a benevolent mind, may be more pleasing than a strict adherence to the occurrences of common life, and to what the painters call *il custumi.* We shall therefore dismiss it with a candid acknowledgement, that several passages of it affected us to an uncommon degree, which is a greater recommendation than any mechanical properties of writing.[56]

Twenty-five years later, Smith's *Celestina* enjoyed the same immunity, with a *Critical* reviewer contending that although "fastidious criticism may point out . . . little errors, the feeling heart will, on various occasions, acknowledge our Author's power of affecting it by frequent tears."[57] The "feeling heart," in other words, overrules the faulting head.

But not universally or unequivocally. Robert Mayo has amply documented reviewers' objections to several characteristic features of novels by would-be imitators of Richardson, including "their sentimental excesses, particularly their abiding preoccupation with love, their absurd predilection for the epistolary form, and their infatuation with faultless characters."[58] And as I have shown, imitations of Sterne attracted even greater venom, especially "the large quantities of that insipid trash, called *Sentimental Letters, Sentimental Effusions,* etc. etc. which had been poured upon us, under the sanction of Yorick's name, or by an affectation of his light and desultory manner of writing, without one grain of his wit or acuteness."[59] Given the nature of the exemplary models, it is not surprising that critics identified a poorly developed or virtually nonexistent plot—unless it was compensated for by the strengths of a Richardson or a Sterne—as a glaring deficiency in most sentimental fiction. A *Critical* commentator, for instance, complains that *The History of Miss Sommerville*, "as usual, is carried on in the epistolary manner, and is, in the first volume at least, much fuller of sentiment than of business."[60] Two years later, admiration for *The Man of Feeling,* the quintessential sentimental novel, does not prevent a reviewer for the *Critical* from cautioning that there "is not indeed fable enough in this volume to keep up the attention of the majority of novel readers; there is not business enough in it for the million."[61] While characteristically implying that a more sophisticated audience would respond more sympathetically, the statement also unintentionally suggests a link between the masses and the critics—a common expectation of "business" that critics do not abandon when evaluating novels less accomplished than Mackenzie's.

Both the quality and quantity of sentiment itself—usually understood as moral or emotional reflection by characters—also underwent regular scrutiny, offering numerous occasions for critical disapproval. Most troubling was the preponderance of mannered or affected sentiment. Although a critic for the *Monthly* generally recommends Mackenzie's *The Man of the World,* he does notice "affectation in some of his [Mackenzie's] sentiments";[62] and twenty-five years later, another *Monthly* critic applauds George Walker's *Cinthelia* for dispensing with "that lofty strain of high-flown sentiment, and that affected refinement of manners, which shine with tinsel glare in many of our modern productions."[63] Frequency of sentiment could also become cumbersome and distracting, as a *Critical* reviewer observes, "Circumstances, in themselves affecting, simply related, have a stronger hold upon the affections, than the endless repetition of exclamatory periods and over-wrought sentiment."[64] More baldly, the reviewer of *Munster Abbey* decides that "by endeavoring to put sentiment into the mouth of his characters on the most trifling occasions, the author often renders his work ridiculous."[65] As early as Melmoth's *Travels for the Heart* (1777), a *Critical* reviewer stresses the superiority of indirection and understatement for appealing to a reader's sensibility: "Never perhaps is the human heart assailed with so much success, as by those who conceal their purpose of affecting it with any impression; while an open attack, unless conducted with peculiar dexterity, . . . is more apt to excite insensibility, than to triumph over the passions."[66]

Here, as with Gothic fiction, reviewers recognized the dangers of excess, which can exhaust sympathy and attention. In *The Tears of Sensibility*, according to a *Monthly* critic, the author "deals only in those virtues and vices which astonish and exercise our sensibility in the extreme. He therefore defeats his own purpose. A tale made up wholly of wonders, never excites admiration."[67] On the same basis, a *Critical* reviewer finds fault with *The Recess:* "The great, though not the only source from which pleasure is derived, in consequence of the representation of distressing scenes, is the emotion, or rather the employment of the mind, on subjects which interest it. When this employment is too long continued, fatigue rather than gratification is the consequence."[68] Once again, an implied golden mean emerged as a standard of literary value, eminently sensible but also problematic insofar as it remained conveniently impossible to specify, inherently conservative, and potentially inhibiting to more daring novelists to whom critical approval might matter.

Reviewers were powerless, on the other hand, to inhibit opportunists from abusing the relatively flexible vocabulary generated by and for discourse on the genre. A *Critical* reviewer's sarcastic assessment of *The Birmingham Counterfeit*, subtitled "A Sentimental Romance," captures the problem and the outrage particularly well, scornfully mimicking the Shandean proclivity for the dash in the process:

> The epithet *sentimental* is used now so frequently, that we are at a loss to guess what idea some writers have of it. We have here a *sentimental* Romance. What sort of romance, gentle reader, do you expect this to be?—Why a romance that has sentiments—The arch rogue of an author! So then, other romances are destitute of sentiment—By no means, tho' this may abound with more refined sentiment than others—*Rem ara tetiqisti.*—Now you've hit the nail on the head.—Well, let's open this volume, and have a taste of this refined sentiment.— So! what story have we here—Oh! It relates to Isabella, a young lady, whose lover not having been permitted by his friends to marry her, shot himself.[69]

Perhaps a source for Clara Reeve (whose complaint I have already examined), this reviewer deplores the use of an attractive label to cloak ineptitude—a license that predictably extended to the term *sensibility* as well. In a review of *The Natural Son*, a *Monthly* critic laments "the present latitude allowed to the word *sensibility;* under which licentious livers and licentious writers now shelter propensities that used to receive harsher names."[70] A less strident critic remarks with bewilderment that it is "not easy to discover what writers mean by the word *sensibility*. It has an imposing sound, and its acceptation is too frequently arbitrary."[71] Yet, in a silence tantamount to unconscious complicity, the reviewers never offered a single definition of their own. The omission might imply, once again, a critically educated audience for which definition would be unnecessary; but it might also signify an unwillingness or inability to rectify a wider audience's uncritical attraction to labels like "sentiment" or "sensibility."

* * *

In the hands of the reviewers themselves, the label "humorous" could be equally misleading, since they devoted little attention to the theory and practice of humor per se. Aside from invocations of Fielding and Smollett as touchstones or expressions of regret for the decline of humor that accompanied the rise of pathos,[72] discourse on the comic novel centered almost exclusively upon the value of nature and probability. The former, mentioned more commonly in earlier reviews, generally denoted "an acquaintance with the living world, with modern manners, and the real character of mankind."[73] Deeming such an acquaintance essential, a *Monthly* reviewer faults Goldsmith's *Vicar of Wakefield* for exhibiting only a "limited judgment of men, manners, and characters" as they appear in real life.[74] Distinctions between critical and popular standards seem to have collapsed a few years later in a *Critical* reviewer's approving analysis of the power of the natural: "Whether novel-writing ought to observe epic or dramatic rules, is of very little consequence to the public. Like the modern taste in gardening, it is often most pleasing when it appears to be the result of nature."[75] As the previous chapter suggests, when demands for novelty led readers to devalue mimesis, reviewers usually remained adamant defenders of probability—going so far as to argue that probability "alone can give due operation to fictitious narrative."[76] A nearly universal mimetic orientation rendered outright defenses of probability unnecessary and infrequent, but a few critics did directly link a probable narrative to the reader's presumed desire to suspend disbelief. In a review of *Female Friendship,* a *Monthly* critic articulates the connection in the context of a novel that fails to make it:

> When a person sits down with a novel in his hand, he knows he is
> going to read a fiction; but if it be well written, he soon forgets that
> circumstance, under an agreeable imposition; and becomes interested
> in the narrative, as a history of real events: others on the contrary,
> like the above curious composition, are so honestly framed, as continu-
> ally to keep the Reader in mind that they are *downright lies*
> throughout.[77]

A few numbers later, the reviewer of *Hadleigh Grove* concurs, with
the observation that multiple improbabilities prevent the reader
from "being well beguiled into a temporary belief of the adventures related."[78] Whether a reader need always desire to be so
beguiled is a question conveniently left unaddressed.

I have already shown to some extent, however, that adherence
to a representational theory did not blind critics to the potential
crudity or banality of indiscriminate imitation of nature. Smollett's
1763 review of *Jeremiah Grant* calls for selection:

> Provided the author takes nature for his guide, and has taste enough
> to select her in her most agreeable attitudes, he need not fear going
> astray. We say, taste enough to regulate his choice, because it is possible
> to be very natural and very insipid, to be very natural and very shock-
> ing. A man may paint a hogstye, or a dunghill, very naturally, without
> giving pleasure to the spectator; and describe with scrupulous exact-
> ness many scenes and incidents that produce nothing but yawning
> and disgust.[79]

It was not only both extremes that generated disapproval: a work
like Lennox's *Life of Harriot Stuart*, wherein "the manners of her
persons, together with the incidents of her story, are most of them
within the bounds of nature, and agreeable to what we daily see
in common life," could, nonetheless, afford "nothing great, or
noble, or useful, or very interesting."[80] *The History of Eliza* may
win the reviewer's admiration for an accurate portrayal of "common life," but he also comments that the characters are conven-
tionally perfect and the plot perfectly conventional.[81]

Written well before the vogue of the supernatural, these reviews
indicate that probability without imagination could receive the
same kind of scorn as morality without entertainment—or originality without realism. The overwhelming number of mediocre
natural novels, moreover, caused—or, at least, encouraged—the
tendency (noted by recent scholars and readily apparent by the
time of the flowering of the Gothic) to lessen the stress on verisimilitude.[82] And even the strongest advocates of probability still

gave due recognition to compensatory merits. Goldsmith's deficient acquaintance with real life and manners does not disguise his "extraordinary natural talents";[83] and despite its "super human characters, its forced situations, [and] its improbable circumstances," Brooke's *Juliet Grenville* is considered "indubitably a work of genius, and of uncommon merit."[84] Searching for unqualified success—especially in the face of so much failure—could only invite despair; therefore, practical critics quite naturally appreciated the attractive qualities of novels that may have lacked other desired characteristics.

* * *

Compensatory tendencies extended from analysis of genre to more specific attention to formal matters, most noticeably—but, perhaps, least significantly—in the frequent superficial catalogues that evaluated several components of a given text, usually in a paragraph or less. Some lists, like the *Critical* commentator's review of *The Fault Was All His Own* (which surprisingly forwent any punning on the title), confined faults and virtues to narrative craft:

> This writer seems to have taken little pains, either in planning or executing her work. The story is irregular, and productive of few interesting events. The characters are imperfectly delineated, and the business assigned to them seldom has importance enough to excite the reader's curiosity or concern. Yet these letters are not destitute of merit. They are interspersed with many sprightly sentiments and sensible reflections, and bear the marks of a promising genius.[85]

Others, predictably enough, juxtaposed form and morality. Clara Reeve's *The Exiles,* for instance, may seem "new, . . . probable, correct, and interesting" to a *Critical* reviewer; but from "a moral view," the reviewer must "object to the necessity which there appears to be for so much deceit."[86] Cursory notices like these enabled reviewers to dispose of novels unworthy of extended critical treatment—or possibly of even a complete reading.

Despite its obvious shortcomings, the catalogue form did provide the most succinct summary of formal properties that reviewers valued at a given time, since a brief notice was not likely to challenge a broad consensus. A *Monthly* commentator's review of *The Denial* exemplifies one common practice—namely, to begin, not with the text in question, but with generalizations about what makes a good novel:

The story of a novel should be formed of a variety of interesting
incidents; a knowledge of the world, and of mankind, are essential
requisites in the writer; the characters should be always natural; the
personages should talk, think, and act, as becomes their respective
ages, situations, and characters; the sentiments should be moral,
chaste, and delicate; the language should be easy, correct, and elegant,
free from affectation, and unobscured by pedantry; and the narrative
should be as little interrupted as possible by digression and episodes
of every kind.[87]

At the opposite extreme, a reviewer for the *Critical* lambasts *An
Interesting Sketch of Genteel Life* for failing in every category:
"There is in these volumes much business with little incident;
and a great many persons without interest. The author has no
invention; the characters are not discriminated with art or knowledge; and the language, though easy, is often colloquial and vulgar."[88] Finally, a commentator reviewing *The Parsonage House*
anatomizes the middling novel. Exhibiting neither Richardson's
knowledge of the heart nor Fielding's humor, the novel according
to the commentator nonetheless demonstrates "real merit, as it is
written in an easy and unaffected style, abounds in good and
virtuous sentiments, and conveys some useful lessons of instruction." Its incidents, "though not numerous, are natural," its characters generally "well supported," and its story "sufficiently
interesting to engage the attention, without too deeply affecting
the hearts and passions of its readers."[89] All three approaches
concur in assumptions about plot, character, and language that
were, indeed, the most commonly held by reviewers. More detailed
analysis of each element, however, complicated and destabilized
the unitary critical position implied in the form and content of
the catalogues.

Without directly endorsing the Aristotelian hierarchy that in-
sisted upon the preeminence of plot—a conviction like that of the
reviewer of *Constance* that it is "from incidents and situations, that
our greatest interest and entertainment are derived"[90]— many
critics did adopt the Aristotelian stress on unity. Phrases like
"unity of design,"[91] "unity of plan,"[92] or "unity of circumstance,"[93]
which appeared prominently in reviews near the end of the century, underscore the durability of the concept—not to mention
the improvisation with terminology common in a relatively un-
regulated critical discourse. A generalization in a 1796 review in
the *Critical* typifies the predominant attitude: "To improve or to
please readers of any taste, the story should be formed on some
consistent plan, having in view a certain *end:* the incidents, how-

ever unusual, should rise in a regular gradation, without any force or distortion, out of each other, all tending to the proposed end."[94] Consequently, narratives were commonly criticized for being conducted "in an unconnected and abrupt manner,"[95] or for being "too much broken and unconnected to be interesting."[96] Agreement on ends, however, did not preclude dispute over means. Broadly skeptical of most novelists' ability to sustain an intricate, diffuse plot, many reviewers demanded simplicity and clarity;[97] but others could not help admiring complexity, whether it be called "contrivance"[98] or "an artificial plot unravelled with skill."[99] These latter critics, more sanguine about the possibilities of the genre, wisely refrained from following criteria that guaranteed nothing more than respectable mediocrity.

More unexpectedly, responses to specific impediments to unity also reveal some divisions. Reviewers, particularly for the *Critical*, often derided frequent shifting of scenes,[100] an overabundance of characters and stories,[101] interpolated tales,[102] unnecessary digressions,[103] and superfluous subplots.[104] While an early work like Haywood's *Betsy Thoughtless* might be criticized for lacking "those entertaining introductory chapters, and digressive essays, which . . . so agreeably relieve us from that over-stretch and languor of attention, which a continual string of mere narrative commonly produces,"[105] by the time of *The Recess*, a *Monthly* commentator places greater emphasis on the gratification of suspense, which would cause readers to consider even Fielding's introductions as "tedious and provoking interruptions to the main story."[106] Yet, a few reviewers of the 1790s articulated a less rigid conception of narrative design. Inchbald's deceptively titled *A Simple Story*—which is actually comprised of two stories concerning a single protagonist's relationship with his eventual wife, and, a generation later, with his daughter—is considered by a *Critical* commentator as having "a peculiar unity, superior to that of some even of our best novels."[107] A reviewer for the *Monthly*, meanwhile, approves of Charlotte Smith's use of digressive asides in *The Wanderings of Warwick:* "In the course of the story, Mrs. Smith has not neglected to introduce, after her usual manner, such miscellaneous reflections on interesting topics . . . as every intelligent reader will think a sufficient compensation for a short interruption of the fictitious narrative."[108] Mindful of the weight of previous critical opinion, the former reviewer does not abandon but refines the notion of unity; and the latter does not dismiss mere narrative but carefully justifies interruption. As is so often the case, temperate language served to mask a marked departure from prevailing opinions.

This particular departure had its roots in critical intolerance for the uniformity and simplemindedness that often accompanied unity and simplicity, as well as respect for works of genius that ignored or subverted accepted structural principles. A deluge of formulaic narratives leads a *Critical* reviewer to issue a sarcastic "skeleton of a modern novel":

> A hero and a heroine, each endowed with every perfection, must see each other by chance, and become instantly enamoured. They must labour through two or three volumes; and if no churlish father, or ambitious aunt, is in the way, they must have a reasonable quantity of doubt and suspicion, infused by false friends. The lady, too, may be forced away by a disappointed lover, and rescued miraculously. At last, one or the other must be near death, either by accident or premeditated violence, and may recover or not, according to the disposition of the author.[109]

At the opposite extreme, in *Eloisa* (the title given to the English translation of *La nouvelle Héloïse*), Rousseau "despises the common aids of plot, incident, and contrivance, but effects all his purposes by mere strength of genius and variety of colouring,"[110] to the obvious satisfaction of the *Critical* commentator. A number earlier, an even more notorious despiser of rules, Sterne, receives more grudging—but no less telling—admiration for the third and fourth volumes of *Tristram Shandy:*

> The reader will not expect that we should pretend to give a detail of a work, which seems to have been written without any plan, or any other design than that of showing the author's wit, humour, and learning, in an unconnected effusion of sentiments and remarks, thrown out indiscriminately, as they rose in his imagination. Nevertheless, incoherent and digressive as it is, the book certainly abounds with pertinent observations on life and characters, humorous incidents, poignant ridicule, and marks of taste and erudition.[111]

Both untalented conformists and great wits who gloriously offended complicated any absolute preference for a unified plot.

Ruminations on unity comprised virtually the entire discourse on plot, which received less attention—at least in quantitative terms—than character. A few commentators forthrightly asserted the priority of character over plot for effective fiction. For one of these, the *Monthly* reviewer of *Agnes de Courci*, the author's excessive concern with design in an obviously "well-wrought story" serves the reader poorly:

The *inventive* faculty of its authoress is not to be disputed: but *character,* that great, that almost indispensable requisite in all such perform- ances as the present, is seldom to be found in it. The reader's attention is so much taken up by the events, that the *personages,* who should undoubtedly be the *first,* become the *secondary,* consideration with him, and thus the very *essence* of such a composition (which, like the dra- matic, consists in a true and faithful display of *manners*) is, in some degree, destroyed.[112]

For the most part, though, more practical motives underlay a sustained focus on character. While reviewers could merely note— but never hope to illustrate—intricacies of structure, they could readily entertain their readers by describing—or by quoting— novelists' descriptions of appealing, innovative, and—most espe- cially—eccentric characters like Sterne's Toby and Trim, Smol- lett's Bramble and Lismahago, Burney's Madam du Val and Captain Mirvan, and several of the characters in Cumberland's *Arundel.*[113] Whatever the critic's intentions, remarks about the faults in the plots of a Sterne or a Cumberland could never regis- ter with the same force upon a reader as extended, amusing, character sketches; therefore, character inevitably assumed a pre- eminent place. But not without cost: the relative ease and obvious appeal of description discouraged moving beyond perfunctory approval of the character described to more speculative commen- tary on process or method. Characteristic of attempts at a broader view is a *Monthly* commentator's comparison of the "three great novel-writers" Richardson, Fielding, and Sterne, to Reynolds, Le Brun, and Hogarth—the "first for truth and beauty of colouring, the second for a lively display of the passions, and the third for caricatura."[114] However apt the analogy, it remains largely impres- sionistic and superficial.

Slightly more elaborate criteria for evaluating characterization, derived primarily from dramatic criticism, did appear with rela- tive consistency—namely, variety, contrast, and discrimination. Largely unsympathetic to Richardson, the *Monthly* reviewer of a professed imitation, *Sir William Harrington,* nonetheless admits that Richardson's excellence "lay in admirably drawing, varying, contrasting, and supporting his characters."[115] Responding to *Ce- cilia,* a *Critical* commentator credits Burney for her skillful use of contrast and her consequent success at "one of the most difficult tasks which a novel-writer has to perform, . . . the invention and colouring of new characters";[116] while a *Monthly* reviewer notes the contrast between Monckton and Belfield and concludes that the characters are "nicely discriminated, and properly supported."[117] And Holcroft, in his review of Cumberland's *Henry,* insists that characters be differentiated by the language that they use in dialogue.[118] Like the rest of the commentary on characterization, these rules treated character externally, forgoing any examination of interior life or of psychological complexity. Safely derivative—morally and ideologically neutral—they predictably engendered little dispute.

Whenever moral considerations entered the discourse, so did complications—as remarks on the relative merits of perfect and mixed characters indicate. In his review of *Amelia,* Cleland—ironically enough, given his own creation of a character like Fanny Hill—lavishly praises a heroine who "is painted, in fine, as the model of female perfection; formed to give the greatest and justest idea of domestic happiness."[119] But the majority of subsequent critics rejected such paragons on the very grounds that Fielding did in *Tom Jones*—namely, that inimitability precludes moral efficacy. *The History of George Ellison, Juliet Grenville,* and *The History of Miss Greville* were all censured for their saintly heroes and heroines,[120] because perfection "is not the lot of humanity, and frail nature can only contemplate, with astonishment, such ideal greatness, such imaginary goodness."[121] Opposing perfection proved easier, however, than specifying the limits of imperfection. The *Critical* reviewer of *Elfrida* seems to accept—and even advocate— a preponderance of vice over virtue, holding that the "great merit" of the work consists in the portrayal of a character "in which envy, jealousy, and a sarcastic ill-humour, are combined with some degree of generosity, and a heart not wholly insensible to gratitude."[122] A few years later, an advocate for a more realistic portrayal of women advances more conservative proportions:

> We wish to see a female character drawn with faults and virtues, to see her feel the effects of misconduct, which does not proceed from a bad heart or corrupted inclinations, but to see her in the end happy, in consequence of her reformation: in short, to see a female Jones, or another Evelina, with faults equally embarrassing, yet as venial.[123]

The emphasis on reformation points to an unambiguous standard; but the conflation of Tom Jones's sometimes serious transgressions with Evelina's minor social faux pas would permit, perhaps unintentionally, considerable latitude in characterization. Criticism that consisted largely of responses to individual characters invited novelists to test the extent of that latitude.

Attraction to realism also fostered some support for the depiction of what reviewers called "low life"—commonly, if mistakenly, considered to have begun with Fielding. Insistent elitism, however, generated opposition. On the one hand, a *Critical* reviewer is pleased that the author of *Arthur O'Bradley* "draws low characters with tolerable justice"[124] and another regrets the absence, in *Lumley House*, of "those little characteristic details of lower life, which evince a deep knowledge of the human heart."[125] On the other hand, as early as 1750, a *Monthly* critic approvingly notes, in a review of *The Adventures of Mr. Loveill*, that the "objection made to most of the celebrated performances of this kind, those of the inimitable Mr. Fielding himself not excepted, has been that the scenes were laid in low life."[126] With an indirect jab at Fielding, a *Critical* commentator commends the style of Lennox's *Henrietta* for "sinking no where below the level of genteel life, a compliment which cannot be paid to one of the most celebrated novel-writers we have."[127] At the end of the century, a reviewer for the *Monthly* opens the door—but only slightly—insisting that "low characters are to be tolerated in novels only when they display considerable wit or drollery, and some striking peculiarity"[128]—in other words, only when the "low characters" are amusing eccentrics. In each instance, the reviewer imputes artistic deficiency or lowness to novels that represent the lower social classes.

Equally damning, from a modern perspective, is the suggestion—contained within the phrase "low life"—that immorality accompanies material or social inferiority. Ironically, it is a defender of Fielding—the *Critical* reviewer of *Timothy Ginnadrake*—who connects the two further: considering whether or not Fielding's influence as a "biographer in low life" has been salutary, the reviewer concludes that Fielding himself "and a few other expert labourers" deserve credit for "portraying various scenes of life, which did not fall within the plans of those biographers whose heroes rank among the kings and princes of the earth," but that "a numerous tribe" of unscrupulous, profiteering, and untalented imitators have taken to "exhibiting scenes of weakness and folly, and marking them with approbation,"[129] thus increasing the ignorance and corrupting the morals of their readers. Altering the criteria for judgment from social status to moral status, however illogical, implies that they are interchangeable. Consciously or not, concerns about appealing to a limited circle of readers—and reinforcing an attitude of social and cultural superiority within that circle—undoubtedly contributed to all too decorous complaints about lowness from on high.

Since the reviewers, unlike contemporary theorists, seldom invested language with any moral or social significance—a word, not to mention a concept, like *phallogocentrism* would have astounded them—their commentary on language normally reflected an unusually high degree of consensus. Balance—absent in its larger sense as the product of contesting perspectives or opinions— emerged in a different form through the common advocacy of moderation and the common shunning of extremes. The most frequent target was excessive embellishment, with critics excoriating novelists—especially, for some reason, during the 1770s—for "quaintness of expression,"[130] for "prettiness of phrase and expression,"[131] for "affected phrases, whimsical conceits, and gaudy ornaments,"[132] and, more particularly, for indiscriminate appropriation of foreign phrases and idioms, especially Gallicisms.[133] The point at which ornaments became gaudy or embellishment became affectation—a fundamentally subjective determination— could not be specified; but reviewers routinely advocated erring on the side of caution. Responding unfavorably to what he calls "poetical prose, which wants only measure to constitute verse," a *Critical* reviewer observes that it "is not the least of the objections to it that it soon swells into bombast, or, *sermoni propior,* creeps into humble prose; that without a cultivated taste, and sound judgment, it cannot be with ease and propriety sustained."[134] Six years later, the reviewer of *Edward* echoes both the warning and the characteristic exemption allowed only to genius: "What is unnatural is seldom interesting; and the inflated poetical style in a prosaic narrative can seldom, but in the hand of a master, reach the heart."[135]

Another comment on unnatural poetic style focuses the criticism more specifically on the issue of decorum. In an analysis of a passage from Robinson's *Vancenza,* a *Critical* commentator finds Robinson's "partiality for the ornamental language of poetry" inappropriate for the rendering of psychological detail: "Polished and figurative language like this is the production of a mind at ease; and the passage we have quoted is written in a moment of the most poignant agony, at a time when the tears flowing, had, in a great degree, defaced the manuscript, and the passage was, on that account, 'with difficulty decyphered'."[136] More pointed than many broad judgments about propriety—like the *Monthly* reviewer's opinion that the diction in *The Quaker* is "in general too splendid for the title it assumes, and too much ornamented for epistolary writing"[137]—this critic insists upon language that mirrors the emotional state of the speaker—or, in this case, the correspondent—thereby inducing empathy within the reader. In a very different context, a common impulse drives Samuel Johnson's famous censure of Shakespeare's unnatural, discordant flights of language in his tragic scenes—Johnson's belief that when Shakespeare "endeavoured, like other tragick writers, to catch opportunities of amplification, and instead of inquiring what the occasion demanded, to show how much his stores of knowledge could supply, he seldom escapes without the pity or resentment of his reader."[138] I draw the parallel to Johnson's controversial position in order to question the assumptions the reviewer seems to have shared with him and with many advocates of decorum. However improbable, "polished" language might communicate a letter writer's "poignant agony" powerfully—in much the same way as an elaborate conceit might vivify a dramatic character's emotions. Absolute mimetic fidelity in language is unnecessary for audiences who routinely accept and expect generic conventions.

Given suspicion of embellishment and adherence to decorum, expressions of distaste for mannerism come as no surprise. In a rebuke to the most idiosyncratic and the most gifted mannerist of the period, the *Critical* commentator's analysis of books 7 and 8 of *Tristram Shandy* concludes that the "principal part of the work before us is its manner, which is either above or below criticism; for if it is level with it, it becomes a kind of impassive object, upon which the artillery of criticism must be discharged in vain."[139] Both timing and tone complicate this critique, however. Forthright disapproval of Sterne's manner came from a *Critical* reviewer only after the similar stylistic eccentricities of the previous six volumes had met with acceptance or even endorsement.[140] Nearly a quarter of a century later, a reviewer of *James Wallace*, labeling Bage a mannerist, voiced the by-then common complaint that "peculiarities which may at first please, disgust by repetition."[141] In Sterne's case, perhaps only considerable repetition could destroy the novelty and generate contempt. Moreover, the sense of futility that accompanies the contempt—contained within the metaphor of impotent critical artillery—reveals more than purely aesthetic reasons for discouraging mannerism. When novels flout stylistic conventions, they also vitiate the conventional notions of—and vocabulary about—style, on which reviewers depend. Then, as now, revising both was more difficult and less attractive than rejecting unique, experimental prose.

Compromised motives should not eliminate genuine sympathy for the reviewers, considering the frequency with which they encountered numbingly poor prose, written with blithe neglect of grammar and idiom. At its worst, affectation went hand in hand with incorrectness, as illustrated in the comments of a reviewer, with a gift for understatement, concerning a novel with the wonderfully ironic title *The Observant Pedestrian:*

> We would admonish the writer to trust less, in future, to "the inspiration of the heart," and to attend more, if not to elegance, to propriety and correctness of composition. The orthography is in many places defective, and the rules of grammar but seldom attended to. The periods are too long, ill-constructed, and defective in unity. The metaphors are mixed and confused, the style frequently affected, and the language, from a want of due regard to the arrangement of words, obscure. Some attention to philology is absolutely necessary to an author.[142]

In many reviews, the most effective form of criticism was to let the offending texts speak for themselves, presumably allowing readers to draw their own conclusions—but, more accurately, persuading them to ratify the critic's judgment. After claiming that *Sentimental Lucubrations,* a Shandean imitation, contains "many passages and idioms . . . which debase the language,"[143] a *Monthly* reviewer lists several of the "passages and idioms," just as a *Critical* reviewer provides selections from *The Hermitage* that reveal "such an unlucky mixture of *high* and *low* words, oddly grouped, that we cannot help smirking at the injudicious combination."[144]

The decorous sensibility that rejected both the inappropriate use of so-called high words and the mixture of high and low also recognized the dangers of language that was *too* common, even if it was technically correct. In 1761, a *Critical* reviewer complains that the author of *Sophronia* "seems to have forgotten the adage, *familiarity breeds contempt.* Striving to be natural, he descends to a meanness of expression and triteness of reflection, which, we fear, will incur the censure of fastidious readers."[145] "Meanness of expression" could violate decorum as easily as inflated poetical prose: in *The Nabob,* the reviewer sometimes meets with "inelegant expressions, and the writer frequently approaches the borders of vulgarity. This is the more inexcusable, because the characters which he describes required more delicate language."[146] Monotony, a particular kind of meanness, provoked the most commonly recurring stylistic complaint about epistolary fiction. Frustrations of several generations of reviewers lay beneath a *Monthly* commentator's opinion that the epistolary style "is of all others the most difficult to sustain with spirit and propriety. As each person has a particular character of thought, and manner of expressing himself, it is necessary for an author to command a sufficient variety of style, suitable to the actors whom he employs."[147] Needless for the reviewer to say, most epistolary writers fell far short of the goal.

The often elusive ideal lay in the middle—in a style at once unaffected and sophisticated. Consistent approval of language that was "easy,"[148] "artless,"[149] or "familiar"[150] was accompanied by the recognition that attaining these qualities requires considerable talent, as a *Critical* reviewer's commendation of Goldsmith's style in *The Vicar of Wakefield* makes abundantly clear: "He appears to tell his story with so much ease and artlessness that one is almost tempted to think, one could have told it every bit as well without the least study; yet so difficult is it to hit off this mode of composition with any degree of mastery, that he who should try would probably find himself deceived."[151] Subsequent reviewers adopted the more apt term *elegance* to characterize such artful simplicity.[152] Richard Graves's *Plexippus* "is written in elegant language, without the affectation of ornament,"[153] Mrs. Gunning's style in *Love at First Sight* "possesses, on the whole, an ease and familiarity approaching to elegance,"[154] and Goldsmith's prose itself is cited as an "elegant, unornamented" model.[155] By the time of widespread acceptance of the luxuriant language of Gothic description, significant theoretical challenges to a definition of elegance as a means that shunned extremes still arose rarely. But rarity did not necessarily preclude cogency: a *Monthly* reviewer advances a powerful defense of what he—unlike reviewers for the *Critical*—considers "richness and fancy" of language in *Vancenza:*

> Style, like dress, admits of various degrees of ornament, between the limits of perfect plainness and finished elegance, each of which has its proper use and peculiar excellence; and it would be as absurd to expect all writers to express themselves with the same style, as to require all men to appear in an uniform habit. Simplicity and ease in language are characters, which, when they do not degenerate into insipidity and negligence, will be always pleasing: but it would be carrying the matter too far, to measure the merit of all writers by this standard.[156]

Even when reviewers consciously embraced a criterion both conservative and conducive to their often burdensome task, uniformity was impossible and dissent inevitable.

A stubborn refusal to evaluate all writers or all novels by a single standard represents—more than any standards they may have developed—the chief legacy of the reviewers. Critical dogmatism would have suffocated novelists and a reading public so thoroughly open to experimentation. The victory of diversity over consistency may strike the theoretical purist as contributing to a hopelessly compromised poetics, but it more than compensates for that in its support of a genre forever in the process of re-imagining itself.

Postscript

Critics uneasy with reductive and exclusive theories of the novel have recently found much comfort in Bakhtin's concept of heteroglossia. Regarding the novel more as a disruptive and vitalizing force than as a distinct genre, Bakhtin has argued that it "parodies other genres. . . ; it exposes the conventionality of their forms and their language; it squeezes out some genres and incorporates others into its own peculiar structure, re-formulating and re-accentuating them."[1] Novels liberate literary discourse by appropriating and organizing heteroglossia, or a "diversity of social speech types . . . and a diversity of individual voices" (262). By means of "authorial speech, the speeches of narrators, inserted genres, [and] the speech of characters" (263), the voices within a novel enter into dialogue with each other and resist the monologizing tendencies of the epic and other established genres. Theory that "works confidently and precisely" for these genres, where "there is a finished and already formed object, definite and clear" (8), cannot account for what is perpetually "a genre-in-the-making" (11).

What I have attempted to sketch in this book is nothing less than a critical heteroglossia that inheres in and animates early criticism of the novel in the same way as heteroglossia does the novel itself. Dialogue, within and among novelists and critics, favored options over absolutes, heterogeneity over consensus—thus enabling the genre that we twentieth-century readers think of as having risen in the eighteenth century to continue rising and to remain a genre in the making. Any lingering desire on our part for monologic unity or rules merely reflects the degree to which we have internalized New Critical or structuralist paradigms— paradigms that Bakhtinian analysis would reject as inadequate for thinking about the novel and that I reject as inadequate for thinking about this criticism. Throughout the eighteenth century, neither moralism, on the one hand, nor popularity, on the other (potent forces though they were), could reduce the discourse to a monologue—a result in which I, as a reader attracted by the richness and variety of the fiction that the discourse supported, can only rejoice.

161

Notes

Preface

1. See Lennard Davis, *Factual Fictions: The Origins of the English Novel* (New York: Columbia University Press, 1983).

2. See Michael McKeon, *The Origins of the English Novel, 1660–1740* (Baltimore: Johns Hopkins University Press, 1987).

3. See, for example, Jane Spencer, *The Rise of the Woman Novelist* (Oxford: Basil Blackwell, 1986); Dale Spender, *Mothers of the Novel: 100 Good Women Writers Before Jane Austen* (London: Pandora Press, 1986); and Mary Anne Schofield and Cecilia Macheski, eds., *Fettr'd or Free? British Women Novelists, 1670–1815* (Athens: Ohio University Press, 1986).

4. See Nancy Armstrong, *Desire and Domestic Fiction: A Political History of the Novel* (Oxford: Oxford University Press, 1987).

5. See John Bender, *Imagining the Penitentiary: Fiction and the Architecture of the Mind in Eighteenth-Century England* (Chicago: University of Chicago Press, 1987).

6. See Terry Castle, *Masquerade and Civilization: The Carnivalesque in Eighteenth-Century English Culture and Fiction* (Stanford: Stanford University Press, 1986).

7. See Carol Kay, *Political Constructions: Defoe, Richardson, and Sterne in Relation to Hobbes, Hume, and Burke* (Ithaca: Cornell University Press, 1988).

Chapter 1. Why, How, and Whence Novels?

1. Jacques Derrida, *Dissemination*, trans. Barbara Johnson (Chicago: University of Chicago Press, 1981), 7. Further page references to this work appear parenthetically in the text.

2. Irene Simon, "Early Theories of Prose Fiction: Congreve and Fielding," in *Imagined Worlds: Essays on Some English Novels and Novelists in Honor of John Butt*, ed. Maynard Mack and Ian Gregor (London: Metheun, 1968), 19.

3. William Congreve, *Incognita* (London, 1692), A5r–A5v. Further page references to this work appear parenthetically in the text.

4. Samuel Johnson, *Lives of the English Poets*, ed. G. B. Hill (Oxford: Clarendon Press, 1905), 2:214.

5. See Maximillian Novak, "Congreve's *Incognita* and the Art of the Novella," *Criticism* 11 (1969): 330; see also Maximillian Novak, *William Congreve* (New York: Twayne, 1971), 63.

6. John Richetti, *Popular Fiction Before Richardson* (Oxford: Clarendon Press, 1969), has argued that Congreve viewed the effects of the two genres as the same but was "saying that the novel is to be preferred because its effects make better sense morally and rationally; the reader's participation in a novel is not

a gratuitous emotional experience but a valid and useful exercise of his moral and emotional capacities" (175). I see a difference in kind as well as in degree: surely wonder and delight are distinct responses—as Congreve applied them to tragedy and comedy and as Burke would later apply them to the sublime and the beautiful.

7. McKeon, *Origins of English Novel*, has demonstrated the ways in which numerous authorial intrusions undercut not only the narrator's posture as a "neutral witness and transparent recorder of what has happened" (62–63) but also the narrator's protestations of truth and plausibility.

8. Novak, *Congreve*, has observed that Congreve "was making claims to skillful and artistic construction and to esthetic rather than moral standards" (65).

9. See the dedicatory epistles to *The Fair Jilt* (1688), *The History of the Nun* (1689), *The Lucky Mistake* (1689), and the opening of *Oroonoko* (1688), in vol. 5 of *Works of Aphra Behn*, ed. Montague Summers (London: Heinemann, 1915; reprint, New York: Phaeton Press, 1967).

10. See McKeon, *Origins of English Novel*, 111–13, on the problematic claims to historicity in *Oroonoko* and *The Fair Jilt;* see also Davis, *Factual Fictions*, 106–10.

11. For instance, Robert Adams Day, *Told in Letters: Epistolary Fiction Before Richardson* (Ann Arbor: University of Michigan Press, 1966), has called it "the most interesting and detailed piece of theorizing on the qualities of the new 'novel'" (98).

12. John L. Sutton, Jr., "The Source of Mrs. Manley's Preface to *Queen Zarah,*" *Modern Philology* 82 (1984): 167–72.

13. Mary Delariviere Manley, *The Secret History of Queen Zarah and the Zarazians,* in vol. 1 of *The Novels of Mary Delariviere Manley*, ed. Patricia Köster (Gainesville, FL: Scholar's Facsimiles and Reprints, 1971), A2v. Further page references to this work appear parenthetically in the text.

14. Richetti, *Popular Fiction Before Richardson*, 126.

15. Sutton, "Preface to *Queen Zarah,*" 169.

16. Pierre Daniel Huet, "The History of Romances," in *Novel and Romance: 1700–1800*, ed. Ioan Williams (London: Routledge and Kegan Paul, 1970), 49. As Williams has noted, Stephen Lewis translated the essay in 1715; and it was used by Samuel Croxall as a preface for his *Select Collection of Novels and Romances*, published in 1720. Some quoted excerpts, phrases, and words that would normally begin with a lowercase letter commence with a capital letter because those letters were capitalized in mid-sentence in the original.

17. Huet, "The History of Romances," 49.

18. Cf. Huet, "The History of Romances": "Probability, which is not always observed in History, is essential to a Romance" (48).

19. Davis, *Factual Fictions*, 111.

20. In *Popular Fiction Before Richardson*, Richetti has said that the "emphasis is on that participation which the plausible provides rather than on the moral and intellectual superiority of the real as such" (178).

21. Manley may well have been attracted to this phrase, given her classification of *Queen Zarah* as a "secret history."

22. Manley, *Novels of Manley*, 1:527.

23. Manley, *Novels of Manley*, 2:740.

24. Davis, *Factual Fictions*, 118.

25. Mary Davys, *The Reform'd Coquet* (London, 1724; reprint, New York: Garland Press, 1973), ix–xii.

26. Davys, *Works* (London: 1725), 1:vii. Further page references to this work appear parenthetically in the text.

27. Richetti, *Popular Fiction Before Richardson,* 211.

28. Jane Barker, *Exilius; or, The Banished Roman* (London, 1715; reprint, New York: Garland Press, 1973), A2v. Further page references to this work appear parenthetically in the text.

29. See William McBurney, "Edmund Curll, Mrs. Jane Barker, and the English Novel," *Philological Quarterly* 37 (1958): 388.

30. Samuel Johnson, review of *Miscellanies,* by Elizabeth Harrison, *The Literary Magazine* (Sept.–Oct. 1756): 282.

31. Elizabeth Rowe, *Friendship in Death,* 3d ed. (London, 1733), A3v. Further page references to this work appear parenthetically in the text.

32. Penelope Aubin, *The Noble Slaves* (London, 1722), xi. Cf. Penelope Aubin, *The Life of Madam de Beaumont, a French Lady* (London, 1721; reprint, New York: Garland, 1973), vii; and Penelope Aubin, *The Strange Adventures of the Count de Vinevil and His Family* (London, 1721; reprint, New York: Garland, 1973), 6.

33. Aubin, *Count de Vinevil,* 6. Further page references to this work appear parenthetically in the text.

34. Aubin, *The Noble Slaves,* xii.

35. See Penelope Aubin, *The Life and Adventures of the Lady Lucy* (London, 1726; reprint, New York: Garland, 1973), ix–x; and Penelope Aubin, *The Life and Adventures of the Young Count Albertus* (London: 1728; reprint, New York: Garland, 1973), 3.

36. Richetti, *Popular Fiction Before Richardson,* considered Aubin to be "claiming a moral truth, a Christian 'realism' in the strict philosophical sense of the word" (219); but the language suggests to me a more provisional move.

37. Penelope Aubin, preface to *Charlotta du Pont,* in *Eighteenth-Century British Novelists on the Novel,* ed. George L. Barnett (New York: Appleton-Century-Crofts, 1968), 21. Cf. Aubin, *The Noble Slaves,* xi.

38. Aubin, *The Noble Slaves,* 202.

39. *The Rambler,* vol. 3 of *The Yale Edition of the Works of Samuel Johnson,* ed. W. J. Bate and A. D. Strauss (New Haven: Yale University Press, 1969), 310–23.

40. Aubin seldom offered extended, detailed portraits of vice; therefore, the problem of the negative example was comparatively rare. See William McBurney, "Mrs. Penelope Aubin and the Early Eighteenth-Century Novel," *Huntington Library Quarterly* 20 (1957): 260.

41. Aubin, *Lady Lucy,* ix–x.

42. Ibid., x.

43. Probability and poetic justice anchored the 1739 preface to Aubin's collected works. The anonymous author of the preface also praised Aubin for "a Purity of Style and Manners," the recommendation of "all the Duties of Social Life," a "polite and unaffected Style," a "Variety of Incidents, which flow naturally from her Subjects," and "very instructive Observations and Reflections." Wolfgang Zach, "Mrs. Aubin and Richardson's Earliest Literary Manifesto (1739)," *English Studies* 62 (1981): 271–85, in a suggestive—but highly circumstantial—reading of the preface, which he reproduced, has contended that these precepts surpassed Aubin's theory and practice and represented, instead, the earliest "manifesto" of a more notable moralistic successor, Samuel Richardson.

44. *The Dunciad,* vol. 5 of *Poems of Alexander Pope,* ed. James Sutherland (New Haven: Yale University Press, 1943), 303–4.

45. George Whicher's *The Life and Romances of Eliza Haywood* (New York:

Columbia University Press, 1915)—the first book-length treatment of Haywood—has been supplanted by two recent studies: Mary Anne Schofield, *Quiet Rebellion: The Fictional Heroines of Eliza Haywood* (Washington, DC: University Press of America, 1982) and Mary Anne Schofield, *Eliza Haywood* (Boston: Twayne, 1985).

46. Eliza Haywood, *The Injur'd Husband*, in *Works* (London, 1744), 2:F2r. Cf. the preface to Eliza Haywood's *Adventures of Eovaai* (London, 1736).

47. Haywood, *Works*, 2:F2r. Cf. The dedication to Eliza Haywood's *The Rash Resolve; or, The Untimely Discovery* (London, 1724).

48. See Schofield, *Eliza Haywood*.

49. Whicher, *Life and Romances of Haywood*, 17.

50. Haywood, *The Fair Hebrew* (London, 1729), x. Cf. Eliza Haywood's *The Life of Madam de Villesache* (London, 1727), iv. The exception that Whicher has noted is Eliza Haywood's *The Surprise* (London, 1724). He has quoted from the dedication, addressed to Sir Richard Steele: "The little History I presume to offer, being composed of Characters full of Honour and Generosity." (18) Other exceptions include the later domestic fiction: in the preface to *The Fortunate Foundlings* (London, 1744), Haywood announced that her purpose was to encourage virtue by imitation.

51. Richetti, *Popular Fiction Before Richardson*, 219–20.

52. Eliza Haywood, *The Mercenary Lover; or, The Unforunate Heiresses* (London, 1726; reprint, New York: Garland, 1973), 8. Cf. the prefaces to Haywood's *The Fair Hebrew* and *Adventures of Eovaai, Princess of Ijaveo*.

53. Haywood, *The Fortunate Foundlings*, A2r.

54. Davis, *Factual Fictions*, has read disavowal of authorship as a statement about novelists' "difficulties in finding their place in the midst of a discourse that was in the active process of rupture" (192).

55. Eliza Haywood, *Lasselia; or, The Self-Abandon'd* (London, 1723), vi–vii. Any further page references to this work appear parenthetically in the text.

56. Richetti, *Popular Fiction Before Richardson*, 187.

57. See Rudolph G. Stamm, "Daniel Defoe: An Artist in the Puritan Tradition," *Philological Quarterly* 15 (1936): 225–46.

58. See Maximillian Novak, "Defoe's Theory of Fiction," *Studies in Philology* 61 (1964): 650–68.

59. Ian A. Bell, *Defoe's Fiction* (Totowa, NJ: Barnes and Noble, 1985), 120.

60. David Blewett, *Defoe's Art of Fiction* (Toronto: University of Toronto Press, 1979), 15. Davis, *Factual Fictions*, has seen Defoe's progress differently—as a move "from a pure assertion of veracity to a highly qualified and contextualized one" (166).

61. Laura Curtis, *The Elusive Daniel Defoe* (London: Vision Press, 1984), 103.

62. Daniel Defoe, *The Life and Strange Surprizing Adventures of Robinson Crusoe of York, Mariner*, ed. J. Donald Crowley (London: Oxford University Press, 1972), 1. Further page references to this work appear parenthetically in the text.

63. Davis, *Factual Fictions*, 166.

64. Daniel Defoe, *The Farther Adventures of Robinson Crusoe*, ed. George A. Aitken (London: J. M. Dent, 1895; reprint, New York: AMS Press, 1974), vii. Further page references to this work appear parenthetically in the text.

65. See Curtis, *The Elusive Daniel Defoe*, 103; see also Davis, *Factual Fictions*, 161.

66. Blewett, *Defoe's Art of Fiction*, 16.

67. Daniel Defoe, *The History of the Life and Surprizing Adventures of Mr. Dun-

can Campbell (Oxford: D. A. Talboys, 1841; reprint, New York: AMS Press, 1973), xxxviii.

68. For details, see W. T. Hastings, "Errors and Inconsistencies in Defoe's *Robinson Crusoe,*" *Modern Language Notes* 27 (1912): 161; see also Charles E. Burch, "British Criticism of Defoe as a Novelist, 1719–1860," *Englische Studien* 67 (1932): 178.

69. Charles Gildon, "An Epistle to Daniel Defoe," in *Robinson Crusoe Examined and Criticized,* ed. Paul Dottin (London: Dent, 1923), 23. Further page references to this work appear parenthetically in the text.

70. Davis, *Factual Fictions,* 156, has noted that Gildon's attack on the fictionality of *Crusoe* was rare, given common knowledge that Defoe's avowals of truth were a convention.

71. According to Davis, *Factual Fictions,* 157, Defoe regarded the story as at once true and false—as both a fiction with a true existence and a true story with a fictional structure.

72. Both Dottin, *Crusoe Examined and Criticized,* 59, and Novak, "Defoe's Theory of Fiction," 654, have discussed Defoe's debt to Gildon for the term *allegory.*

73. Daniel Defoe, *Serious Reflections during the Life and Surprising Adventures of Robinson Crusoe,* ed. George A. Aitken (London, J. M. Dent, 1895; reprint, New York: AMS Press, 1974), x. Further page references to this work appear parenthetically in the text.

74. See Davis, *Factual Fictions,* 159–61.

75. Novak, "Defoe's Theory of Fiction," 665. Cf. Stamm, "Daniel Defoe," 244.

76. I borrow the classification from Paula Backscheider, chap. 5 in *Daniel Defoe: Ambition and Innovation* (Lexington: University Press of Kentucky, 1986).

77. Daniel Defoe, *Memoirs of a Cavalier,* ed. James T. Boulton (London: Oxford University Press, 1972), 1. Further page references to this work appear parenthetically in the text.

78. See Novak, "Defoe's Theory of Fiction," 651.

79. Defoe, *The History and Remarkable Life of the Truly Honourable Colonel Jacque,* ed. Samuel Holt Monk (London: Oxford University Press, 1965), 1. Further page references to this work appear parenthetically in the text. Novak, "Defoe's Theory of Fiction," has called the preface "Defoe's most outspoken defense of fiction" (666), but I regard it as characteristically self-serving.

80. Novak, "Defoe's Theory of Fiction," has accepted at face value Defoe's "vindication of the work as a depiction of social evils" (666).

81. Daniel Defoe, *The Fortunes and Misfortunes of the Famous Moll Flanders,* ed. G. A. Starr (London: Oxford University Press, 1971), 1. Further page references to this work appear parenthetically in the text.

82. Daniel Defoe, *Roxana, The Fortunate Mistress,* ed. Jane Jack (London: Oxford University Press, 1964), 1. Further page references to this work appear parenthetically in the text.

83. Bell, *Defoe's Fiction,* 115, has noted the allusiveness of the title page to *Moll Flanders,* which connects it to novels like those by Manley and Haywood— as well as the tendency of the preface to withdraw that connection.

84. See Davis, *Factual Fictions,* 165.

85. In fact, Defoe, *Moll Flanders,* emphasizes penitence so insistently that he alters the usual formulation of poetic justice: "There is not a superlative Villain brought upon the Stage, but either is brought to an unhappy End, or brought to be a Penitent" (3). Ever desirous, though, to pique the reader's curiosity, he

then turns the tables and announces that in later years Moll "was not so extraordinary a Penitent, as she was at first" (3).

86. As Starr, *Moll Flanders*, 385n. has noted, Defoe made the same point in *The Family Instructor* through a comparison of the reception of *Paradise Lost* and *Paradise Regained.*

Chapter 2. Cracking Facades of Authority

1. Samuel Richardson to Aaron Hill, 1741, *Selected Letters of Samuel Richardson,* ed. John Carroll (Oxford: Clarendon Press, 1964), 42.

2. Samuel Richardson, *Pamela; or, Virtue Rewarded* (London: 1740), 1:vi. See T. C. Duncan Eaves and Ben D. Kimpel, *Samuel Richardson: A Biography* (Oxford: Clarendon Press, 1971), 91.

3. Samuel Richardson, *Pamela; or Virtue Rewarded,* 3d ed. (London: 1741), 1:vi.

4. Samuel Richardson, *Clarissa; or, The History of a Young Lady,* ed. Angus Ross (Harmondsworth: Penguin Books Ltd., 1985), 36. This is the most accessible contemporary text of Richardson's first edition, published in 1747–48.

5. Richardson to Lady Bradshaigh, 8 February 1754, *Letters of Richardson,* 280.

6. Richardson to William Warburton, 19 April 1748, ibid., 85.

7. See Elizabeth Bergen Brophy, *Samuel Richardson: The Triumph of Craft* (Knoxville: University of Tennessee Press, 1974), 31; see also Davis, *Factual Fictions,* 180.

8. Samuel Johnson to Samuel Richardson, 26 September 1753 (qtd. in T. C. Duncan Eaves, "Dr. Johnson's Letters to Richardson," *PMLA* 75 [1960]: 377).

9. See William Beatty Warner, pt. 2 of *Reading "Clarissa": The Struggles of Interpretation* (New Haven: Yale University Press, 1979); see also Terry Castle, chap. 7 in *Clarissa's Ciphers: Meaning and Disruption in Richardson's "Clarissa"* (Ithaca: Cornell University Press, 1982).

10. Carroll, *Letters of Richardson,* 35.

11. Both Brophy, *Samuel Richardson,* and Donald L. Ball, *Samuel Richardson's Theory of Fiction* (The Hague: Mouton, 1971), have attempted to combine Richardson's scattered comments into a coherent theory and to apply that theory to the novels. 12. Samuel Richardson, *Clarissa; or, The History of a Young Lady,* ed. William King and Adrian Bott (Oxford: Basil Blackwell, 1929–31), 1:xv. This is the most accessible contemporary text that incorporates the revisions Richardson made in the third edition, published in 1751. Alan D. McKillop, *Samuel Richardson, Printer and Novelist* (Chapel Hill: University of North Carolina Press, 1936), 126–27, has largely accepted Richardson's explanation for the restorations. Warner, *Reading "Clarissa,"* 195, however, has laid bare the ideological motives that prompted Richardson's restorations and outright additions.

13. Richardson, *Sir Charles Grandison,* ed. Jocelyn Harris (London: Oxford University Press, 1972), 1:4. Further page references to this work appear parenthetically in the text.

14. Richardson to Edward Young, 1744, *Letters of Richardson,* 61.

15. Richardson to Aaron Hill, 26 January 1746–47, 7 November 1748, *Letters of Richardson,* 84, 89.

16. Richardson to Edward Moore, 1748, *Letters of Richardson*, 118.

17. Richardson to Thomas Edwards, 20 November 1752, *Letters of Richardson*, 220.

18. See Jerry C. Beasley, *Novels of the 1740s* (Athens: University of Georgia Press, 1982), who has said that "Richardson was above all things a deliberate didactic writer, his aims exactly coinciding with those of many lesser pious biographers and storytellers whose works were as current as his own" (155).

19. Richardson, *Pamela*, 3d ed., 1:xvi. Cf. the "Concluding Note" to Richardson's *Sir Charles Grandison.*

20. Richardson, "Hints of Prefaces to *Clarissa,*" in "*Clarissa*: Prefaces, Hints of Prefaces, and Postscript," intro. R. F. Brissenden, *Augustan Reprint Society* 103 (1964): 4. Further page references to this work appear parenthetically in the text.

21. Richardson, *Clarissa*, ed. Ross, 1389.

22. William B. Warde, Jr. "Revisions of the Published Texts of Samuel Richardson's Preface to *Clarissa,*" *South-Central Bulletin* 30 (1970): 233, has noted that Richardson also argued that the novel was not designed only to amuse, partly in response to Warburton's preface to volume 3, which stressed entertainment.

23. Richardson, *Clarissa*, ed. King and Bott, 1:xv.

24. T. C. Duncan Eaves and Ben D. Kimpel, "An Unpublished Pamphlet by Samuel Richardson," *Philological Quarterly* 63 (1984), began their analysis of Richardson's pamphlet defending the fire scene in *Clarissa* by examining "Richardson's usual double preoccupation when discussing his novels: he is concerned about their moral effect and at the same time about dramatic effectiveness and plausibility, especially when it depends upon consistency of characterization" (406).

25. Sheldon Sacks, *Fiction and the Shape of Belief: A Study of Henry Fielding, With Glances at Swift, Johnson, and Richardson* (Berkeley: University of California Press, 1964), 237.

26. Richardson, *Pamela* (London, 1740), 1:iv.

27. Richardson, *Clarissa*, ed. King and Bott, 1:xv, xiv.

28. Richardson to Aaron Hill, 1741, *Letters of Richardson*, 41.

29. Richardson, *Clarissa*, ed. King and Bott, 8:308.

30. See Ronald S. Crane, "Richardson, Warburton, and French Fiction," *Modern Language Review* 17 (1922): 17–23. Crane has detailed Warburton's subsequent antipathy toward Richardson and attraction to Fielding.

31. Richardson, *Clarissa*, ed. Ross, 35.

32. Richardson, *Clarissa*, ed. King and Bott, 1:xiv. See also George Sherburn, "Samuel Richardson's Novels and the Theatre: A Theory Sketched," *Philological Quarterly* 41 (1962): 325–29.

33. Richardson, *Pamela*, 3rd. ed., 1:xvii.

34. Richardson to Lady Bradshaigh, 15 December 1748, *Letters of Richardson*, 104.

35. Ibid., 108.

36. See Alan D. McKillop, *Samuel Richardson*, 147, on this attitude as it is reflected in the postscript.

37. Richardson, *Clarissa*, ed. Ross, 1496–97.

38. Richardson, *Clarissa*, ed. King and Bott, 8:318, 314.

39. Beasley, *Novels of the 1740s*, 149. Duncan Eaves and Kimpel, *Samuel Richardson: A Biography*, 220, moving in a different—but equally unflattering—direc-

tion, have concluded that someone else may have had a hand in writing the postscript, since it seems above Richardson.

40. Richardson, *Clarissa*, ed. King and Bott, 8:319.

41. Brissenden, introduction to *"Clarissa*: Preface, Hints of Prefaces, and Postscript," iii. Cf. Brophy, *Samuel Richardson*, 27.

42. Richardson to Aaron Hill, 10 May 1748, *Letters of Richardson*, 87.

43. Richardson, *Clarissa*, ed. King and Bott, 8:325.

44. Richardson, *Clarissa*, ed. King and Bott, 8:325.

45. Richardson, *Pamela*, 3rd. ed., 1:xviii.

46. William Warburton, "Preface to Volume III of *Clarissa*," in *Novel and Romance: 1700–1800*, ed. Ioan Williams (London: Routledge and Kegan Paul, 1970), 124.

47. Richardson, *Clarissa*, ed. King and Bott, 8:326.

48. Ian Watt, *The Rise of the Novel: Studies in Defoe, Richardson, and Fielding* (Berkeley: University of California Press, 1957), 192.

49. Richardson, *Clarissa*, ed. Ross, 36.

50. Ibid., 1495.

51. See Warner, *Reading "Clarissa,"* 237.

52. Richardson to Aaron Hill, 29 October 1746, *Letters of Richardson*, 71.

53. Richardson to William Duncombe, 22 October 1751, *Letters of Richardson*, 194. Cf. *Letters of Richardson*, 185, 195, 235.

54. See Frederick W. Hillis, "The Plan of *Clarissa*," *Philological Quarterly* 45 (1966): 236–48; see also Edward Copeland, "Allegory and Analogy in *Clarissa:* The 'Plan' and the 'No-Plan,'" *ELH* 39 (1972): 254–65.

55. Richardson, *Pamela* (London, 1740), 1:v.

56. See Bernard Kreissman, *Pamela-Shamela: A Study of the Criticisms, Burlesques, Parodies, and Adaptations of Richardson's "Pamela"* (Lincoln: University of Nebraska Press, 1960).

57. Richardson to George Cheyne, 31 August 1741, *Letters of Richardson*, 50. This letter has been discussed by Ball, *Samuel Richardson's Theory of Fiction* 45, and by Eaves and Kimpel, *Samuel Richardson: A Biography*, 143.

58. Quoted in Eaves and Kimpel, "Unpublished Pamphlet by Samuel Richardson," 402.

59. Ibid., 404.

60. Ibid., 407.

61. *Gentleman's Magazine* 19 (June–July 1749): 348.

62. Ibid., 348.

63. Richardson, *Clarissa*, ed. King and Bott, 1:xiii–xiv.

64. Quoted in Eaves and Kimpel, "Unpublished Pamphlet by Samuel Richardson," 204.

65. See Eaves and Kimpel, *Samuel Richardson: A Biography*, 696; see also McKillop, "The Personal Relations between Fielding and Richardson," *Modern Philology* 28 (1931): 429.

66. Eaves and Kimpel, *Samuel Richardson: A Biography*, 397.

67. McKillop, *Samuel Richardson*, 129.

68. Richardson to Aaron Hill, 18 November 1748, *Letters of Richardson*, 101. Terry Eagleton, *The Rape of Clarissa: Writing, Sexuality, and Class Struggle in Samuel Richardson* (Minneapolis: University of Minnesota Press, 1982), 7, has cited this letter to argue that Richardson was, in fact, preempting modern critics who inevitably search for faults in Clarissa's character.

69. Richardson to Hester Mulso, 11 July 1751, *Letters of Richardson*, 185.

70. Richardson, *Clarissa*, ed. Ross, 36.

71. Richardson, *Clarissa*, ed. King and Bott, 8:307.

72. Ibid., 8:320–21.

73. Eaves and Kimpel, *Samuel Richardson: A Biography*, 316.

74. For similarities between the two, see William Park, "Fielding *and* Richardson," *PMLA* 81 (1966): 381–88; and William Park, "What Was New About the 'New Species of Writing'?" *Studies in the Novel* 2 (1970): 112–30. See also Beasley, *Novels of the 1740s*, 23–42.

75. Park, "Fielding *and* Richardson," 384.

76. Henry Fielding, *The History of Tom Jones, A Foundling*, ed. Fredson Bowers (Middletown, CT: Wesleyan University Press, 1975), 1:1. Further page references to this work appear parenthetically in the text.

77. Henry Fielding, *Amelia*, ed. Martin C. Battestin (Middletown, CT: Wesleyan University Press, 1983), 3–4. Further page references to this work appear parenthetically in the text.

78. Henry Fielding, *The Covent-Garden Journal*, ed. G. E. Jensen (New York: Russell and Russell, 1964), 193–94.

79. Henry Fielding, *The Journal of a Voyage to Lisbon* New York: Dutton, 1932), 189. Further page references to this work appear parenthetically in the text. The *Journal* was first published in 1755.

80. Fielding, *The History of the Adventures of Joseph Andrews*, ed. Martin Battestin (Middletown, CT: Wesleyan University Press, 1967), 10. Further page references to this work appear parenthetically in the text.

81. Homer Goldberg, "Comic Prose Epic or Comic Romance: The Argument of the Preface to *Joseph Andrews*," *Philological Quarterly* 43 (1964): 206.

82. Mark G. Sokolyansky, "Poetics of Fielding's Prose Epics," *Zeitschrift fur Anglistik und Americanistik* 22 (1974): 251–65, has demonstrated how Fielding used the terms *novel* and *romance* in a deprecating fashion to attack the fiction of the late seventeenth and early eighteenth centuries. Yet Arthur L. Cooke, "Henry Fielding and the Writers of Heroic Romance," *PMLA* 62 (1947): 984–94, has noted that Fielding's critical comments often resembled those of the romance writers.

83. Maurice Johnson, *Fielding's Art of Fiction* (Philadelphia: University of Pennsylvania Press, 1961), 84.

84. McKeon, *Origins of English Novel*, 404–5. Cf. John J. Burke, Jr., "History Without History: Fielding's Theory of Fiction," in *A Provision of Human Nature*, ed. Donald Kay (Montgomery: University of Alabama Press, 1977), 45–64.

85. McKeon, *Origins of English Novel*, 404–5.

86. Ethel Thornbury, *Henry Fielding's Theory of the Comic Prose Epic* (Madison: University of Wisconsin Press, 1931).

87. See J. Paul Hunter, *Occasional Form: Henry Fielding and the Chains of Circumstance* (Baltimore: Johns Hopkins University Press, 1975), 134; see also Ronald Paulson, "Models and Paradigms: Fielding's *Joseph Andrews*, Hogarth's *Good Samaritan*, and Fénelon's *Télémaque*," *Modern Language Notes* 91 (1976): 1186–1207.

88. E. T. Palmer, "Fielding's *Joseph Andrews*: A Comic Epic in Prose," *English Studies* 52 (1971): 331–39. Most of Palmer's parallels are farfetched—and, at times, he has taken Fielding's comments out of context.

89. Mark Spilka, "Fielding and the Epic Impulse," *Criticism* 11 (1968): 69.

90. Watt, *Rise of the Novel*, 239–59.

91. Goldberg, "Comic Prose Epic or Romance," 193–215.

92. Sheridan Baker, "Fielding's Comic-Epic-in-Prose Romances Again," *Philological Quarterly* 58 (1979): 63–81.

93. Wayne C. Booth, *The Rhetoric of Fiction* (Chicago: University of Chicago Press, 1961), 83.

94. Fielding, *The Covent-Garden Journal*, 186.

95. See Lyall H. Powers, "The Influence of the *Aeneid* on Fielding's *Amelia*," *Modern Language Notes* 71 (1956): 330–36; see also Sheridan Baker, "Fielding's *Amelia* and the Materials of Romance," *Philological Quarterly* 41 (1962): 437–49.

96. Henry Fielding, "Preface to *The Adventures of David Simple*," in *The Criticism of Henry Fielding*, ed. Ioan Williams (London: Routledge and Kegan Paul, 1970), 264.

97. Fielding to Samuel Richardson, 15 October 1748, *Criticism of Henry Fielding*, 189. For the background of this letter, see E. L. McAdam, Jr., "A New Letter from Fielding," *Yale Review* 38 (1948): 304–6.

98. Henry Fielding, *The Jacobite's Journal and Related Writings*, ed. W. B. Coley (Middletown, CT: Wesleyan University Press, 1975), 119.

99. Fielding, *Covent-Garden Journal*, 181.

100. For the fullest discussion of Fielding's use of this term, see John S. Collidge, "Fielding and 'Conservation of Character,'" *Modern Philology* 57 (1960): 245–59.

101. Robert V. Wess, "The Probable and the Marvellous in *Tom Jones*," *Modern Philology* 68 (1970): 33.

102. Fielding, *Criticism of Henry Fielding*, 265.

103. Recent critics who have remarked on the inconsistency include Lance St. John Butler, "Fielding and Shaftesbury Reconsidered: The Case of *Tom Jones*," in *Henry Fielding: Justice Observed*, ed. K. G. Simpson (Totowa, NJ: Barnes and Noble, 1985), 63–64; see also Patrick Reilly, "Fielding's Magisterial Art," in *Henry Fielding: Justice Observed*, 95–96.

104. See Martin Battestin, "*Tom Jones:* The Argument of Design," in *The Augustan Milieu: Essays Presented to Louis A. Landa*, ed. Henry Knight Miller, Eric Rothstein, and G. S. Rousseau (Oxford: Clarendon Press, 1970), 316–17; see also Douglas Lane Patey, *Probability and Literary Form: Philosophic Theory and Literary Practice in the Augustan Age* (Cambridge: Cambridge University Press, 1984), 206.

105. See Ronald S. Crane, "The Concept of Plot and the Plot of *Tom Jones*," in *Critics and Criticism, Ancient and Modern* (Chicago: University of Chicago Press, 1952), 638; see also Wess, "The Probable and Marvellous," 44. Sacks, *Fiction and Shape of Belief*, 107, makes a similar point about the ending of *Joseph Andrews*.

106. See, for example, Robert E. Moore, "Dr. Johnson on Fielding and Richardson," *PMLA* 66 (1951): 162–81; Ian Donaldson, "The Clockwork Novel: Three Notes on an Eighteenth-Century Analogy," *Review of English Studies*, 2d ser., 21 (1970): 14–22; and Russell A. Hunt, "Johnson on Fielding and Richardson: A Problem in Literary Moralism," *Humanities Association Review* 27 (1976): 410–20.

107. See Robert D. Mayo, *The English Novel in the Magazines, 1740–1815* (Evanston, IL: Northwestern University Press, 1962), 93–100; see also Robert Alter, "On the Critical Dismissal of Fielding: Post-Puritanism in Literary Criticism," *Salmagundi* 1 (1966): 11–28.

108. Samuel Johnson, *The History of Rasselas, Prince of Abissinia*, ed. Geoffrey Tillotson and Brian Jenkins (London: Oxford University Press, 1971), 21.

109. *Johnson on Shakespeare*, vol. 7 of *The Yale Edition of the Works of Samuel Johnson*, ed. Arthur Sherbo (New Haven: Yale University Press, 1969), 48.

110. *The Works of Samuel Johnson*, ed. Sir John Hawkins (London: Buckland, Rivington, and Sons, 1787), 1:217.

111. For elaboration, see Carey McIntosh, *The Choice of Life: Samuel Johnson and the World of Fiction* (New Haven: Yale University Press, 1973), 6.

112. *The Rambler*, vol. 3 of *Yale Edition of Works*, ed. W. J. Bate and A. D. Strauss, (1969), 19.

113. Hester Thrale Piozzi, "Anecdotes of the Late Samuel Johnson," in *Johnsonian Miscellanies*, ed. G. B. Hill (Oxford: Clarendon Press, 1897), 1:332.

114. McIntosh, *Samuel Johnson and Fiction*, has called *Rambler* No. 4 "only one skirmish in the intermittent feud between naturalism and moralism in Johnson's writings" (8).

115. While here Johnson was referring to youthful or naive readers, he generally viewed all minds as susceptible to the power of art. See Leopold Damrosch, *The Uses of Johnson's Criticism* (Charlottesville: University of Virginia Press, 1976), who has written: "Art is received not with rational analysis . . . but with emotional rapture, in a kind of paralysis of the will" (111). Damrosch has rightly credited Johnson for his appreciation of the potency of art—an appreciation rare among didactic critics.

116. Johnson, *Yale Edition of Works*, 3:21–22.

117. Ibid., 24. Cf. *Rambler* No. 77: "It has been apparently the settled purpose of some writers, whose powers and acquisitions place them high in the ranks of literature, to set fashion on the side of wickedness; to recommend debauchery, and lewdness, by associating them with qualities most likely to dazzle the discernment, and attract the affections; and to show innocence and goodness with such attendant weaknesses as necessarily expose them to contempt and derision" (4:42). James B. Misenheimer, "Dr. Johnson's Concept of Literary Fiction," *Modern Language Review* 62 (1967), has summarized Johnson's position: literature "must show man what things are possible in this world and convince him that the achievement of these is often worth the work and the sacrifice and the discipline that is required. Through the power of the negative example, it must reflect, too, the less admirable qualities of man; and here Johnson asserts the responsibility of the author to exploit these qualities and undesirable propensities in such a way that the reader will strive to shun rather than to emulate them" (604).

118. Johnson, *Yale Edition of Works*, 4:153. Such flattery would be customary in the introduction of a guest author, but this is more than mere courtesy.

119. Johnson quoted in *Miscellanies*, 2:251. Moore, "Johnson on Fielding and Richardson," 168, has noted that Johnson confined his comments on Richardson almost exclusively to *Clarissa* and that Johnson's view of Richardson was heavily colored by that novel.

120. Johnson, *Lives of English Poets*, 2:67.

121. James Boswell, *The Life of Samuel Johnson*, ed. G. B. Hill, rev. L. F. Powell (Oxford: Clarendon Press, 1934), 2:173–74.

122. Johnson, *Yale Edition of Works*, 7:339.

123. Ibid., 7:71.

124. Johnson, *Lives of English Poets*, 2:278.

125. Ibid., 2:135.

126. Boswell, *Life of Johnson*, 4:53.

127. Johnson, *Lives of English Poets*, 2:358.

128. Johnson, *Yale Edition of Works,* 7:66.

129. Ibid., 7:523.

130. Ibid.

131. Ibid.; see also McIntosh, *Johnson and World of Fiction,* 9.

132. Johnson, *Yale Edition of Works,* 3:24.

133. Damrosch, *Uses of Johnson's Criticism,* 120, has made a similar point in regard to Johnson's treatment of Shakespeare, contending that Johnson was more successful at relating morality and criticism in the *Lives of English Poets* than in his preface and notes to Shakespeare.

134. Shirley White Johnston, "The Unfurious Critic: Samuel Johnson's Attitudes Toward His Contemporaries," *Modern Philology* 77 (1979): 18–25, has connected Johnson's refusal to evaluate his contemporaries in print to the absence of published commentary on Richardson and Fielding.

135. Johnson, *Yale Edition of Works,* 7:60.

136. Ibid., 3:16–18.

137. Ibid., 3:19.

138. Ibid., 3:21.

139. Ibid., 3:24.

140. Ibid., 3:21.

141. Ibid., 3:24–25.

142. Johnston, "Johnson's Attitudes Toward Contemporaries," has correctly observed that the anecdotal materials "simply do not yield a disinterested, balanced account" (19). I cannot, however, accept her proscriptive conclusion that one should not devote serious attention to these materials.

143. Boswell, *Life of Johnson,* 2:48–49.

144. Donaldson, "Clockwork Novel," 16. Cf. Moore, "Johnson on Fielding and Richardson," 169.

145. See Watt, *Rise of the Novel,* 261–89.

146. Mark Kinkead-Weekes, "Johnson on 'The Rise of the Novel,'" in *Samuel Johnson: New Critical Essays,* ed. Isobel Grundy (Totowa, NJ: Barnes and Noble, 1984), 79.

147. See Moore, "Johnson on Fielding and Richardson," 172–75; see also Kinkead-Weekes, "Johnson on 'Rise of Novel,'" 76.

148. McIntosh, *Johnson and World of Fiction,* has observed that "few great writers are as deficient in negative capability as Johnson" (45).

149. See Watt, *Rise of the Novel,* 261; see also Kinkead-Weekes, "Johnson on 'Rise of Novel,'" 75.

150. Johnson, *Yale Edition of Works,* 8:974.

151. Ibid., 8:884.

152. Ibid., 8:836.

153. Ibid., 7:61–62.

154. Jean Hagstrum, *Samuel Johnson's Literary Criticism* (Minneapolis: University of Minnesota Press, 1952), 71–72, has elaborated upon both meanings but has minimized the inherent contradictions. In a different context, Johnson actually complimented Fielding for his "characters of manners," positing them as the standard against which Burney's Mr. Smith should be judged: "Oh, Mr. Smith, Mr. Smith is the man. . . . Harry Fielding never drew so good a character" (Johnson qtd. in *Miscellanies,* 1:72). The compliment was especially extravagant, since Johnson once admitted to never having read *Evelina* through. See also W. J. Bate, *Samuel Johnson* (New York: Harcourt Brace Jovanovich, 1977), 488.

155. Johnson, *Yale Edition of Works,* 8:653.

156. Ibid., 8:745.

157. Johnson, *Lives of English Poets*, 2:67.

158. See John A. Dussinger, "Richardson and Johnson: Critical Agreement on Rowe's *The Fair Penitent*," *English Studies* 49 (1968): "Johnson's belief that domestic tragedy has more affective appeal than heroic tragedy because the spectator can more immediately identify himself with the protagonist is a principal tenet Richardson had followed in *Clarissa*" (47). Cf. McIntosh, *Johnson and World of Fiction*, 24.

159. Johnson, quoted in *Miscellanies*, 1:297.

160. Boswell, *Life of Johnson*, 3:43.

161. Johnson to Samuel Richardson, 9 March 1751, *Letters of Samuel Johnson*, ed. R. W. Chapman (Oxford: Clarendon Press, 1952), 1:36. Johnson practiced what he preached; when compiling his *Dictionary*, he relied on a collection of quotations from *Clarissa*, which was begun by Solomon Lowe and completed by Richardson himself. See William R. Keast, "The Two *Clarissa*s in Johnson's *Dictionary*," *Studies in Philology* 54 (1957): 429–39.

162. See my note, Joseph F. Bartolomeo, "Johnson, Richardson, and the Audience for Fiction," *Notes and Queries*, n.s., 33 (1986): 517.

163. Boswell, *Life of Johnson*, 2:175.

Chapter 3. Respect, Readers, or Both?

1. Henry Brooke, *The Fool of Quality; or, The History of Henry Earl of Moreland* (London, 1766), 1:B3.

2. Catherine Parry, *Eden Vale* (London, 1784), 1:1.

3. See *Sophronia; or, Letters to the Ladies* (London, 1761), iii; Albinia Gwynn, *The Rencontre; or, Transition of a Moment* (Dublin, 1785), 1:iii; and Charlotte Smith, *Marchmont* (London, 1796), 1:v.

4. Harriet Lee, *The Errors of Innocence* (London, 1786), 1:iii.

5. Richard Graves, *The Spiritual Quixote*, ed. Clarence Tracy (London: Oxford University Press, 1967), 4.

6. Robert Bage, *Mount Henneth*, vol. 9 of *Ballantyne's Novelist's Library* (London: 1824), 113.

7. I borrow the term from Leslie M. Thompson and John R. Ahrens, "Criticism of English Fiction 1780–1810: The Mysterious Powers of the Pleading Preface," *Yearbook of English Studies* 1 (1971): 125–34. Cf. J. M. S. Tompkins, *The Popular Novel in England 1770–1800* (London: Constable and Co., 1932; reprint, Lincoln: University of Nebraska Press, 1961), 17.

8. *Memoirs of Harriot and Charlotte Meanwell* (London, 1757), 1.

9. See Eliza Parsons, *The History of Miss Meredith* (London, 1790), 1:iv–vi; see also Eliza Parsons, *The Mysterious Warning: A German Tale* (London, 1796), 1:1.

10. Patricia Meyer Spacks, *Imagining a Self: Autobiography and Novel in Eighteenth-Century England* (Cambridge: Harvard University Press, 1976), 89, 59.

11. See, for example, Elizabeth Helme, *Louisa; or, The Cottage on the Moor* (London, 1787), 1:x; Elizabeth Sophia Tomlins, *Rosalind de Tracy* (London, 1798), 1:iii; and Jane West, *A Gossip's Story, And A Legendary Tale*, 4th ed. (London, 1799), 1:xiii.

12. Frances Burney, *Evelina; or, The History of a Young Lady's Entrance Into the World*, ed. Edward Bloom (London: Oxford University Press, 1968), 14.

13. Elizabeth Inchbald, *A Simple Story*, ed. J. M. S. Tompkins (London: Oxford University Press, 1967), 2.

14. Dale Spender, *Mothers of the Novel*, 206.

15. Lee, *Errors of Innocence*, 1:vi.

16. Burney, *Evelina*, 1–3.

17. Anne Ehrenpreis, introduction to *The Old Manor House*, by Charlotte Smith (London: Oxford University Press, 1969), viii–ix.

18. Smith, *Marchmont*, 1:xiii.

19. Charlotte Smith, *The Young Philosopher* (London, 1798), 1:vii.

20. Charlotte Smith, *The Banished Man* (London, 1794), 1:ix.

21. *The History of Lord Clayton and Miss Meredith* (London, 1769), 1:A2r.

22. Sophia Lee, *The Life of a Lover* (London, 1804), 1:x.

23. Helenus Scott, *The Adventures of a Rupee* (London, 1782), xiv. Cf. Sarah Fielding's humorous description of classes of readers with differing personalities and depths of penetration, in the preface to *The History of the Countess of Dellwyn* (London, 1759), 1:xxxiii ff.

24. Elizabeth Griffith, *The Delicate Distress* (London, 1769), 1:vii–viii.

25. George Hadley, *Argal: or, The Silver Devil* (London, 1793), 1:vi–vii.

26. Robert Bage, *Man As He Is* (London, 1792), 1:iv.

27. Thomas Holcroft, *Alwyn: or, The Gentleman Comedian* (London, 1780), 1:viii.

28. These objections are catalogued in John Tinnon Taylor, *Early Opposition to the English Novel* (New York: King's Crown Press, 1943).

29. Helen Maria Williams, *Julia* (London, 1790), 1:iii.

30. Smith, *Marchmont*, 1:xvi.

31. Thomas Amory, *The Life of John Buncle, Esq.* (London, 1756), 1:vi.

32. Charles Johnstone, *The History of Arsaces, Prince of Betlis* (London, 1774), 1:vi.

33. Thomas Leland, *Longsword, Earl of Salisbury* (London, 1762), 1:A2r.

34. Lee, *Errors of Innocence*, 1:iv.

35. Tobias Smollett, *The Adventures of Ferdinand Count Fathom*, ed. Damian Grant (London: Oxford University Press, 1971), 3.

36. Charles Johnstone, *The History of John Juniper, Esq., Alias Juniper Jack* (London, 1781), 1:3.

37. See B. Slepian and L. J. Morrissey, "What is *Fanny Hill*?" *Essays in Criticism* 14 (1964): 74. Cf. Malcolm Bradbury, "*Fanny Hill* and the Comic Novel," *Critical Quarterly* 13 (1971): 274.

38. See, for example, *Sophronia* (1761); Amory, *John Buncle* (1756); Parry, *Eden Vale* (1784); Jane West, *The Advantages of Education* (London, 1793); and Parsons, *The Mysterious Warning* (1796).

39. Edward Bancroft, *The History of Charles Wentworth, Esq.* (London, 1770), 1:A2r–A2v.

40. Ibid., 1:A3v.

41. William Godwin, *Things As They Are: or, The Adventures of Caleb Williams*, ed. David McCracken (London: Oxford University Press, 1970), 11. Some critics regard the preface as a promise that the novel leaves unfulfilled; but in the introduction, McCracken has argued cogently that Godwin's announced intention was sincere and that—at least, in part—the novel realizes it. Cf. David McCracken, "Godwin's Literary Theory: The Alliance Between Fiction and Political Philosophy," *Philological Quarterly* 49 (1970): 113–33.

42. Thomas Holcroft, *Memoirs of Bryan Perdue* (London: 1805), 1:iii. For an extensive analysis of Holcroft's use of fiction for political ends, see Rodney M.

Baine, *Thomas Holcroft and the Revolutionary Novel* (Athens: University of Georgia Press, 1965).

43. Clara Reeve, *The Old English Baron, A Gothic Story*, ed. James Trainer (London: Oxford University Press, 1967), 4. Cf. Clara Reeve's preference for Richardson over Fielding in *The Progress of Romance* (London, 1785), 1:139.

44. Charles Jenner, *The Placid Man; or, Memoirs of Sir Charles Belville* (London, 1770; reprint, New York: Garland, 1974), 2:3.

45. Ibid., 2:4–5.

46. See Taylor, *Opposition to English Novel*, 111.

47. Maria Edgeworth, *Castle Rackrent*, ed. George Watson (London: Oxford University Press, 1964), 2.

48. Frances Sheridan, *Memoirs of Miss Sidney Biddulph* (London: 1761), 1:6.

49. *Sophia* (London, 1788), 1:vii.

50. Burney, *Evelina*, 7.

51. See Tompkins, *Popular Novel in England*, 19.

52. Tobias Smollett, *The Adventures of Roderick Random*, ed. Paul-Gabriel Boucé (London: Oxford University Press, 1979), xliv–xlv.

53. *The Generous Briton; or, The Authentic Memoirs of William Goldsmith, Esq.* (London, 1765), 1:ix.

54. Smith, *The Young Philosopher*, 1:iv.

55. Jenner, *The Placid Man*, 2:175–76.

56. West, *A Gossip's Story*, 1:xi–xiii.

57. Richard Cumberland, *Henry* (London, 1795), 2:7.

58. Horace Walpole, *The Castle of Otranto*, ed. W. S. Lewis (Oxford: Oxford University Press, 1964), 7.

59. Ibid., 7–8.

60. Reeve, *The Old English Baron*, iii.

61. Ibid.

62. Walpole to William Cole, 22 August 1778, *Horace Walpole's Correspondence*, ed. W. S. Lewis (New Haven: Yale University Press, 1937), 3:110; and Walpole to William Mason, 8 April 1778, *Correspondence* (1955), 27:381. See also Devendra P. Varma, *The Gothic Flame* (London: Arthur Barker Ltd., 1957), 77–78.

63. Leland, *Longsword*, 1:A2r. Cf. Clara Reeve, *Memoirs of Sir Roger de Clarendon* (London, 1793): ". . . historical facts have not been falsified, and . . . the characters with which liberties have been taken are such as have been barely named in history" (1:vi).

64. Sophia Lee, *The Recess; or, A Tale of Other Times* (London, 1785), 1:A2r.

65. Tompkins, *Popular Novel in England*, has cited the example of *The Amicable Quixote*, whose author "declares that his interest is in exploring character and tracing its 'undiscovered lineaments,' but lacking the skills to engage his characters in action, makes a rather disappointing business of his researches" (177).

66. For an exhaustive consideration of the issue, see W. J. Bate, *The Burden of the Past and the English Poet* (New York: W. W. Norton and Co., 1972). Poets would seem to have had much more reason to feel that their genre was attenuated; but it is useful to recall that, after 1750, the novel was generally regarded as being in inexorable decline.

67. Burney, *Evelina*, 9.

68. Ibid.

69. Sarah Fielding and Jane Collier, *The Cry: A New Dramatic Fable* (London, 1754), 1:14.

70. Godwin, *The Enquirer: Reflections on Education, Manners, and Literature* (Philadelphia, 1797), 366.

71. Godwin, *St. Leon: A Tale of the Sixteenth Century*, vol. 5 of *Bentley's Standard Novels* (London, 1831), ix.

72. Ibid.

73. Gwynn, *The Rencontre*, vi–vii.

74. Jenner, *The Placid Man*, 1:76, 75.

75. Ibid., 1:75.

76. See Taylor, *Opposition to English Novel*, 66, for the primarily moralistic—but also artistic—complaints against the emphasis on love.

77. Smith, *The Banished Man*, 1:vi–vii. However, as Katharine M. Rogers, "Inhibitions on 18th-Century Women Novelists: Elizabeth Inchbald and Charlotte Smith," *Eighteenth-Century Studies* 11 (1977): 73, has noted, Smith did not succeed in her professed attempt.

78. Charlotte Smith, *Desmond* (London, 1792), 1:iii.

79. Both McCracken, "Godwin's Literary Theory," and C. R. Kropf, "*Caleb Williams* and the Attack on Romance," *Studies in the Novel* 8 (1976): 81–87, have attested to Godwin's serious purpose. They would presumably dispute his later characterization of *Caleb Williams* as "a mighty trifle" and "a book to amuse boys and girls in their vacant hours." See William Godwin, *Fleetwood; or, The New Man of Feeling*, vol. 22 of *Bentley's Standard Novels* (London, 1832), 341.

80. Walpole, *Castle of Otranto*, 12. Elizabeth Napier, *The Failure of Gothic* (Oxford: Clarendon Press, 1987), has observed that in "seeking to define that newness," Walpole "falls back on old definitions of romance and the serio-comic" (75) and is ultimately unable to arrive at a coherent justification.

81. Laurence Sterne, *The Life and Opinions of Tristram Shandy, Gentleman*, ed. Ian Campbell Ross (Oxford: Oxford University Press, 1983), 58, 225.

82. Mary Wollstonecraft, *Mary: A Fiction* (London, 1788), A1v.

83. Herbert Lawrence, *The Contemplative Man; or, The History of Christopher Crab, Esq.* (London, 1771), 1:213.

84. Griffith, *The Delicate Distress*, 1:ix–x.

85. Pierre Henri Treyssac de Vergy, *The Mistakes of the Heart* (London, 1769), 1:A3r–A3v.

86. William Combe, *Letters from Eliza to Yorick* (London, 1775), xii. As the title suggests, this is a spurious sequel to Sterne's *Journal to Eliza*.

87. See Courtney Melmoth, *Emma Corbett; or, The Miseries of the Civil War*, 3d ed. (London, 1781), 1:v; see also Helme, *Louisa*, 1:ix.

88. Griffith, *The History of Lady Barton* (London, 1771), 1:x–xi.

89. Wollstonecraft, *The Wrongs of Woman; or, Maria*, in *Posthumous Works of the Author of A Vindication of the Rights of Woman*, ed. William Godwin (London, 1798), 1:b4v.

90. Lee, *Life of a Lover*, 1:vi.

91. For the most recent attempt, see Janet Todd, *Sensibility: An Introduction* (London and New York: Methuen, 1986).

92. Clara Reeve, *The School for Widows*, (London, 1791), 1:vi.

93. *Monthly Review*, 2d ser., 5 (August 1791): 467.

94. Smollett, *Roderick Random*, xliii.

95. Smollett, *Ferdinand Count Fathom*, 2. For Smollett's move away from satire, see Tuvia Bloch, "Smollett's Quest for Form," *Modern Philology* 65 (1967): 103–13; see also John M. Warner, "Smollett's Development as a Novelist," *Novel* 5 (1972): 148–61. Bloch has viewed the transformation as a result of Smollett's

failure to sustain Fielding's ironic vision, while Warner has seen the development as more gradual and deliberate.

96. Walpole, *Castle of Otranto*, 4. As Arthur L. Cooke has noted, "Some Side Lights on the Theory of the Gothic Romance," *Modern Language Quarterly* 12 (1951): 430, Walpole hinted at the possible cathartic effects of his genre, an obvious enough connection with drama—but one unnoticed and unmade by his successors.

97. In his private correspondence, Walpole pushed the comparison with drama no further. Reacting to Warburton's observation that the plan of *Otranto* was modeled on the five-act structure of drama, he rejoins that this was "an intention I am sure I do not pretend to have conceived, nor indeed can I venture to affirm that I had any intention at all but to amuse myself" (see Walpole to Robert Jephson, 27 January 1780, *Correspondence*, 41: 410). Such an admission is in keeping with Walpole's repeated characterization of *Otranto* as a jeu d'esprit, written hurriedly and begun "without knowing in the least what I intended to say or relate" (see Walpole to William Cole, 9 March 1785, *Correspondence*, 1: 88).

98. Smollett, *Ferdinand Count Fathom*, 2. Rufus Putney, "The Plan of *Peregrine Pickle*," *PMLA* 60 (1945): 1051–65, has argued that Smollett put this concept into practice before offering it as a generalization.

99. Holcroft, *Alwyn*, 1:vi. Tompkins, *Popular Novel in England*, 330, was the first to notice this unusual emphasis on form in Holcroft's preface.

100. Cumberland, *Henry*, 2:216.

101. Godwin, *Fleetwood*, 337.

102. Smollett, *The Adventures of Peregrine Pickle*, ed. James L. Clifford (London: Oxford University Press, 1964), 682–83.

103. Sterne, *Tristram Shandy*, 57–59.

104. Lawrence, *The Contemplative Man*, 1:196.

105. Francis Coventry, *The History of Pompey the Little; or, The Life and Adventures of a Lap-Dog*, ed. Robert Adams Day (London: Oxford University Press, 1974), xliv.

106. See Smollett, *Ferdinand Count Fathom*, 3; Bancroft, *Charles Wentworth*, 1:A3r; Cumberland, *Henry*, 3:113; and Courtney Melmoth, *The Tutor of Truth* (Dublin, 1784), 1:vii.

107. Jenner, *The Placid Man*, 2:173–74; Hadley, *Argal*, 1:v; Mary Hays, *Memoirs of Emma Courtney* (London, 1796; reprint, New York, 1802), 1:4.

108. Wollstonecraft, *Posthumous Works*, 1:b4v–b5r.

109. Fielding and Collier, *The Cry*, 1:14.

110. Burney, *Camilla; or, A Picture of Youth*, ed. Edward and Lillian Bloom (London: Oxford University Press, 1972), 1.

111. Godwin, *Fleetwood*, 339.

112. Tompkins, *Popular Novel in England*, for instance, has traced a growing movement in characterization from "types" to "individuals" (177).

113. Melmoth, *Family Secrets, Literary and Domestic* (London, 1797), 1:iii.

114. Amory, *John Buncle*, 1:ix.

115. Reeve, *The Exiles; or, Memoirs of the Count de Cronstadt* (London, 1788), 1:iii.

116. Graves, *The Spiritual Quixote*, 7.

117. Bage, "Ballantyne's Novelist's Library," 9:114.

118. Ibid.

119. Reeve, *The Exiles*, 1:xii.

120. Frances Burney to Doctor Burney, 8 November 1796, vol. 3 of *Journals*

and Letters of Fanny Burney, ed. Joyce Hemlow, Patricia Boutilier, and Althea Douglas (Oxford: Clarendon Press, 1973), 3:222.

121. For details, see Appendix B in Burney, *Journals and Letters,* 3:368.

122. Ibid., 3:299.

123. Ibid., 3:221.

Chapter 4. Hierarchies of Fiction for a Cultural Elite

1. Jane Austen, *Northanger Abbey,* ed. John Davie (London: Oxford University Press, 1971), 32.

2. *Monthly Review* 73 (December 1785): 418. (*The Monthly Review* is hereafter abbreviated as *MR.*)

3. *MR* 16 (February 1757): 178.

4. *Critical Review* 35 (June 1773): 475. (*The Critical Review* is hereafter abbreviated as *CR.*)

5. *CR* 44 (November 1777): 397.

6. *MR,* 2d ser., 5 (July 1791): 338.

7. *MR* 4 (March 1751): 356.

8. *MR,* 2d ser., 6 (November 1791): 287.

9. *CR,* 2d ser., 8 (May 1793): 44.

10. *CR* 34 (1772): A2r.

11. *CR* 34 (1772): A2r.

12. *CR,* 2d ser., 12 (November 1794): 360.

13. See, for example, the reviews of volumes 3 and 4 of Charles Johnstone's *Adventures of a Guinea, CR* 20 (August, 1765): 120; Anne Yearsley's *The Royal Captives, CR,* 2d ser., 14 (August 1795): 390; and Robert Bage's *Barham Downs, CR* 58 (July 1784): 75.

14. *MR* 66 (March 1782): 237.

15. *CR* 67 (May 1789): 237.

16. *CR* 5 (January 1758): 31.

17. *CR* 32 (August 1771): 154.

18. *CR* 7 (February 1754): 174. Cf. *CR* 32 (November 1771): 372.

19. *CR* 26 (November 1768): 360. Such reactions opened the reviewers to attacks for not reading the novels they reviewed, and their equivocal responses to the attacks suggest that they may have indeed been reviewing blindly. See *CR* 5 (January 1758): 31; *CR* 7 (February 1759): 174; and *CR* 32 (August 1771): 154.

20. *CR,* 2d ser., 10 (February 1794): 235–36.

21. *CR* 31 (April 1771): 315. Cf. *CR* 15 (January 1765): 77.

22. *CR* 58 (August 1784): 155.

23. *MR* 60 (June 1779): 480.

24. *MR,* 2d ser., 19 (January 1796): 88.

25. *CR* 2 (November 1756): 379.

26. See Johnson, *Rambler* No. 4 (31 March 1750), *Yale Edition of Works,* 3:21.

27. *CR* 7 (February 1759): 174.

28. *MR* 81 (July 1789): 78.

29. *MR* 44 (June 1771): 498. Cf. *MR* 48 (February 1773): 154.

30. *MR* 48 (May 1773): 417.

31. *MR* 45 (July 1771): 74.

32. *CR* 41 (March 1776): 241.

33. *MR* 52 (April 1775): 360.

34. *MR*, 2d ser., 23 (April 1797): 211.

35. *CR* 29 (February 1770): 148.

36. *MR* 14 (May 1756): 445.

37. W. Denham Sutcliffe, "English Book Reviewing, 1749–1800" (Ph.D. diss., Oxford University, 1942), 368.

38. Thomas Ord Treadwell, "The English Novel in the Monthly Reviews: 1770–1800," (Ph.D. diss., Columbia University, 1974), 283.

39. Robert Mayo, *English Novel in Magazines,* has hypothesized that the reviewers' frequent satiric thrusts were "welcomed by the readers of the reviews, who expected to be entertained, and to have their moral and social prejudices flattered, by crisp comments and facetious sallies" (193).

40. *MR* 43 (October 1770): 326. Cf. *CR* 5 (February 1758): 172–73; *CR* 10 (July 1760): 79; and *CR* 29 (June 1770): 474.

41. *MR*, 2d ser., 2 (August 1790): 465. Cf. *CR* 37 (June 1774): 475.

42. J. M. S. Tompkins, *Popular Novel in England,* has maintained that this occurred largely at the end of the century; but the practice was more consistent than she has implied.

43. *MR* 27 (December 1762): 472.

44. *MR*, 2d ser., 8 (July 1792): 339–40.

45. *CR* 37 (April 1774): 317.

46. See Edward A. Bloom, "'Labours of the Learned': Neoclassic Book Reviewing Aims and Techniques," *Studies in Philology* 54 (1957): 562; see also Thompson and Ahrens, "Criticism of English Fiction," 132.

47. *CR*, 2d ser., 4 (March 1792): 352.

48. See Rogers, "Inhibitions on Women Novelists," 476.

49. *CR* 13 (May 1762): 435.

50. *MR* 35 (December 1766): 485. Cf. *CR* 34 (December 1772): 473; and *CR* 56 (December 1783): 476.

51. *CR* 57 (May 1784): 253.

52. *MR* 47 (September 1772): 151.

53. *CR* 29 (June 1770): 474 (qtd. in Tompkins, *Popular Novel in England,* 125).

54. *CR*, 2d ser., 1 (February 1791): 207.

55. *CR*, 2d ser., 1 (April 1791): 435.

56. See Tompkins, *Popular Novel in England,* 125–27; see also Spencer, *Rise of Woman Novelist,* 79, 98–100.

57. *MR* 67 (December 1782): 453.

58. *CR* 70 (October 1790): 424–25.

59. *CR*, 2d ser., 26 (August 1799): 451.

60. *CR*, 2d ser., 1 (February 1791): 207.

61. *MR*, 2d ser., 9 (December 1792): 406.

62. *MR* 67 (December 1782): 456.

63. *MR* 24 (January 1761): 102–16. However, Alan B. Howes, *Yorick and the Critics: Sterne's Reputation in England, 1760–1868* (New Haven: Yale University Press, 1958), 13, has noted that the review furnished generous excerpts and was carried on in a generally bantering tone.

64. *MR* 26 (January 1762): 31–32. The *Critical* was consistently more favorable toward *Tristram Shandy,* but Sterne's derision of Smollett in *A Sentimental Journey* ensured harsher treatment for that novel.

65. *CR*, 2d ser., 19 (February 1797): 196–97.

66. See *MR*, 2d ser., 14 (August 1794): 485, for its review of Roche's *Maid*

of the Hamlet; see also *CR*, 2d ser., 13 (February 1795): 139, on Holcroft's *Hugh Trevor,* for late, detailed examples.

67. *MR* 52 (April 1775): 275. Cf. *MR* 74 (October 1786): 315; and *MR* 79 (December 1788): 558.

68. *MR* 32 (June 1765): 481.

69. *MR* 68 (February 1783): 91.

70. *MR*, 2d ser., 2 (July 1790): 353.

71. *MR*, 2d ser., 12 (November 1793): 338.

72. *CR*, 2d ser., 13, (March 1795): 275.

73. *CR* 32 (March 1772): 255. Cf. *CR* 63 (January 1787): 77; *CR* 67 (January 1789): 77; *MR* 36 (February 1767): 172; and *MR* 68 (June 1783): 539.

74. *MR* 41 (July 1769): 76.

75. *CR* 57 (March 1784): 235.

76. See, for example, *CR* 59 (January 1785): 67; see also *MR*, 2d ser., 22 (February 1797): 221.

77. *MR* 80 (January 1789): 60.

78. *CR* 36 (December 1773): 444. Mayo, *English Novel in Magazines,* has credited John Cleland with initiating the practice of giving "primacy both qualitatively and quantitatively to the literary aspects" of novels over the moral aspects (197).

79. *MR* 20 (May 1759): 428. Tompkins, *Popular Novel in England,* 71, has exaggerated in claiming that *no* reviewer complained about interpolated moralizing.

80. *CR* 8 (April 1759): 372. Philip J. Klukoff, "Smollett and the *Critical Review:* Criticism of the Novel 1756–1763," *Studies in Scottish Literature* 4 (1966): 95–96, has observed that the reviewer of *Rasselas* preferred morality communicated through a structurally vivid presentation that appealed to the imagination over intellectualized moral preachment.

81. *MR*, 2d ser., 15 (October 1794): 149.

82. *MR* 40 (June 1769): 477.

83. *MR* 45 (October 1771): 332.

84. *MR* 44 (March 1771): 262.

85. *MR* 57 (September 1777): 249.

86. *MR* 66 (May 1782): 394.

87. *CR* 36 (July 1773): 74.

88. *CR* 70 (September 1790): 339.

89. *CR* 67 (April 1789): 554.

90. *CR* 45 (June 1778): 474.

91. *MR* 16 (May 1757): 452.

92. Tompkins, *Popular Novel in England,* 68.

93. *CR*, 2d ser., 15 (September 1795): 120.

94. *MR* 49 (November 1773): 409.

95. *MR* 53 (December 1775): 515–16.

96. *CR* 36 (September 1773): 236.

97. *MR* 57 (July 1777): 74.

98. *CR* 32 (November 1771): 372; and *CR* 70 (July 1790): 81.

99. *CR* 32 (August 1771): 81–82.

100. Johnson, *Lives of English Poets,* 1:20.

101. *CR*, 2d ser., 1 (February 1791): 207.

102. *CR* 22 (April 1766): 272.

103. *CR* 62 (September 1786): 199.

104. *CR* 70 (October 1790): 454.

105. *MR* 71 (September 1784): 224.

106. *MR*, 2d ser., 2 (August 1790): 462–63.

107. *MR*, 2d ser., 1 (March 1790): 332.

108. *MR* 22 (June 1760): 548.

109. *CR* 11 (May 1761): 394–95.

110. See, for example, *MR* 20 (January 1759): 81; *MR* 34 (March 1766): 240; *CR* 50 (September 1780): 168; and, especially, the review of *Evelina, CR* 46 (September 1778): 202.

111. *CR* 43 (June 1777): 473.

112. *MR* 40 (May 1769): 424.

113. *CR* 54 (August 1782): 152.

114. See *CR*, 2d ser., 4 (May 1792): 472; see also *MR*, 2d ser., 8 (May 1792): 107.

115. *CR*, 2d ser., 3 (September 1791): 116.

116. *CR*, 2d ser., 21 (October 1797): 229.

117. In regard to poetry, see Bate, *The Burden of the Past*, and Harold Bloom, *The Anxiety of Influence: A Theory of Poetry* (New York and London: Oxford University Press, 1973), for the issue of coming to terms with intimidating predecessors.

118. *CR* 12 (1761): 204. Klukoff, "Smollet and *Critical Review*," 99, has offered a more extended analysis of the comparison.

119. *MR* 25 (September 1761): 260.

Chapter 5. The Balanced Critical Practices of Practical Critics

1. *MR*, 2d ser., 21 (October 1796): 156.

2. *CR* 11 (June 1761): 469.

3. *MR* 22 (May 1761): 58.

4. *CR* 17 (April 1764): 298.

5. *MR* 26 (April 1762): 254.

6. *MR* 20 (April 1759): 380.

7. *CR* 27 (March 1769): 179.

8. *CR* 57 (March 1784): 235.

9. *MR* 51 (November 1774): 401.

10. This ongoing popularity was lamented by a *Critical* reviewer in the same year (*CR* 38 [August 1774]: 157) and by a *Monthly* reviewer a generation later (*MR*, 2d ser., 15 [October 1794]: 226).

11. *MR*, 2d ser., 9 (November 1792): 338.

12. *MR* 49 (November 1773): 410.

13. *MR* 26 (April 1762): 254.

14. *MR*, 2d ser., 15 (November 1794): 219.

15. *CR*, 2d ser., 11 (August 1794): 360. Tompkins, *Popular Novel in England*, 250, has attributed this review to Coleridge—an attribution disputed by Charles I. Patterson, "The Authenticity of Coleridge's Reviews of Gothic Romances," *JEGP* 50 (1951): 517–21.

16. *CR*, 2d ser., 12 (November 1794): 360.

17. *CR*, 2d ser., 11 (August 1794): 360. As Mayo has observed, the reviewer "allowed a memory of the old categories to haunt his visit to the castle" (206)—

demanding unity, real life, and strongly marked characters. Similar admiration for the explained supernatural can be found in the reviews of *The Romance of the Forest* (*CR*, 2d ser., 4 [April 1792]: 459) and *The Sorcerer* (*CR*, 2d ser., 17 [May 1796]: 113).

18. *CR*, 2d ser., 13 (March 1795): 345.

19. *MR*, 2d ser., 15 (April 1795): 466–67.

20. *CR*, 2d ser., 15 (September 1795): 119–20. In the view of Tompkins, *Popular Novel in England,* the critic advocated romance as "the natural result of human curiosity and the love of novelty" (216); but the remarks about repetition call such a reading into question.

21. *CR*, 2d ser., 23 (June 1798): 166. Derek Roper, *Reviewing Before the Edinburgh, 1788–1802* (Newark: University of Delaware Press, 1976), has detailed the decline in the popularity of Gothic fiction among reviewers in the mid-1790s.

22. *CR* 62 (July 1786): 38.

23. *MR*, 2d ser., 30 (September 1799): 96. Tompkins, *Popular Novel in England,* 221–22, has discussed the remarks on terror by Anna Laetitia Aikin (later Mrs. Barbauld)—the amplification of Burke perhaps most significant for Gothic fiction.

24. *CR* 19 (January 1765): 51. Cf. *MR* 32 (May 1765): 394.

25. *CR*, 2d ser., 11 (August 1794): 362.

26. *MR*, 2d ser., 22 (January 1797): 91.

27. Ibid., 93.

28. *MR*, 2d ser., 24 (October 1797): 199.

29. *MR*, 2d ser., 14 (August 1794): 465.

30. *MR*, 2d ser., 9 (November 1792): 337.

31. *CR*, 2d ser., 19 (February 1797): 195. Treadwell, "Novel in Monthly Reviews," has considered the review a "damning indictment" (278) of the genre; but Roper, *Reviewing Before the Edinburgh,* 143, has offered a more nuanced reading.

32. *CR*, 2d ser., 19 (February 1797): 195.

33. *CR*, 2d ser., 21 (October 1797): 195.

34. *CR*, 2d ser., 14 (July 1795): 353.

35. *CR*, 2d ser., 17 (May 1796): 113.

36. *CR*, 2d ser., 17 (February 1797): 194. Treadwell, "Novel in Monthly Reviews," 278, has examined the passage from a similar perspective.

37. *MR*, 2d ser., 21 (October 1796): 156.

38. *MR*, 2d ser., 18 (October 1795): 229.

39. *CR*, 2d ser., 20 (July 1797): 353.

40. *MR*, 2d ser., 19 (March, 1796): 351.

41. *CR*, 2d ser., 19 (February 1797): 194.

42. See Treadwell, "Novel in Monthly Reviews," 25.

43. *CR* 13 (March 1762): 252–53.

44. *CR* 55 (March 1783): 233.

45. Ibid., 234.

46. *CR* 61 (March 1786): 215.

47. *MR* 75 (August 1786): 135.

48. Ibid., 134. In a later number, however, *MR* 77 (September 1787), a reviewer forthrightly admits that the proper combination of fact and fiction represents a considerable challenge: "To blend truth and fiction in such a manner as that work shall have no dissimilar parts, to give the latter the garb and appearance of the former, is not, perhaps, an easy task. Nature must be observed and

studied: men and manners must be steadily and attentively contemplated: and though in such a composition, portraits may be highly coloured, though there may be sometimes an exaggeration of character,—yet an air of verisimilitude and probability should pervade and distinguish the whole" (190).

49. See Treadwell, "Novel in Monthly Reviews," 261.

50. *CR* 68 (November 1789): 409. A few months later, the reviewer of *The Statue Room*, *CR* 69 (April 1790), cited this review as a touchstone for critical judgment: "When we spoke with complacency of historical novels, we excepted those abounding with anachronisms, which contradicted history in its most material circumstances, and in every respect was insignificant" (477). The standard was neither permanent nor absolute, however. See *CR*, 2d ser., 21 (October 1797): "We are not fastidious in works of this kind, as to expect a close adherence to *costume*" (235).

51. *CR* 69 (June 1790): 413.

52. *MR*, 2d ser., 2 (June 1790): 414.

53. *CR*, 2d ser., 17 (May 1796): 114.

54. *MR*, 2d ser., 29 (May 1799): 90.

55. William Park, "Changes in the Criticism of the Novel After 1760," *Philological Quarterly* 46 (1967): 39–40.

56. *CR* 22 (September 1766): 204.

57. *CR*, 2d ser., 3 (November 1791): 319.

58. Mayo, *English Novel in Magazines*, 200.

59. *MR* 65 (July 1781): 65.

60. *CR* 27 (May 1769): 482.

61. *CR* 31 (June 1771): 482.

62. *MR* 48 (April 1773): 268.

63. *MR*, 2d ser., 25 (May 1798): 107.

64. *CR*, 2d ser., 13 (March 1795): 346.

65. *CR*, 2d ser., 22 (February 1798): 237.

66. *CR* 44 (November 1777): 349.

67. *MR* 48 (May 1773): 319.

68. *CR* 61 (March 1786): 218.

69. *CR* 33 (April 1772): 325.

70. *MR*, 2d ser., 2 (August 1790): 426.

71. *CR*, 2d ser., 21 (December 1797): 471.

72. See Tompkins, *Popular Novel in England*, 112.

73. *MR* 35 (October 1766): 287.

74. *MR* 34 (May 1766): 407.

75. *CR* 28 (August 1769): 132.

76. *CR* 54 (October 1782): 320.

77. *MR* 42 (January 1770): 70.

78. *MR* 49 (December 1773): 508.

79. *CR* 15 (January 1763): 13. For the attribution to Smollett, see James G. Basker, *Tobias Smollett: Critic and Journalist* (Newark: University of Delaware Press, 1988), 271.

80. *MR* 4 (December 1750): 160.

81. *CR* 22 (December 1766): 434.

82. See Mayo, *English Novel in Magazines*, 199; see also Park, "Criticism of the Novel," 41.

83. *MR* 34 (May 1766): 407.

84. *MR* 50 (January 1774): 15.

85. *CR* 31 (May 1771): 397.

86. *CR* 67 (January 1789): 75.

87. *MR*, 2d ser., 3 (December 1790): 400.

88. *CR* 53 (March 1782): 234.

89. *CR* 50 (November 1780): 373.

90. *CR* 60 (November 1785): 394.

91. *MR* 77 (August 1787): 163; *MR*, 2d ser., 10 (March 1793): 298. For additional examples, see Treadwell, "Novel in Monthly Reviews," 231.

92. *MR*, 2d ser., 3 (September 1790): 91.

93. *CR*, 2d ser., 17 (July 1796): 351.

94. *CR*, 2d ser., 17 (July 1796): 351.

95. *MR* 35 (August 1766): 97.

96. *MR* 59 (November 1778): 392.

97. See Claude E. Jones, "The English Novel: A 'Critical' View, Part I," *Modern Language Quarterly* 19 (1958): 159.

98. *CR* 30 (August 1779): 146.

99. *CR* 68 (August 1789): 163.

100. *CR* 32 (December 1771): 449.

101. See *CR* 51 (April 1781): 284; see also *CR* 34 (July 1772): 77.

102. *CR* 30 (December 1770): 459.

103. See *CR* 29 (January 1770): 43; see also *CR* 67 (January 1789): 78.

104. *CR*, 2d ser., 18 (November 1796): 341.

105. *MR* 5 (October 1751): 394.

106. *MR* 68 (May 1783): 456. A reviewer of Cumberland's *Henry*, *MR*, 2d ser., 17 (June 1795) shares this opinion on Fielding's introductory chapters and is even harder on Cumberland's, judging them as "dedicated to the egotism of the author" (135).

107. *CR*, 2d ser., 1 (February 1791): 207.

108. *MR*, 2d ser., 14 (August 1794): 113.

109. *CR* 59 (April 1785): 316.

110. *CR* 12 (September 1761): 240.

111. *CR* 11 (April 1761): 238. Jones, "The English Novel," is correct in claiming that, in general, the critics "could see the limitations" (159) of the often eccentric methods of the best writers; but such an awareness did not unduly compromise their respect.

112. *MR*, 2d ser., 1 (February 1790): 216. Cf. *MR* 76 (April 1787): 326.

113. See *CR* 9 (January 1760): 67; *CR* 32 (August 1771): 81–82; *CR* 46 (September 1788): 203; and *CR* 67 (January 1789): 78.

114. *MR* 76 (April 1787): 325.

115. *MR* 44 (March 1771): 262.

116. *CR* 54 (December 1782): 414. Cf. *CR* 52 (August 1781), where the reviewer also praises characters that are "well-supported" and "happily contrasted" (155).

117. *MR* 67 (December 1782): 456.

118. *MR*, 2d ser., 17 (1795): 136–37. See Treadwell, "Novel in Monthly Reviews," 228.

119. *MR* 5 (December 1751): 515.

120. *CR* 21 (April 1765): 281; *MR* 50 (January 1774): 15; and *CR* 64 (September 1787): 201.

121. *CR* 21 (April 1765): 281.

122. *CR* 62 (July 1786): 68.

123. *CR* 65 (June 1788): 486.
124. *CR* 28 (July 1769): 69. Cf. *CR* 17 (June 1764): 480.
125. *CR* 63 (May 1787): 391.
126. *MR* 3 (May 1750): 58.
127. *CR* 5 (February 1758): 130. Treadwell, "Novel in Monthly Reviews," has traced the reviewers' objections to their distaste for violations of decorum, wherein "low" characters speak in "high" style (228).
128. *MR*, 2d ser., 27 (November 1798): 333.
129. *CR* 34 (July 1772): 52.
130. *MR* 20 (January 1759): 189.
131. *MR* 48 (January 1773): 71. Cf. *CR* 28 (August 1769): 142.
132. *MR* 58 (January 1778): 85.
133. See *CR* 31 (February 1771): 160; *MR* 44 (January 1771): 91; and *CR* 48 (November 1779): 339.
134. *CR* 60 (October 1785): 318. Cf. *MR* 65 (November 1781): 390. According to Tompkins, *Popular Novel in England,* since the reviewers were "anxious to classify and delimit the functions of poetry and prose once for all," they "did not approve of this overlapping and infiltration of one into the other" (363). In the 1790s, however, several reviewers did commend the poetry that was interspersed within narratives.
135. *CR*, 2d ser., 2 (July 1791): 356.
136. *CR*, 2d ser., 4 (March 1792): 270. Cf. *CR*, 2d ser., 3 (November 1791), on the use of poetry in Smith's *Celestina:* "Poetry is the production of a mind that has regained some share of ease; it is incompatible with deep distress, and more so with an anxious, uneasy suspense" (320).
137. *MR* 74 (April 1786): 306.
138. Johnson, *Yale Edition of Works,* 7:73.
139. *CR* 19 (January 1765): 65.
140. See Howes, *Yorick and the Critics,* 1–17, for details on the reception of the previous volumes.
141. *CR* 67 (January 1789): 76.
142. *CR*, 2d ser., 15 (November 1795): 341.
143. *MR* 42 (March 1770): 181.
144. *CR* 35 (January 1773): 79.
145. *CR* 11 (May 1761): 420.
146. *MR* 74 (January 1786): 72. When decorum was not an issue, a *Monthly* reviewer, *MR*, 2d ser., 11 (June 1793), did commend Charlotte Smith's "imitation of the ordinary language of people in different classes of the inferior ranks" (151).
147. *MR*, 2d ser., 22 (January 1797): 91. Cf. *MR* 38 (April 1768): 335; *MR* 48 (March 1773): 183; *CR* 59 (June 1785): 475; and *CR* 63 (February 1787): 160.
148. See *MR* 20 (1759): 428; *CR* 17 (May 1764): 400; *MR* 50 (March 1774): 176; and *MR* 58 (January 1778): 85.
149. *CR* 21 (June 1766): 439.
150. *CR*, 2d ser., 21 (September 1797): 43.
151. *CR* 21 (June 1766): 439–40.
152. Park, "Criticism of the Novel," 41, has claimed that *elegance* replaced the other terms; but this is not consistently the case.
153. *CR* 70 (July 1790): 97.
154. *CR*, 2d ser., 21 (September 1797): 43.

155. *MR* 64 (June 1781): 466.
156. *MR,* 2d ser., 7 (March 1792): 298–99.

Postscript

1. M. M. Bakhtin, *The Dialogic Imagination: Four Essays,* ed. Michael Holquist, trans. Caryl Emerson and Michael Holquist (Austin: University of Texas Press, 1981), 5. Further page references to this work appear parenthetically in the text.

Bibliography

Primary Material

The Amicable Quixote; or, The Enthusiasm of Friendship. London, 1788.

Amory, Thomas. *The Life of John Buncle, Esq.* 2 vols. London, 1756.

Aubin, Penelope. *The Life and Adventures of the Lady Lucy.* London, 1726.

———. *The Life of Madam de Beaumont, a French Lady.* 1721. Reprint. New York: Garland, 1973.

———. *The Noble Slaves.* London, 1722.

———. *The Strange Adventures of the Count de Vinevil and His Family.* 1721. Reprint. New York: Garland, 1973.

Austen, Jane. *Northanger Abbey.* Edited by John Davie. London: Oxford University Press, 1971.

Bage, Robert. *Man As He Is.* 4 vols. London, 1792.

———. *Mount Henneth.* Vol. 9 of *Ballantyne's Novelist's Library.* London, 1824.

Bancroft, Edward. *The History of Charles Wentworth, Esq.* 3 vols. London, 1770.

Barker, Jane. *Exilius; or, The Banished Roman.* 1715. Reprint. New York: Garland, 1973.

Barnett, George L., ed. *Eighteenth-Century British Novelists on the Novel.* New York: Appleton-Century-Crofts, 1968.

Bate, W. J., ed. *Criticism: The Major Texts.* New York: Harcourt Brace Jovanovich, 1970.

Behn, Aphra. *Works of Aphra Behn.* Edited by Montague Summers. 6 vols. London: Heinemann, 1915. Reprint. New York: Phaeton Press, 1967.

Boileau-Despreaux, Nicholas. *Les Héros de Roman.* Edited by Thomas F. Crane. Boston: Atheneum Press, 1902.

Boswell, James. *The Life of Samuel Johnson.* Edited by G. B. Hill. Revised by L. F. Powell. 6 vols. Oxford: Clarendon Press, 1934–1950.

Brooke, Henry. *The Fool of Quality; or, The History of Henry Earl of Moreland.* 5 vols. London, 1766–1770.

Burney, Frances. *Camilla; or, A Picture of Youth.* Edited by Edward and Lillian Bloom. London: Oxford University Press, 1972.

———. *Evelina; or, The History of a Young Lady's Entrance Into the World.* Edited by Edward Bloom. London: Oxford University Press, 1968.

———. *Journals and Letters of Fanny Burney.* Vol. 3. Edited by Joyce Hemlow, Patricia Boutilier, and Althea Douglas. Oxford: Clarendon Press, 1973.

———. *The Wanderer; or, Female Difficulties.* 5 vols. London, 1814.

Cleland, John. *Memoirs of a Woman of Pleasure.* Edited by Peter Sabor. London: Oxford University Press, 1985.

Combe, William. *Letters from Eliza to Yorick*. London, 1775.

Congreve, William. *Incognita; or, Love and Duty Reconciled*. London, 1692.

Coventry, Francis. *The History of Pompey the Little; or, The Life and Adventures of a Lap-Dog*. Edited by Robert Adams Day. London: Oxford University Press, 1974.

The Critical Review. 1–70 (1756–1790).

The Critical Review. 2d ser. 1–27 (1790–1799).

Cumberland, Richard. *Henry*. 4 vols. London, 1795.

Davys, Mary. *The Reform'd Coquet*. 1724. Reprint. New York: Garland, 1973.

———. *Works*. 4 vols. London, 1725.

Defoe, Daniel. *The Farther Adventures of Robinson Crusoe*. Edited by George A. Aitken. London: J. M. Dent, 1895. Reprint. New York: AMS Press, 1974.

———. *The Fortunes and Misfortunes of the Famous Moll Flanders*. Edited by G. A. Starr. London: Oxford University Press, 1971.

———. *The History and Remarkable Life of the Truly Honourable Colonel Jacque*. Edited by Samuel Holt Monk. London: Oxford University Press, 1965.

———. *The History of the Life and Surprizing Adventures of Mr. Duncan Campbell*. Oxford: D. A. Talboys, 1841. Reprint. New York: AMS Press, 1973.

———. *The Life and Strange Surprizing Adventures of Robinson Crusoe of York, Mariner*. Edited by J. Donald Crowley. London: Oxford University Press, 1972.

———. *Memoirs of a Cavalier*. Edited by James T. Boulton. London: Oxford University Press, 1972.

———. *Roxana, The Fortunate Mistress*. Edited by Jane Jack. London: Oxford University Press, 1964.

———. *Serious Reflections during the Life and Surprising Adventures of Robinson Crusoe*. Edited by George A. Aitken. London: J. M. Dent, 1895. Reprint. New York: AMS Press, 1974.

Dodd, William. *The Sisters; or, The History of Lucy and Caroline Sanson*. London, 1754.

Edgeworth, Maria. *Castle Rackrent*. Edited by George Watson. London: Oxford University Press, 1964.

Fielding, Henry. *Amelia*. Edited by Martin C. Battestin. Middletown, CT: Wesleyan University Press, 1983.

———. *The Covent-Garden Journal*. Edited by G. E. Jensen. New York: Russell and Russell, 1964.

———. *The History of Tom Jones, A Foundling*. Edited by Fredson Bowers. 2 vols. Middletown, CT: Wesleyan University Press, 1975.

———. *The History of the Adventures of Joseph Andrews*. Edited by Martin Battestin. Middletown, CT: Wesleyan University Press, 1967.

———. *The Jacobite's Journal and Related Writings*. Edited by W. B. Coley. Middletown, CT: Wesleyan University Press, 1975.

———. *The Journal of a Voyage to Lisbon*. New York: Dutton, 1932.

Fielding, Sarah. *The History of the Countess of Dellwyn*. 2 vols. London, 1759.

———, and Jane Collier. *The Cry; A New Dramatic Fable*. 3 vols. London, 1754.

The Generous Briton; or, The Authentic Memoirs of William Goldsmith, Esq. 2 vols. London, 1765.

The Gentleman's Magazine. 19 (June–July 1749).

Gildon, Charles. *Robinson Crusoe Examined and Criticized.* Edited by Paul Dottin. London: Dent, 1923.

Godwin, William. *The Enquirer: Reflections on Education, Manners, and Literature.* Philadelphia, 1797.

———. *Fleetwood; or, The New Man of Feeling.* Vol. 22 of *Bentley's Standard Novels.* London, 1832.

———. *St. Leon: A Tale of the Sixteenth Century.* Vol. 5 of *Bentley's Standard Novels.* London, 1831.

———. *Things As They Are; or, The Adventures of Caleb Williams.* Edited by David McCracken. London: Oxford University Press, 1970.

Goldsmith, Oliver. *Collected Works.* Edited by Arthur Friedman. 5 vols. Oxford: Clarendon Press, 1966.

Graves, Richard. *The Spiritual Quixote.* Edited by Clarence Tracy. London: Oxford University Press, 1967.

Griffith, Elizabeth. *The Delicate Distress.* 2 vols. London, 1769.

———. *The History of Lady Barton.* 3 vols. London, 1771.

Gwynn, Albinia. *The Rencontre; or, Transition of a Moment.* Dublin, 1785.

Hadley, George. *Argal; or, The Silver Devil.* 2 vols. London, 1793.

Hawkins, Sir John, ed. *The Works of Samuel Johnson.* London, 1787.

Hays, Mary. *Memoirs of Emma Courtney.* 2 vols. 1796. Reprint. New York, 1802.

Haywood, Eliza. *Adventures of Eovaai, Princess of Ijaveo.* London, 1736.

———. *The Fair Hebrew.* London, 1729.

———. *The Fortunate Foundlings.* London, 1744.

———. *Lasselia; or, The Self-Abandon'd.* London, 1723.

———. *The Life of Madam de Villesache.* London, 1727.

———. *The Mercenary Lover; or, The Unfortunate Heiresses.* 1726. Reprint. New York: Garland, 1973.

———. *The Rash Resolve; or, The Untimely Discovery.* London, 1724.

———. *The Surprise; or, Constancy Rewarded.* London, 1724.

———. *Works.* 4 vols. London, 1744.

Helme, Elizabeth. *Louisa; or, The Cottage on the Moor.* 2 vols. London, 1787.

Hill, G. B., ed. *Johnsonian Miscellanies.* 2 vols. Oxford: Clarendon Press, 1897.

The History of Lord Clayton and Miss Meredith. 2 vols. London, 1769.

Holcroft, Thomas. *Alwyn; or, The Gentleman Comedian.* 2 vols. London, 1780.

———. *Memoirs of Bryan Perdue.* 3 vols. London, 1805.

Inchbald, Elizabeth. *A Simple Story.* Edited by J. M. S. Tompkins. London: Oxford University Press, 1967.

Jenner, Charles. *The Placid Man; or, Memoirs of Sir Charles Belville.* 2 vols. London, 1770. Reprint. New York: Garland, 1974.

Johnson, Samuel. *The History of Rasselas, Prince of Abissinia.* Edited by Geoffrey Tillotson and Brian Jenkins. London: Oxford University Press, 1971.

———. *Johnson on Shakespeare.* Vols. 7–8 of *The Yale Edition of the Works of Samuel Johnson.* Edited by Arthur Sherbo. New Haven: Yale University Press, 1969.

————. *Letters of Samuel Johnson.* Edited by R. W. Chapman. 3 vols. Oxford: Clarendon Press, 1952.

————. *Lives of the English Poets.* Edited by G. B. Hill. 3 vols. Oxford: Clarendon Press, 1905.

————. *The Rambler.* Vols. 3–5 of *The Yale Edition of the Works of Samuel Johnson.* Edited by W. J. Bate and A. D. Strauss. New Haven: Yale University Press, 1969.

Johnstone, Charles. *The History of Arsaces, Prince of Betlis.* 2 vols. London, 1774.

————. *The History of John Juniper, Esq., Alias Juniper Jack.* 3 vols. London, 1781.

Lawrence, Herbert. *The Contemplative Man; or, The History of Christopher Crab, Esq.* 2 vols. London, 1771.

Lee, Harriet. *The Errors of Innocence.* 5 vols. London, 1786.

Lee, Sophia. *The Life of a Lover.* 6 vols. London, 1804.

————. *The Recess; or, A Tale of Other Times.* 3 vols. London, 1785.

Leland, Thomas. *Longsword, Earl of Salisbury.* 2 vols. London, 1762.

The Literary Magazine. Edited by Donald L. Eddy. 3 vols. New York: Garland, 1978.

Manley, Mary Delariviere. *The Novels of Mary Delariviere Manley.* Edited by Patricia Köster. 2 vols. Gainesville, FL: Scholar's Facsimiles and Reprints, 1971.

————. *The Power of Love.* London, 1741.

Melmoth, Courtney [Samuel Jackson Pratt]. *Emma Corbett.* 3 vols. 3d ed. London, 1781.

————. *Family Secrets, Literary and Domestic.* 5 vols. London, 1797.

————. *The Tutor of Truth.* 2 vols. Dublin, 1784.

Memoirs of Harriot and Charlotte Meanwell. London, 1757.

The Monthly Review. 1–89 (1749–1789).

The Monthly Review. 2d ser. 1–30 (1790–1799).

Parry, Catherine. *Eden Vale.* 2 vols. London, 1784.

Parsons, Eliza. *The History of Miss Meredith.* 2 vols. London, 1790.

————. *The Mysterious Warning: A German Tale.* 2 vols. London, 1796.

Pope, Alexander. *The Dunciad.* Vol. 5 of *Poems of Alexander Pope.* Edited by James Sutherland. New Haven: Yale University Press, 1943.

Reeve, Clara. *The Exiles; or, Memoirs of the Count de Cronstadt.* 3 vols. London, 1788.

————. *Memoirs of Sir Roger de Clarendon.* 3 vols. London, 1793.

————. *The Old English Baron, A Gothic Story.* Edited by James Trainer. London: Oxford University Press, 1967.

————. *The Progress of Romance.* 2 vols. London, 1785.

————. *The School for Widows.* 3 vols. London, 1791.

Richardson, Samuel. *Clarissa; or, The History of a Young Lady.* Edited by Angus Ross. Harmondsworth: Penguin Books Ltd., 1985.

————. *Clarissa; or, The History of a Young Lady.* Edited by William King and Adrian Bott. 8 vols. Oxford: Basil Blackwell, 1929–31.

————. "*Clarissa:* Preface, Hints of Prefaces, and Postscript." Introduction by R. F. Brissenden. *Augustan Reprint Society* 103 (1964).

————. *Pamela; or, Virtue Rewarded.* London, 1740.

————. *Pamela.* 3d ed. London, 1741.

————. *Selected Letters of Samuel Richardson.* Edited by John Carroll. Oxford: Clarendon Press, 1964.

————. *Sir Charles Grandison.* Edited by Jocelyn Harris. 3 vols. London: Oxford University Press, 1972.

Rowe, Elizabeth. *Friendship in Death.* 3d ed. London, 1733.

Scott, Helenus. *The Adventures of a Rupee.* London, 1782.

Sheridan, Frances. *Memoirs of Miss Sidney Biddulph.* 3 vols. London, 1761.

Smith, Charlotte. *The Banished Man.* 4 vols. London, 1794.

————. *Desmond.* 3 vols. London, 1792.

————. *Marchmont.* 4 vols. London, 1796.

————. *The Old Manor House.* Edited by Anne Henry Ehrenpreis. London: Oxford University Press, 1969.

————. *The Young Philosopher.* 4 vols. London, 1798.

Smollett, Tobias. *The Adventures of Ferdinand Count Fathom.* Edited by Damian Grant. London: Oxford University Press, 1971.

————. *The Adventures of Peregrine Pickle.* Edited by James L. Clifford. London: Oxford University Press, 1964.

————. *The Adventures of Roderick Random.* Edited by Paul-Gabriel Boucé. London: Oxford University Press, 1979.

Sophia; or, The Embarrassed Wife. 2 vols. 2d ed. London, 1788.

Sophronia; or, Letters to the Ladies. London, 1761.

Sterne, Laurence. *Letters of Laurence Sterne.* Edited by Lewis P. Curtis. Oxford: Clarendon Press, 1935.

————. *The Life and Opinions of Tristram Shandy, Gentleman.* Edited by Ian Campbell Ross. Oxford: Oxford University Press, 1983.

Tomlins, Elizabeth Sophia. *Rosalind de Tracy.* 3 vols. London, 1798.

de Vergy, Pierre Henri Treyssac. *The Mistakes of the Heart.* 3 vols. London, 1769.

Walpole, Horace. *The Castle of Otranto.* Edited by W. S. Lewis. Oxford: Oxford University Press, 1964.

————. *Horace Walpole's Correspondence.* Edited by W. S. Lewis. 44 vols. New Haven: Yale University Press, 1937–1983.

West, Jane. *The Advantages of Education.* 2 vols. London, 1793.

————. *A Gossip's Story, And A Legendary Tale.* 2 vols. 4th ed. London, 1799.

Williams, Helen Maria. *Julia.* 2 vols. London, 1790.

Williams, Ioan, ed. *Novel and Romance: 1700–1800.* London: Routledge and Kegan Paul, 1970.

————. *The Criticism of Henry Fielding.* London: Routledge and Kegan Paul, 1970.

Wollstonecraft, Mary. *Mary: A Fiction.* London, 1788.

————. *Posthumous Works of the Author of A Vindication of the Rights of Woman.* Edited by William Godwin. 2 vols. London, 1798.

Secondary Material

Alter, Robert. *Fielding and the Nature of the Novel.* Cambridge: Harvard University Press, 1968.

————. "On the Critical Dismissal of Fielding: Post-Puritanism in Literary Criticism." *Salmagundi* 1 (1966): 11–28.

Armstrong, Nancy. *Desire and Domestic Fiction: A Political History of the Novel.* Oxford: Oxford University Press, 1987.

Alvarez, A. "The Delinquent Aesthetic." *Hudson Review* 19 (1967): 590–600.

Anderson, Paul B. "Delariviere Manley's Prose Fiction." *Philological Quarterly* 13 (1934): 168–88.

Backscheider, Paula. *Daniel Defoe: Ambition and Innovation.* Lexington: University Press of Kentucky, 1986.

Baine, Rodney M. *Thomas Holcroft and the Revolutionary Novel.* Athens: University of Georgia Press, 1965.

Baker, Sheridan. "Fielding's *Amelia* and the Materials of Romance." *Philological Quarterly* 41 (1962): 437–49.

————. "Fielding's Comic-Epic-in-Prose Romances Again." *Philological Quarterly* 58 (1979): 63–81.

Bakhtin, M. M. *The Dialogic Imagination: Four Essays.* Edited by Michael Holquist. Translated by Caryl Emerson and Michael Holquist. Austin: University of Texas Press, 1981.

Ball, Donald L. *Samuel Richardson's Theory of Fiction.* The Hague: Mouton, 1971.

Bartolomeo, Joseph F. "Johnson, Richardson, and the Audience for Fiction." *Notes and Queries.* n.s., 33 (1986): 517.

Basker, James G. *Tobias Smollett: Critic and Journalist.* Newark: University of Delaware Press, 1988.

Bate, W. J. *The Achievement of Samuel Johnson.* New York: Oxford University Press, 1955.

————. *The Burden of the Past and the English Poet.* New York: W. W. Norton and Co., 1972.

————. *Samuel Johnson.* New York: Harcourt Brace Jovanovich, 1977.

Battestin, Martin C. *The Moral Basis of Fielding's Art.* Middletown, CT: Wesleyan University Press, 1959.

Beasley, Jerry C. *Novels of the 1740s.* Athens: University of Georgia Press, 1982.

Bell, Ian A. *Defoe's Fiction.* Totowa, NJ: Barnes and Noble, 1985.

Bender, John. *Imagining the Penitentiary: Fiction and the Architecture of the Mind in Eighteenth-Century England.* Chicago: University of Chicago Press, 1987.

Bissell, Frederick Olds, Jr. *Fielding's Theory of the Novel.* Ithaca: Cornell University Press, 1933.

Blewett, David. *Defoe's Art of Fiction.* Toronto: University of Toronto Press, 1979.

Bloch, Tuvia A. "Smollett's Quest for Form." *Modern Philology* 65 (1967): 103–13.

Bloom, Edward A. "'Labors of the Learned': Neoclassic Book Reviewing Aims and Techniques." *Studies in Philology* 54 (1957): 537–63.

Bloom, Harold. *The Anxiety of Influence: A Theory of Poetry.* New York and London: Oxford University Press, 1973.

Boege, Fred W. *Smollett's Reputation as a Novelist.* Princeton: Princeton University Press, 1947. Reprint. New York: Octagon Books, 1969.

Booth, Wayne C. *The Rhetoric of Fiction.* Chicago: University of Chicago Press, 1961.

Bradbury, Malcolm. "*Fanny Hill* and the Comic Novel." *Critical Quarterly* 13 (1971): 263–75.

Brophy, Elizabeth Bergen. *Samuel Richardson: The Triumph of Craft.* Knoxville: University of Tennessee Press, 1974.

Burch, Charles E. "British Criticism of Defoe as a Novelist, 1719–1860." *Englische Studien* 67 (1932): 178–98.

Burke, John J., Jr. "History Without History: Fielding's Theory of Fiction." In *A Provision of Human Nature.* Edited by Donald Kay. Montgomery: University of Alabama Press, 1977.

Castle, Terry. *Clarissa's Ciphers: Meaning and Disruption in Richardson's "Clarissa."* Ithaca: Cornell University Press, 1982.

———. *Masquerade and Civilization: The Carnivalesque in Eighteenth-Century English Culture and Fiction.* Stanford: Stanford University Press, 1986.

Colby, Elbridge. *A Bibliography of Thomas Holcroft.* New York: New York Public Library, 1922.

Collidge, John S. "Fielding and 'Conservation of Character.'" *Modern Philology* 57 (1960): 245–59.

Cooke, Arthur L. "Henry Fielding and the Writers of Heroic Romance." *PMLA* 62 (1947): 984–94.

———. "Some Side Lights on the Theory of the Gothic Romance." *Modern Language Quarterly* 12 (1951): 429–36.

Crane, Ronald S. "The Concept of Plot and the Plot of *Tom Jones.*" In *Critics and Criticism, Ancient and Modern.* Chicago: University of Chicago Press, 1952.

———. *The Idea of the Humanities and Other Essays.* Chicago: University of Chicago Press, 1967.

———. "Richardson, Warburton, and French Fiction." *Modern Language Review* 17 (1922): 17–23.

Curtis, Laura. *The Elusive Daniel Defoe.* London: Vision Press, 1984.

Damrosch, Leopold. *The Uses of Johnson's Criticism.* Charlottesville: University of Virginia Press, 1976.

Davis, Lennard. *Factual Fictions: The Origins of the English Novel.* New York: Columbia University Press, 1983.

Day, Robert Adams. *Told in Letters: Epistolary Fiction Before Richardson.* Ann Arbor: University of Michigan Press, 1966.

Derrida, Jacques. *Dissemination.* Translated by Barbara Johnson. Chicago: University of Chicago Press, 1981.

Donaldson, Ian. "The Clockwork Novel: Three Notes on an Eighteenth-Century Analogy." *Review of English Studies,* 2d ser., 21 (1970): 14–22.

Duff, Dolores D. C. "Materials Toward a Biography of Mary Delariviere Manley." Ph.D. diss., Indiana University, 1965.

Dussinger, John A. "Richardson and Johnson: Critical Agreement on Rowe's *The Fair Penitent.*" *English Studies* 49 (1968): 45–47.

Eagleton, Terry. *The Rape of Clarissa: Writing, Sexuality, and Class Struggle in Samuel Richardson.* Minneapolis: University of Minnesota Press, 1982.

Eaves, T. C. Duncan. "Dr. Johnson's Letters to Richardson." *PMLA* 75 (1960): 377–81.

————, and Ben D. Kimpel. "*Richardsoniana*." *Studies in Bibliography* 14 (1961): 232–34.

————. *Samuel Richardson: A Biography.* Oxford: Clarendon Press, 1971.

————. "An Unpublished Pamphlet by Samuel Richardson." *Philological Quarterly* 63 (1984): 401–9.

Foster, James R. *History of the Pre-Romantic Novel in England.* New York: Modern Language Association, 1949.

Frye, Northrop. "Towards Defining an Age of Sensibility." *ELH* 23 (1956): 144–52.

Galloway, W. F. "The Conservative Attitude Toward Fiction, 1770–1830." *PMLA* 55 (1940): 1041–59.

Goldberg, Homer. "Comic Prose Epic or Comic Romance: The Argument of the Preface to *Joseph Andrews*." *Philological Quarterly* 43 (1964): 193–215.

Grundy, Isobel, ed. *Samuel Johnson; New Critical Essays.* Totowa, NJ: Barnes and Noble, 1984.

Hagstrum, Jean. *Samuel Johnson's Literary Criticism.* Minneapolis: University of Minnesota Press, 1952.

Hastings, W. T. "Errors and Inconsistencies in Defoe's *Robinson Crusoe*." *Modern Language Notes* 27 (1912): 161–66.

Heidler, Joseph Bunn. *The History, from 1700 to 1800, of English Criticism of Prose Fiction.* N.p.: University of Illinois Press, 1928.

Hilbish, Florence M. A. *Charlotte Smith: Poet and Novelist.* Philadelphia: University of Pennsylvania Press, 1941.

Hillis, Frederick W. "The Plan of *Clarissa*." *Philological Quarterly* 45 (1966): 236–48.

Howes, Alan B. *Yorick and the Critics: Sterne's Reputation in England, 1760–1868.* New Haven: Yale University Press, 1958.

Hunt, Russell A. "Johnson on Fielding and Richardson: A Problem in Literary Moralism." *Humanities Association Review* 27 (1976): 410–20.

Hunter, J. Paul. *Occasional Form: Henry Fielding and the Chains of Circumstance.* Baltimore: Johns Hopkins University Press, 1975.

Iser, Wolfgang. *The Implied Reader: Patterns of Communication in Prose Fiction from Bunyan to Beckett.* Baltimore: Johns Hopkins University Press, 1974.

Johnson, Maurice. *Fielding's Art of Fiction.* Philadelphia: University of Pennsylvania Press, 1961.

Johnston, Shirley White. "The Unfurious Critic: Samuel Johnson's Attitudes Toward His Contemporaries." *Modern Philology* 77 (1979): 18–25.

Jones, Claude E. "The English Novel: A 'Critical' View, Part I." *Modern Language Quarterly* 19 (1958): 147–59.

————. "The English Novel: A 'Critical' View, Part II." *Modern Language Quarterly* 19 (1958): 213–24.

Kay, Carol. *Political Constructions: Defoe, Richardson, and Sterne in Relation to Hobbes, Hume, and Burke.* Ithaca: Cornell University Press, 1988.

Keast, William R. "The Two *Clarissa*s in Johnson's *Dictionary*." *Studies in Philology* 54 (1957): 429–39.

Klukoff, Philip J. "Smollett and the *Critical Review*: Criticism of the Novel 1756–1763." *Studies in Scottish Literature* 4 (1966): 89–100.

Kreissman, Bernard. *Pamela-Shamela: A Study of the Criticisms, Burlesques, Parodies, and Adaptations of Richardson's "Pamela."* Lincoln: University of Nebraska Press, 1960.

Kropf, C. R. "*Caleb Williams* and the Attack on Romance." *Studies in the Novel* 8 (1976): 81–87.

Mayo, Robert D. *The English Novel in the Magazines, 1740–1815.* Evanston, IL: Northwestern University Press, 1962.

McAdam, E. L., Jr. "A New Letter from Fielding." *Yale Review* 38 (1948): 304–06.

McBurney, William H. "Edmund Curll, Mrs. Jane Barker, and the English Novel." *Philological Quarterly* 37 (1958): 385–99.

———. "Mrs. Penelope Aubin and the Early Eighteenth-Century Novel." *Huntington Library Quarterly* 20 (1957): 245–67.

McCracken, David. "Godwin's Literary Theory: The Alliance Between Fiction and Political Philosophy." *Philological Quarterly* 49 (1970): 113–33.

McIntosh, Carey. *The Choice of Life: Samuel Johnson and the World of Fiction.* New Haven: Yale University Press, 1973.

McKeon, Michael. *The Origins of the English Novel, 1660–1740.* Baltimore: Johns Hopkins University Press, 1987.

McKillop, Alan D. "Charlotte Smith's Letters." *Huntington Library Quarterly* 15 (1952): 237–55.

———. *The Early Masters of English Fiction.* Lawrence: University of Kansas Press, 1956.

———. "The Personal Relations between Fielding and Richardson." *Modern Philology* 28 (1931): 423–33.

———. *Samuel Richardson, Printer and Novelist.* Chapel Hill: University of North Carolina Press, 1936.

Miller, Henry Knight, Eric Rothstein, and G. S. Rousseau, eds. *The Augustan Milieu: Essays Presented to Louis A. Landa.* Oxford: Clarendon Press, 1970.

Misenheimer, James B. "Dr. Johnson's Concept of Literary Fiction." *Modern Language Review* 62 (1967): 598–605.

Moore, Robert E. "Dr. Johnson on Fielding and Richardson." *PMLA* 66 (1951): 162–81.

Nangle, Benjamin C. *The Monthly Review First Series, 1749–1789: Index of Contributors and Articles.* Oxford: Clarendon Press, 1934.

———. *The Monthly Review Second Series, 1790–1815: Index of Contributors and Articles.* Oxford: Clarendon Press, 1955.

Napier, Elizabeth R. *The Failure of Gothic: Problems of Disjunction in an Eighteenth-Century Literary Form.* Oxford: Clarendon Press, 1987.

Needham, Gwendolyn B. "Mrs. Manley: An 18th-Century Wife of Bath." *Huntington Library Quarterly* 14 (1951): 259–84.

Novak, Maximillian E. "Congreve's *Incognita* and the Art of the Novella." *Criticism* 11 (1969): 329–42.

———. "Defoe's Theory of Fiction." *Studies in Philology* 61 (1964): 650–68.

———. *William Congreve.* New York: Twayne, 1971.

Palmer, E. T. "Fielding's *Joseph Andrews*: A Comic Epic in Prose." *English Studies* 52 (1971): 331–39.

Park, William. "Changes in the Criticism of the Novel After 1760." *Philological Quarterly* 46 (1967): 34–41.

———. "Fielding *and* Richardson." *PMLA* 81 (1966): 381–88.

———. "*Tristram Shandy* and the New 'Novel of Sensibility.'" *Studies in the Novel* 6 (1974): 268–77.

———. "What Was New About the 'New Species of Writing'?" *Studies in the Novel* 2 (1970): 112–30.

Patey, Douglas Lane. *Probability and Literary Form: Philosophic Theory and Literary Practice in the Augustan Age.* Cambridge: Cambridge University Press, 1984.

Patterson, Charles I. "The Authenticity of Coleridge's Reviews of Gothic Romances." *JEGP* 50 (1951): 517–21.

Paulson, Ronald. "Models and Paradigms: Fielding's *Joseph Andrews*, Hogarth's *Good Samaritan,* and Fénelon's *Télémaque.*" *Modern Language Notes* 91 (1976): 1186–1207.

Piper, William B. "Tristram Shandy's Digressive Artistry," *Studies in English Literature* 1 (1961): 65–76.

Powers, Lyall H. "The Influence of the *Aeneid* on Fielding's *Amelia.*" *Modern Language Notes* 71 (1956): 330–36.

Putney, Rufus. "The Evolution of *A Sentimental Journey.*" *Philological Quarterly* 19 (1940): 349–69.

———. "The Plan of *Peregrine Pickle.*" *PMLA* 60 (1945): 1051–65.

Renwick, W. L. "Comic Epic in Prose." *Essays and Studies by Members of the English Association* 32 (1946): 40–43.

Richetti, John J. "Mrs. Elizabeth Rowe: The Novel as Polemic." *PMLA* 82 (1967): 522–39.

———. *Popular Fiction Before Richardson: Narrative Patterns, 1700–1739.* Oxford: Clarendon Press, 1969.

Roper, Derek. *Reviewing Before the Edinburgh, 1788–1802.* Newark: University of Delaware Press, 1976.

Rogers, Katharine M. "Inhibitions on 18th-Century Women Novelists: Elizabeth Inchbald and Charlotte Smith." *Eighteenth-Century Studies* 11 (1977): 63–78.

Sacks, Sheldon. *Fiction and the Shape of Belief: A Study of Henry Fielding, With Glances at Swift, Johnson, and Richardson.* Berkeley: University of California Press, 1964.

Schofield, Mary Anne. *Eliza Haywood.* Boston: Twayne, 1985.

———. *Quiet Rebellion: The Fictional Heroines of Eliza Haywood.* Washington, DC: University Press of America, 1982.

———, and Cecilia Macheski, eds. *Fettr'd or Free? British Women Novelists, 1670–1815.* Athens: Ohio University Press, 1986.

Sherburn, George. "Samuel Richardson's Novels and the Theatre: A Theory Sketched." *Philological Quarterly* 41 (1962): 325–29.

Simon, Irene. "Early Theories of Prose Fiction: Congreve and Fielding." *Imagined Worlds: Essays on Some English Novels and Novelists in Honor of John Butt.* Edited by Maynard Mack and Ian Gregor. London: Metheun, 1968. 19–35.

Simpson, K. G., ed. *Henry Fielding: Justice Observed.* Totowa, NJ: Barnes and Noble, 1985.

Slepian, B. and L. J. Morrissey. "What is *Fanny Hill?*" *Essays in Criticism* 14 (1964): 65–75.

Snyder, Henry L. "Some New Light on Mrs. Manley." *Philological Quarterly* 52 (1973): 767–70.

Sokolyansky, Mark G. "Poetics of Fielding's Prose Epics." *Zeitschrift fur Anglistik und Americanistik* 22 (1974): 251–65.

Spacks, Patricia Meyer. *Imagining a Self: Autobiography and Novel in Eighteenth-Century England.* Cambridge: Harvard University Press, 1976.

Spencer, Jane. *The Rise of the Woman Novelist.* Oxford: Basil Blackwell, 1986.

Spender, Dale. *Mothers of the Novel: 100 Good Women Writers Before Jane Austen.* London: Pandora Press, 1986.

Spilka, Mark. "Fielding and the Epic Impulse." *Criticism* 11 (1968): 68–77.

Stamm, Rudolph G. "Daniel Defoe: An Artist in the Puritan Tradition." *Philological Quarterly* 15 (1936): 225–46.

Sutcliffe, W. Denham. "English Book Reviewing, 1749–1800." Ph.D. diss., Oxford University, 1942.

Sutton, John L., Jr. "The Source of Mrs. Manley's Preface to *Queen Zarah.*" *Modern Philology* 82 (1984): 167–72.

Taylor, John Tinnon. *Early Opposition to the English Novel.* New York: King's Crown Press, 1943.

Thompson, Leslie M. and John R. Ahrens. "Criticism of English Fiction 1780–1810: The Mysterious Powers of the Pleading Preface." *Yearbook of English Studies* 1 (1971): 125–34.

———. "Satire in Eighteenth-Century Reviews of Fiction: Guffaws of the Grave Reviewer." *Satire Newsletter* 9 (1972): 113–21.

Thornbury, Ethel. *Henry Fielding's Theory of the Comic Prose Epic.* Madison: University of Wisconsin Press, 1931.

Tieje, A. J. "The Expressed Aim of Long Prose Fiction from 1579 to 1740." *JEGP* 11 (1912): 402–32.

Todd, Janet. *Sensibility: An Introduction.* New York: Methuen, 1986.

Tompkins, J. M. S. *The Popular Novel in England 1770–1800.* London: Constable and Co., 1932. Reprint. Lincoln: University of Nebraska Press, 1961.

Treadwell, Thomas Ord. "The English Novel in the Monthly Reviews: 1770–1800." Ph.D. diss., Columbia University, 1974.

Varma, Devendra P. *The Gothic Flame.* London: Arthur Barker Ltd., 1957.

Warde, William B., Jr. "Revisions of the Published Texts of Samuel Richardson's Preface to *Clarissa.*" *South-Central Bulletin* 30 (1970): 232–34.

Warner, John M. "Smollett's Development as a Novelist." *Novel* 5 (1972): 148–61.

Warner, William Beatty. *Reading "Clarissa": The Struggles of Interpretation.* New Haven: Yale University Press, 1979.

Watt, Ian. *The Rise of the Novel: Studies in Defoe, Richardson, and Fielding.* Berkeley: University of California Press, 1957.

Wess, Robert V. "The Probable and the Marvellous in *Tom Jones.*" *Modern Philology* 68 (1970): 32–45.

Whicher, George. *The Life and Romances of Eliza Haywood.* New York: Columbia University Press, 1915.

Zach, Wolfgang. "Mrs. Aubin and Richardson's Earliest Literary Manifesto (1739)." *English Studies* 62 (1981): 271–85.

Index

A New Species of Criticism

Sophia, 75, 77
Sophia, 98
Sophia (Lennox), 121
Sophronia, 158
Sorcerer, The (Weber), 140
Spacks, Patricia Meyer, 90
Spencer, Jane, 122
Spilka, Mark, 70
Spiritual Quixote, The (Graves), 89, 110
Sterne, Lawrence, 19, 103, 105, 108, 144, 145, 153; imitators of, 130, 144; *Tristram Shandy*, 108, 152, 157
St. Leon (Godwin), 102, 103
Strange Adventures of the Count de Vinevil and His Family, The (Aubin), 31
Substantive truth: claim to, 20
Supernaturalism, 100
Sur l'origine des Romans (Huet), 24
Suspense: gratification of, 151
Sutcliffe, W. Denham, 118
Sutton, John L., Jr., 23
Swift, Jonathan: *A Tale of a Tub*, 22

Tale of a Tub, A (Swift), 22
Tears of the Sensibility, The (d'Arnaud), 146
Télémaque (Fénelon), 70
Terror: sublimity linked to, 138. *See also* Gothic novels
Théodore (Corneille), 59
Thomson, James: *The Denial*, 149
Thornbury, Ethel, 70
Thrale, Mrs. Hester, 86
Tillotson, John, 61
Timon of Athens (Shakespeare), 86
Timothy Ginnadrake (Fleming), 155
Toby, 153
Tom Jones (Fielding), 61, 63, 66, 68, 69, 72, 73, 75, 84, 94, 107, 154; Johnson's attack of "compromised" hero in, 172n.117; poetic justice discussed in, 64
Tompkins, J. M. S., 122, 128
Tone, 62
Tragedy: domestic, 86; principal design of, 54; Richardson's notion of, 55
Tragicomedy, 82
Travels for the Heart (Melmouth), 145
Treadwell, Thomas, 118, 120
Trim, 153

Tristram Shandy (Sterne), 108, 123, 152, 157
Triumph of Benevolence, The, 125
Tutor, The, 127

Unfortunate Beauty, The, 128
Unity, 39, 57, 58, 107, 152; of action, 74; of circumstance, 150; of design, 138, 150; of plan, 150

Vancenza (Robinson), 156, 159
Variety: Defoe's use of term for, 39; in Richardson, 56
Varma, Devendra P., 100
Vathek (Beckford), 138
Verisimilitude, 25, 73, 79, 148; and control, 74; in Defoe, 38
Vicar of Wakefield, The (Goldsmith), 147; linguistic style in, 159
Victim of Prejudice, The (Hays), 122
Virgil, 71
Virtue: improvement of, 29
Voluntary Exile, The (Parsons), 140
von Grosse, Marquis: *The Genius*, 130
Voyage to Lisbon, A (Fielding), 64, 68, 69

Walker, George: *Cinthelia*, 145
Walker, Mary: *The Memoirs of the Marchioness de Louvoi*, 127
Walpole, Horace, 101, 104; *The Castle of Otranto*, 100, 106
Wanderings of Warwick, The (Smith), 151
Warburton, William, 49, 56, 85; preface to *Clarissa*, 53
Warner, William, 49
Watt, Ian, 57, 70; *The Rise of the Novel*, 9, 84
Weber, Veit: *The Sorcerer*, 140
Wess, Robert V., 74
West, Jane: *The Advantages of Education*, 99; *A Gossip's Story*, 99, 131
Whicher, George, 33
White, James: *Earl Strongbow*, 143
Wit: Johnson's definition of, 130
Wollstonecraft, Mary, 104; *The Wrongs of Woman*, 108
Women novelists, 9, 23–35, 90, 91; gender bias in characterization of, 108; reviewers' bifurcated response to, 119–21
Works (Davys), 28